# Designing the Physical Education Curriculum

*Promoting Active Lifestyles*

**Judith E. Rink**
*University of South Carolina*

McGraw-Hill
Higher Education

Boston   Burr Ridge, IL   Dubuque, IA   New York   San Francisco   St. Louis
Bangkok   Bogotá   Caracas   Kuala Lumpur   Lisbon   London   Madrid   Mexico City
Milan   Montreal   New Delhi   Santiago   Seoul   Singapore   Sydney   Taipei   Toronto

# McGraw-Hill
# Higher Education

McGraw-Hill Higher Education
A Division of The McGraw-Hill Companies

Published by McGraw-Hill, an imprint of The McGraw-Hill Companies, Inc., 1221 Avenue of the Americas, New York, NY 10020. Copyright © 2009. All rights reserved. No part of this publication may be reproduced or distributed in any form or by any means, or stored in a database or retrieval system, without the prior written consent of The McGraw-Hill Companies, Inc., including, but not limited to, in any network or other electronic storage or transmission, or broadcast for distance learning.

This book is printed on acid-free paper.

1 2 3 4 5 6 7 8 9 0 DOC/DOC 1 0 9 8

ISBN:    978-0-76-741008-3
MHID:    0-76-741008-4

Editor in Chief: *Michael Ryan*
Publisher: *William R. Glass*
Executive Editor: *Christopher Johnson*
Executive Marketing Manager: *Nick Agnew*
Director of Development: *Kathleen Engelberg*
Developmental Editor: *Gary O'Brien for Van Brien & Associates*
Developmental Editor, Technology: *Julia D. Akpan*
Editorial Coordinator: *Sarah B. Hill*
Lead Media Project Manager: *Ron Nelms, Jr.*
Production Editor: *Karol Jurado*
Production Service: *Aaron Downey, Matrix Productions Inc.*
Manuscript Editor: *Jean Dal Porto*
Designer: *Margarite Reynolds*
Production Supervisor: *Louis Swaim*
Composition: *10/12 Times New Roman PS by Aptara, Inc.*
Printing: 45# *New Era Matte Plus, R.R. Donnelley & Sons*

Cover Image: © Susan LeVan/Getty Images

**Library of Congress Cataloging-in-Publication Data**

Rink, Judith.
    Designing the physical education curriculum: promoting healthy lifestyles / Judith Rink. —1st ed.
       p. cm.
    ISBN-13: 978-0-76-741008-3
    ISBN-10: 0-76-741008-4
    1. Physical education and training—Curricula.   2. Curriculum planning.   3. Sports for children—Health aspects. I. Title.
  GV363.R54 2008
  613.7071—dc22                                                  2007018875

The Internet addresses listed in the text were accurate at the time of publication. The inclusion of a Web site does not indicate an endorsement by the authors or McGraw-Hill, and McGraw-Hill does not guarantee the accuracy of the information presented at these sites.

www.mhhe.com

# BRIEF CONTENTS

# CONTENTS

# PREFACE

F
ew physical education programs devote the time and resources to long-term planning and program assessment that are needed to ensure effectiveness. Without identifying and assessing clear goals and objectives, programs with lofty ambitions can drift aimlessly.

In recent years, the general consensus among physical educators has been that the purpose of physical education programs is to teach students how to develop physically active lifestyles. The National Standards for Physical Education, developed by the National Association for Sport and Physical Education (NASPE), defined outcomes that are consistent with that purpose and that provide a blueprint for getting us there. However, standards and goal setting are only a small part of the curriculum planning process. Standards are not curriculum; they are outcomes. There are many ways that programs can achieve those outcomes. There is no single curriculum for the development of a physically active lifestyle. Educators can take different routes to the same outcomes. The process of curriculum design designates how those outcomes are to be achieved by a particular program. Curriculum planning is largely about taking a position on issues and selecting and setting priorities from among many good and oftentimes competing choices.

## Purpose and Organization

The purpose of this book is to provide a framework for using the National Standards for Physical Education to develop a K–12 physical education curriculum. Two foundational chapters are provided. Chapter 1 helps the student situate physical education curriculum within the larger issues and choices related to the purposes of schools and education. Chapter 2 presents a frank and unique discussion of the issues and choices involved in developing programs designed to promote physically active lifestyles.

Chapter 3 addresses the process of designing the curriculum in the long term—over the course of a year or even many years. Unit planning lies somewhere between curriculum planning and lesson planning, and as such it is often a forgotten skill in the development of a teacher's planning abilities. Chapter 4 introduces the student to the decisions that need to be made at the unit level; these decisions increase the chances that the goals of the program will be achieved.

Chapters 5–10 are devoted to planning physical education curriculum at the elementary, middle, and high school levels. The assumption is that decisions at each of these levels are unique and therefore should be treated at a level of specificity not found in much of the literature on designing curriculum. Two separate chapters are used to present curriculum for each of the school levels. The first chapter develops the foundations of curriculum at that level, introduces appropriate content for that level, and presents the key issues that curriculum designers must consider in their planning. The second chapter leads the student through the steps of curriculum planning at that level, providing examples of each of the steps.

Chapters 11 and 12 are devoted to the procedures used in working at a district level to develop and evaluate curriculum with others. The overriding message of this text is that planning and designing curriculum are not easy processes; in fact they are very difficult processes, but they are essential to developing and maintaining effective programs.

The appendix provides an extended sample plan for a high school basketball unit.

Curriculum planning has not been a strong part of the preparation of many physical education teachers. It is often left out of undergraduate preparation programs under the assumption that students aren't ready for the decision making and skills needed to design curriculum. As a profession we can no longer assume that teachers will pick up these skills somewhere in their professional experience. Experience tells us they will not. Unless we make curriculum planning a strong part of both our undergraduate and graduate programs, we will continue to leave to chance perhaps the most important part of the planning process.

## Features

The following pedagogical features are included in the text to enhance teaching and learning:

- At the beginning of each chapter, an **Overview** explains the importance of the chapter and how the chapter material fits within the context of the entire book.
- Following the Overview, a list of chapter **Outcomes** indicates to students what they should know and be able to do after completing the chapter.
- **Text boxes** throughout each chapter highlight and organize material and examples related to chapter content.
- Boxes called **A Time for Reflection** ask students to reflect on their own experiences and examine their perspectives on the subject matter.
- At the end of each chapter, **Checking Your Understanding** questions allow students to make sure they have identified and grasped the important ideas in the chapter.
- **Suggested Reading** gives students resources to enrich their understanding of each chapter.

## Supplements

The Web site that accompanies *Designing the Physical Education Curriculum : Promoting Active Lifestyles* (www.mhhe.com/rink) includes a variety of teaching learning tools. Among the instructor's resources are an Instructor's Manual, a Test Bank, and PowerPoint slides for each chapter. Among the student resources are curriculum framework templates and other tools for designing physical education curricula that align with national standards; students can use these to learn the process of curriculum planning and practice creating their own unit and lesson plans.

## Academic Advisors and Reviewers

The author is indebted to the following authorities, whose excellent critical reviews provided direction for this text:

Kristin Wegner, *Grand Valley State University–Allendale*

Shirley Wintjen, *Delaware State University*

Patricia Sherblom, *University of Texas of the Permian Basin*

Christine Tipps, *University of Wisconsin–Oshkosh*

Steve Stork, *Georgia College & State University*

Paul Brawdy, *St. Bonaventure University*

# CHAPTER 1

# Foundations for Curriculum

## OVERVIEW

Curriculum is a plan for what you will teach and what students will learn. This chapter identifies the need for articulating the goals of your program and long-term planning to achieve those goals. Broad perspectives on how we decide what to teach and who decides what we should teach are discussed.

## OUTCOMES

- Why articulating long-term goals is important.
- Different perspectives on the purposes of schools.
- The role of the federal, state, and local governments in school curriculum.
- The knowledge bases that inform the development of curriculum.

If you were asked what you learned in physical education in your elementary, middle, or high school experiences, what would you say? Some of you might respond that you learned different games in elementary school and different sports in middle and high school. Some of you might have a more extensive or descriptive list of what you learned. Compare your response to the list of national content standards for physical education (Box 1.1). This list of standards represents what the profession says students should know and be able to do as a result of having physical education in the school program. Which of these content standards did you learn in physical education? If you came out of a good physical education program you should be competent in these standards and should be able to describe what you learned more specifically. The experiences of many physical education

## Box 1.1   The National Standards for Physical Education

*Standard 1:* Demonstrates competency in motor skills and movement patterns needed to perform a variety of physical activities

*Standard 2:* Demonstrates understanding of movement concepts, principles, strategies, and tactics as they apply to the learning and performance of physical activities

*Standard 3:* Participates regularly in physical activity

*Standard 4:* Achieves and maintains a health-enhancing level of physical fitness

*Standard 5:* Exhibits responsible personal and social behavior that respects self and others in physical activity settings

*Standard 6:* Values physical activity for health, enjoyment, challenge, self-expression, and/or social interaction

Source: NASPE. (2004). *Moving into the Future: National Standards for Physical Education* (2nd ed.). Reston, VA: NASPE.

students do not measure up to the field's potential to accomplish the standards described by the National Association for Sport and Physical Education (NASPE) (2004).

These national standards have been adopted or adapted by most states and districts in the country in some form. If we assume that the national standards are appropriate expectations for students, there are many reasons why students in physical education programs have not achieved them, including curriculums that don't address the standards or have little chance of accomplishing them, poor teaching, and inadequate resources. In this text we are most concerned with curriculum and the ability of physical education programs to articulate goals and to devise a plan to reach those goals.

One of the primary reasons why physical education programs have not been effective is because they have not articulated a clear set of accomplishable goals. Most physical educators have not taken the time to determine how best to accomplish them. Although physical education is not alone in its failure to articulate in practice a K–12 plan to accomplish clearly articulated goals, physical education is one of the few programs that has left this major responsibility primarily to the practitioner and local school districts. In the past, the lack of a national consensus about what those goals should be was a great inhibitor to clearly articulated goals at the local level. With the contribution of the national standards in 1995 (NASPE) and their revision in 2004, programs now have a great resource from which to begin to design programs.

The problem for the teacher is that although the national standards describe program outcomes in general terms, they do not describe the specific content that needs to be taught to achieve those outcomes or the action steps needed to get there. There are good reasons for not having a policy-making body at the national level describe specific content. The perspective of the national body is that there are many ways to achieve the content, and state and local districts should have the responsibility to choose how to achieve the standards. The disadvantage of not having the national body outline more specific content needed to achieve the standards is that teachers at state and local levels must be well prepared to do both long-term and short-term planning to achieve the standards.

Physical education professionals do not spend a whole lot of time planning what they do. This is particularly true of long-term planning. When they do plan, there is little coordination to the process. Each teacher and each grade level makes independent decisions about what to teach and when to teach it. Sometimes planning for what students will do involves nothing more than a few thoughts on the way to work. More often the result is that there is very little connection between what a student does in physical education from one day to another, one unit to another, or from one year to the next year. Middle school teachers complain that elementary school teachers have not taught students what they need to know and be able to do in order to be successful in the middle school program. High school teachers complain that middle school teachers have not taught students what they need to know and be able to do in a high school program. While students are exposed to a lot, often the same content each year, they do not learn much of what they are exposed to.

---

**A Time for Reflection**

From your own experiences in a teaching practicum or as a student in a physical education class, can you identify teachers you think had very specific goals for their lessons? How do you know? What were the goals of these teachers? Were they related to the national standards? Which ones? Which ones were left out of your experiences?

---

The process of designing programs to accomplish clearly articulated goals is the process of curriculum design. In the very simplest sense, when educators design curriculum they make a decision about what they want students to know and be able to do when they leave their physical education experiences and then they devise a plan that has the potential to get them to those goals through the K–12 program.

## What Is Curriculum?

Although the term *curriculum* itself can mean anything from the guide that sits on the teacher's shelf to all the experiences of the learner under the auspices of the school, the purpose of this book is to help you devise a long-term plan for what students will learn in your program and how they will learn it. The term *curriculum* when used in reference to a subject area like physical education is usually meant to mean the *course of study:* the long-term plan for what students are expected to learn in that subject area organized by grade level. The long-term plan is usually produced in a document called a *curriculum guide*. The term *curriculum plan* will be used throughout the text to refer to the course of study for a physical education program that is included in the curriculum guide.

Curriculum plans are meant to be referred to often in order to plan units of instruction and lesson plans. Units of instruction are plans for the major content areas that make up a curriculum. In high school, these major content areas might be activities like basketball or weight lifting, or content areas like fitness. At the elementary school level, units might be concepts like striking or content areas like creative dance or educational gymnastics. Teachers include units they think will help students meet their curriculum goals. For good programs there is a close match between what is planned, what is taught, what is assessed, and what is learned. This is called *curriculum alignment.* Many curriculum guides sit idle on teacher's shelves and have little influence on what teachers actually do day to day oftentimes because they are not appropriate for the school, don't have realistic expectations, and aren't specific enough to provide real guidance. When a teacher uses the curriculum guide there is no guarantee that he or she is skilled enough to implement it so that students actually learn what was intended. Nevertheless, all good programs start with good plans and the ability to write a good curriculum guide is an essential skill for physical education teachers.

Another important distinction that we need to make when talking about curriculum plans is to recognize that students learn more in schools than what is planned. The curriculum plan and what the teacher sets out to teach is *intended* learning. Students learn a lot that is not intended. If all the posters of basketball players on the gym walls are of males, girls learn that basketball is a boys sport. If fitness is taught in the context of doing exercises, than students learn that physical exercises,

Good sportsmanship skills need to be articulated as outcomes, planned, taught for, and evaluated. (© *image100/PunchStock*)

rather than lifestyle changes and physical activities, are the way to develop fitness. If activities are designed so that the students actually "hate" what they do, students learn that physical activity is not an enjoyable activity The unintended curriculum is sometimes called the *null curriculum, the hidden curriculum,* or the *covert curriculum*. It is called hidden because many times we are not aware that it exists and we are not aware of the unintended impact on students. While what the teacher plans for is *explicit*, the null, hidden, and covert curriculum is usually *implicit*.

---

**A Time for Reflection**

Think back on your school experiences. What do you think you learned (positive or negative) that was not intended by your teachers? Could, or should, the teacher have planned to do something to make what you learned intentional?

---

Most people reading this text have already learned to plan lessons. You have learned how very important it is to have clear lesson objectives and to design learning experiences that help you meet those objectives. Curriculum planning is a similar process but at a much broader level. Although you will have a major responsibility for planning the program you are directly responsible for (elementary, middle; or high school in most cases), your curriculum should in some way be attached to a K–12 perspective. Elementary school, middle school (sometimes junior high school), and high school experiences should be integrated, not only so that students feeding into the same secondary schools from different elementary and middle schools do not come with radically different experiences, but also because a progressive and integrated plan to accomplish long-term goals has the best chance of meeting those goals. There is little sense in teaching volleyball to elementary children if the middle school and high school programs do not offer opportunities for students to more fully develop their skill in this sport. Likewise, it is difficult to teach high school students tennis who have had no striking experiences.

When you plan curriculum you will go through a process that helps you clearly articulate the goals you want to accomplish and devise a workable plan to gradually lead the students from where they currently are to where you want them to be. This plan will result in yearly plans for each grade level that will specify what you will teach, when you will teach it, and how you will assess what you have taught. There are two initial steps in the process of curriculum design. The first is to decide what students should learn in physical education throughout the grade levels, and the second is to decide how to organize what you think students should learn throughout the program. At first glance this would seem like a fairly easy process. All you have to do is decide what you want students to learn and then figure out how to get there. As you might expect, little about educational planning is as easy at it may appear to be.

## Deciding What You Want Students to Learn

Physical education programs are a part of school programs. What to teach in the schools has long been, and will continue to be, a source of controversy and debate in our society. Physical education is very much affected by the decisions made by the public about what to include in the school curriculum and the extent to which different subject areas and content should be included. There is a continuing debate about what the purposes of schools should be. Public attention to what the schools should be teaching is recognition of schools as a powerful source to meet the needs of a society for transmitting and transforming culture.

Schools do have the power to transmit or to transform culture. The problem is that there are many different ideas on what should be transmitted and what needs to be transformed. Closed societies such as communist groups have long used the schools to foster their own political agendas. Current examples of debates about what should be taught in schools involve issues such as abstinence-only in sex education and creationism in the science curriculum. The founders of the United States recognized that a democratic society could only prosper where there was an educated populace of citizens prepared to make good decisions that would benefit both the individual as well as the society as a whole. However, educated people can, and do, disagree.

Physical education is an integral part of the school program and therefore is subject to the same issues regarding the purposes of schools in our society as all other content areas. It is included in the curriculum only because the people who make decisions about the purposes schools should serve have decided that physical education contributes to what they see as the purpose of schools. It is supported in the curriculum only to the extent that the populace feels that the contribution it makes to the education of students relative to the other subject areas competing for curriculum time, warrants support. Physical education can be reduced or removed from the curriculum at any point when the decision makers decide that, relative to the inclusion of other priorities, it does not warrant inclusion.

Physical education programs experienced a major decline of support as emphases on academic achievement gained prominence. However, the recent attention to the obesity epidemic has given physical education increased support as a major player to improve the health and fitness of our children. What physical education does with that increased support will determine whether that support is warranted. Continued support depends on the willingness of physical educators to plan programs that make a difference and can show that they make a difference.

---

**A Time for Reflection**

If you were a taxpayer would you vote to increase the resources of physical education programs and the program time of physical education programs? Why? Why not? Where would you take the time from? On what do you base this decision?

---

## What Purposes Should the Schools Serve?

The direction school curriculum takes is most influenced by the answer given to the question, "What purpose should schools serve?" Although there are many comprehensive lists of what the public expects schools to do, most of them revolve around the following ideas.

Schools should:

1. Impart the knowledge, skills, and attitudes needed to be a productive citizen.
2. Develop fully the potential of each student.
3. Help students to learn about themselves and the world they live in to make it a better place.

It is possible to separate broad curriculum models or directions into an almost infinite number of possibilities. There are three orientations that tend to be most influential in today's perspectives of the school curriculum and physical education: academic mastery, humanistic curriculum, and social reconstruction. Each of these perspectives is based on some assumptions about the role that schools should play in our society. These perspectives influence not only the total curriculum in the schools, but physical education as well.

## Academic Mastery

Academic mastery is probably the most dominant perspective on the purpose of schools. Although schools will serve many other roles, mostly society expects schools to teach students the basics: to read, to write, and to compute. Other subject areas such as social studies, science, the arts, physical education, and health have gradually won a place in the school curriculum, but it is the basic academic areas that have been historically the major mission of the institutions we call schools.

An academic mastery perspective on the purpose of schools expects schools to teach students content. Each content area in the schools, the basic subjects as well as those that have also won a place in the school curriculum, has content that students are expected to master. An academic mastery perspective holds the teaching of that content as the most significant contribution of the schools.

Within an academic mastery perspective decisions have to be made as to which content areas should receive the most program time. Content areas within school curriculums struggle to get the experts' attention for recognition and support of their content. In an academic mastery perspective schools are successful to the extent that they are successful in getting students to master that content.

More recently, the academic content that students are expected to achieve has been more narrowly defined in terms of academic standards. Student achievement in the standards is assessed and students, teachers, and schools are held accountable for these defined outcomes. The ideas of academic mastery have impacted physical education in several ways. First, when academic mastery is defined narrowly in terms of the mastery of core academic subjects, academic subjects become the major priority of schools. Support for other subject areas like physical education programs is reduced. Education resources will flow to what is considered the most important content area. When schools are put under pressure to accomplish particular goals, like academic mastery of basic/core academic subjects, they shift their resources to accomplish those goals. This usually means reducing resources like teachers, class time, facilities, and/or equipment from other areas not considered as important, or perceived as having weak support.

An argument for academic mastery is that PE should
provide students the skills they need to be participants.
(© *image100/PunchStock*)

The idea of academic mastery also impacts what physical education teachers
choose to teach. An academic mastery perspective for the physical education curriculum assumes that your major purpose as a physical education teacher is to teach
physical education content. Teachers who hold different perspectives on the major
purposes of schools are forced to acknowledge that the content of a subject area
may take precedence over other purposes they may deem more appropriate for
schools. At the present time the choice of content in physical education is guided
by the outcomes defined in the national standards (NASPE, 2004) or those accepted
by states or local school districts. A large part of this text will be devoted to helping you define what that content is for physical education.

## Humanistic Curriculum

People whose ideas are more aligned with a humanistic perspective of the purpose
of schooling are concerned that the curriculum fully develop human potential.
Maslow's notion of self-actualization and the fully functioning individual is usually

perceived at the heart of the goals of this orientation as well as affective concerns centering on the personal growth and development of each student (Maslow, 1968). The humanistic curriculum is not without a concern for academic achievement, but accepts responsibility for more fully developing the social and emotional aspects of individuals, their creativity, and higher-order thinking processes, the self.

From an educator's perspective, many of the concerns of the humanist are always part of the decision-making process of what to teach and how to teach it. As educators we have been taught to take a developmental perspective (subject matter should be appropriate to the needs, interests, and abilities of the individual child). In particular periods of history, most recently the 1960s, the humanistic curriculum has been a more dominant model and received much more attention and support of both educators and the public. During these periods, humanistic concerns took priority over the concerns for subject matter mastery. The more explicit humanistic curriculum emphases most evident in the 1960s have been largely replaced by a greater concern for academic standards and mastery. However, recent emphases on character education, conflict resolution, and equity and inclusion are examples of humanistic ideas exerting pressure on traditional academic mastery orientations to curriculum. The reader needs only to return to the national standards for physical education listed in Box 1.1 to recognize the influence of the ideas of the humanist on the goals of physical education. Which of the six standards are those that are most related to a more humanistic purpose of schools?

Although there are few examples of schools and school programs that could be characterized by a dominant emphasis on humanistic concerns, you will find in later chapters that there are many physical educators and a few leaders in physical education who would advocate that a humanistic orientation replace more traditional physical education content.

## Social Reconstruction

Social recontructionists do not have one single agenda, so therefore there is not one single direction a curriculum might take. While more traditional orientations to curriculum are designed to help students "fit into" and "get along" in society, social reconstruction orientations to curriculum are designed to prepare students for a different society and to help students change society. Social reconstructionists want to reconstruct society. They do not necessarily want to transmit a past culture—they want to create a new one. They advocate organizing the curriculum around real life problems that need to be solved to create a better society, and they want to teach students how to engage in a process that would resolve those problems.

Areas that have been identified as needing "fixing" in our present society involve a wide range of issues from ecology to the empowerment of minorities. Concern for equity in the schools and in society has been one of the more popular directions of reconstructionist perspectives on schools. Few school curriculums are organized around the ideas of the social reconstructionist, but many school curriculums do attend to the concerns of this model to varying degrees. Social justice and equity for all students has long been a concern of physical educators, although efforts to operationalize such perspectives have not been made explicit in most physical education curriculum. Physical education national standard five, *Exhibits responsible personal and social behavior that respects self and others in physical activity settings,* implies the notion of inclusion. *Inclusion* is one of those educational terms that have come to mean a concern for equity and the just treatment of people who may be different in some way from you. More commonly, *highlighted differences* refers to people with different ethnic, cultural, and racial backgrounds.

> **A Time for Reflection**
> Reflect on your own beliefs about what schools should accomplish. With which curriculum orientation on the purposes of schools do you see yourself aligned? What physical education learning experiences can you identify that might be most associated with an academic mastery, humanistic, or reconstructionist orientation to physical education curriculum?

## The Eclectic Curriculum

If you had trouble deciding which of the above purposes the schools should most serve, you are not alone. Although you will lean more toward one or another at different points in your career, you will probably find yourself wanting to incorporate aspects of all of the above purposes in your personal philosophy of what education should be about. For the curriculum designer as well as the teacher in the schools, these positions are tensions that are always present, making our jobs one of the most important and most difficult. If we could just worry about how to help students master content and not be concerned with what kind of people our students become, we could do a much better job helping students master content. If we could just worry about developing human potential and not worry about the content they learn, we could do a much better job developing human potential. And if we didn't have to worry at all about whether we were preparing students for a better and more just world, we could do a much better job at all of it. Each of these purposes tug at us from different directions, pulling us sometimes more in one direction than another.

What makes the decisions of educators regarding what to teach and how to teach it even more difficult is the idea that educators are most often not in control of the choices. The sociopolitical climate of any particular time has a great influence on what we expect schools to do. Historically, when the Soviet Union was the first to reach space, calls for increased science in the curriculum were most evident. Schools in the 1950s and 1960s were expected to be the major source of racially integrating our society. The demand for a more high-tech labor force significantly increases the demand for schools that can prepare students for the needs of business. Headlines about violence in the schools significantly increases the need for more humanistic emphases. When the economic leadership of the United States in the world is threatened, schools are asked to produce more scientists. As you will see in the next section, education most often follows the sociopolitical climate of the time and it is other groups, not educators, who are most often the dominant players.

## Who Makes the Decisions?

Decisions as to what should be taught in schools are made at many different levels. State and national governments decide what schools should teach and toward what end. School districts make decisions as to what they will teach, program faculty within a school make decisions, and so do individual teachers. All of these levels of decision making impact what is taught in physical education and how it is taught.

### National Government

Unlike most other countries who have national curriculums, when our government was formed, the Constitution of the United States clearly gave control of the schools to the individual states. We have no national curriculum. Many of our forefathers did not trust government with perhaps one of the most powerful tools for change of government's responsibilities. Although the national government does not have any direct authority over what is taught and how it is taught in the schools, the national government can and does exert a significant influence over schools. The ability of the federal government to exercise power through granting and withholding federal funds (inducement) is the most obvious source of power over state and local schools. When the federal government wants to support a change in the schools it has the power to provide funds for that change and to withdraw federal funds from those schools that do not comply. States are free not to seek or accept funds for changes they do not want to make, but few can risk losing federal funds to do so. The federal government also supports states through research and by developing and providing information to schools on national problems and trends from which schools can make decisions.

### State Government

It is state government that has the most direct power over schools (mandates) and there are two key organizational structures in most states that exert this power. Most states have an *elected board of education,* which has the ability to make policy decisions about what should be taught and how it should be taught in the schools. Most of these boards are composed of citizens who are not educators but have final say over what is taught and how it is taught. Most states also have state departments of education that are technically the professional arm of the state. State departments of education are given the responsibility to direct education within a state. Many state departments of education have limited responsibility for state policy, which usually comes from either legislated mandates to them or from a state board of education.

Until recently most states have primarily transferred their power to control much of what occurs in schools to local school districts. During the latter part of the 1990s, states began a concerted effort to define much more explicitly what they want students to know and be able to do across all schools in the state. Many states have developed state-level assessment materials to determine the extent to which students have accomplished those goals. Many states have also begun to hold schools accountable for reaching those goals to varying degrees. This reform movement has been called the standards, assessment, and accountability movement. It was initiated with a report that suggested that the nation was in trouble because our students could not do what students in other countries could do (*A Nation at Risk,* 1983). As a result, all school content areas, including physical education, developed national content standards. Most states either adapted, or adopted, these national standards and developed policies for state-level assessment and accountability. State-level accountability in many states means that test results are made public for each school. Schools that do not show improvement are subject to state-level intervention to improve that school.

The standards, assessment, and accountability movement has had a profound effect on school curriculum. Schools that are held accountable for academic mastery find it difficult not to teach what they are held accountable for. High-stakes assessment produces change of what is being tested. This change can be as obvious as changes in the amount of program time devoted to a subject or content area within a subject. It can also be as subtle as changes in teachers' lesson plans to spend more time on what "counts." The advantage of high-stakes assessment is that it is more likely that a majority of students will meet minimum standards. The disadvantage is that it often reduces what is taught to what is more easily measured, and important goals of the school curriculum often lying in more humanistic concerns do not receive the attention they probably should.

An unintended consequence of the standards and assessment movement for many program areas that are not considered core academic subject areas and are not included in high-stakes assessment is that they too do not "count." Any subject area not included is likely to find itself in a very defensive position struggling to maintain program time and resources. In many states physical education is one of those subject areas.

## School Districts and Boards of Education

Local control of schools is usually designated to elected district school boards. School boards are elected citizens who hire school district personnel, approve budgets, and in general set policy, priorities, and directions for local schools. These boards are primarily made up of citizens living in a district who are not educators but who have concerns about what their children should learn and how they should learn it. Any decisions or power that is not mandated by the state is under the control of these elected officials. Many of the boards at the district level designate authority for decisions to the professional educators in a district depending on the significant political agendas of the group at any particular time. In effect, the administration of a school district and its teachers serve at the discretion of the people's elected school board.

## Program Faculty

Program faculties in a district are often called upon to design curriculum for a district within the parameters of state and district policy. In the best of circumstances, all the physical educators in a district would get together and make decisions about what was going to be taught at each grade level so that there is some coordination between the elementary, middle, and high school levels. Sometimes a smaller committee is given that responsibility, which means that there then must be an opportunity for the smaller committee to do staff development with those teachers who were not involved in the process. In other academic areas a lot of curriculum development occurs with decisions to use particular textbooks and materials. Because physical education only occasionally uses textbooks, physical educators find themselves having to create curriculum materials from scratch.

The standards and assessment movement has created a great deal of material in physical education at all levels that should facilitate the process of curriculum development, but teachers must have the skills to be able to translate this material into workable curriculum plans and yearly plans for all levels. The curriculum *guide,* which is usually the term given to the document that describes the curriculum plan, is usually approved by the school board. Curriculum guides describe what a program will accomplish and how the content will be organized (scope and sequence) to accomplish the goals/objectives that are specified. They also usually include policy regarding a subject area.

At the present time, many school districts have curriculum guides in physical education, but few districts actually use them or hold students or teachers accountable for them. One big reason for the failure of curriculum guides to actually influence what is taught in the schools is probably the fact that these materials have not been designed with a specificity that actually describes in enough detail what students should know and be able to do at each level. Another big reason for the failure of teachers to actually use curriculum guides to deliver curriculum is that in most cases, there is no assessment or accountability for teachers to do so. No one checks whether teachers are teaching or students are actually learning what is described in many of the guides that sit on teachers' shelves. The intent of this text is to help you design curriculum materials that will be used and can be assessed.

# What Informs Curriculum Decision Making?

While a lot of decision making about what should be taught in the schools is not a "thoughtful" process but rather a reaction to sociopolitical events of the time, educators who make decisions about what to teach and how to teach it are asked to approach the process as professionals with a knowledge base that people who are not trained as professional educators do not have. There are several knowledge bases that inform the process of curriculum development, including educational philosophy, subject matter knowledge, knowledge of learners, knowledge of learning theory, and knowledge related to curriculum design.

## Educational Philosophy

Educational philosophy will play a major role in what you choose to teach and how you choose to teach it. As a teacher you will have a view on what the most important role of the schools should be. Some of you will support an academic mastery perspective, some of you will be more humanistic, and some of you may have an agenda for reconstructing society to make it better. Your position on these issues will play a role in how you design curriculum and how you teach.

As a physical educator you will also find yourself leaning in the direction of one or another of the national standards. Some of you will focus more heavily on giving students actual skills to be a participant in physical activity; some of you will want your programs oriented to helping students make the transition into a physically active lifestyle; some of you will want to develop fitness and the ability to maintain fitness, or to have the knowledge needed to maintain a physically active lifestyle; and some of you will see physical education as a laboratory for personal growth (development of emotional and social skills of students). Although all comprehensive programs will develop aspects of all of these important directions, individual teachers will tend to stretch their curriculums in one direction or another, depending on the value positions that grow out of their philosophy.

## Subject Matter Knowledge

As a physical educator you possess knowledge about the content of physical education as well as the disciplines that affect the learning and teaching of physical education. The course work you took in psychomotor skills (sports, aquatics, gymnastics, dance, educational games, etc.), as well as the knowledge you have and will teach students about physical activity and how to learn motor skills, is the subject matter of physical education. The subject matter of physical education is what we teach and what students learn. Knowledge from course work you took in areas such as exercise physiology, motor, learning/development, and sport psychology is knowledge you have that you will not necessarily teach to students but that you will need to know in order to better teach content. The knowledge we possess as physical educators is related to not only how to perform and how to develop fitness, but knowledge about how to increase the level of performance, how to develop skills and fitness, and how to address affective concerns. You will need to know how to organize the content over 12 years of school in a way that supports learning.

## Knowledge of Learners

Your knowledge of how children learn and develop will help you make good decisions about what to teach children at what ages and how to teach children of different ages. You have to be able to diagnose where students are in the learning process. This knowledge is essential to planning curriculum. Where children are in terms of their motor development, their cognitive development, and their social development are important factors that will determine how you sequence what you will teach and when and how you will teach it. This knowledge is unique to physical educators.

## Knowledge of Learning Theory

Learning is a relatively permanent change in behavior. The teacher's role in school settings is to produce learning. There is no single theory or knowledge base that defines how students learn. Instead, educators are faced with several theories that explain different kinds of learning under different conditions. Most of these theories will take four different perspectives: behaviorism, information processing, constructivism, and social learning theory.

The *behaviorist* describes learning in terms of changing the external conditions to shape behavior. The behaviorist models good behavior, and positively rewards and reinforces appropriate behavior. Behaviorists are concerned that learning be successful and will want to break down skills into small component parts to ensure success throughout the learning process. A lot of your own experiences in school were probably guided by many of these principles. You were rewarded for appropriate behavior and encouraged to act in ways adults felt were most appropriate.

*Information processing* focuses on the internal cognitive processes individuals use to make sense out of their world. The emphasis for the information processor is to make instruction consistent with the manner in which individuals select, interpret, use, and store information. The teacher who is aware of how individuals process information can make that information more meaningful, ensure that individuals attend to what is important, and integrate what they have learned with previous learning. Although a lot of what the information processing learning theory has to say is most important for the delivery of instruction, teachers who plan curriculum will need to incorporate this knowledge base into their curriculum plans.

*Constructivism* is a learning orientation that is associated with cognitive theory. Cognitive theorists focus on how people create meaning from their learning experiences. Constructivists feel strongly that students construct meaning by being actively involved in the learning process rather than being passive receptors of information. For the constructivists, problem solving, creativity, learning how to learn, and learning processes in general that involve the learner at higher levels of cognitive activity have more value than those that do not. Several newer curriculum/instructional orientations to the teaching of games and sport, such as games for understanding, would be considered approaches that rest heavily on constructivist orientations to our content.

*Social learning* theorists essentially believe that all knowledge is socially constructed and therefore emphasize the important nature of active group interaction in learning. Cooperative learning and cooperative games, and to some extent the recent emphasis on sport education, are more recent emphases on education and physical education that rely heavily on placing students in social groups and encouraging cooperative interaction to produce learning.

## Knowledge of Curriculum Design

As a teacher you will have to be skilled at designing curriculum. There is a knowledge base that will help you make good decisions about how to put a plan together to accomplish your purposes in your role as a teacher. This knowledge base will enable you to identify what it is you want to accomplish in terms of curriculum goals, what it is you want to teach to meet those goals, and how best to sequence that content in a defensible plan. Providing you with that knowledge is the purpose of this book.

## Check Your Understanding

1.  Why is it important to articulate the long-term goals of schools?
2.  What are three different perspectives on the purposes of schools?
3.  What role does the federal, state, and local government play in the development of school curriculum?
4.  What knowledge bases inform the development of curriculum?

## References

Maslow, A. (1968). *Toward a Psychology of Being* (2nd ed.). Princeton, NJ: Van Nostrand.

National Commission on Excellence in Education. (1983). *A Nation at Risk: The Imperative for Educational Reform.* Washington, DC.

NASPE. (2004). Moving into the Future: National Content Standards for Physical Education. Reston, VA: NASPE.

## Suggested Reading

*Note:* Many of the topics included in this chapter are current debates for both educators and the public. Excellent current reading on learning theories and the purpose of schools appears on several good Web sites listed below. In addition, a review of current as well as past editions of *Educational Leadership,* the journal of the Association for Supervision and Curriculum Development, continuously publishes articles related to the themes of this chapter.

### Learning Theories

There are many Web sites devoted to the description and understanding of learning theories that can be accessed through a search engine. Among those are www.understanding.com and www.usask.ca/education/.

### Purpose of Schools

*Reinventing Schools: A Conversation with Linda Darling-Hammond,* available at www.ed.psu.edu/insys/esd/darling/purpose.html. AIT Box A 1111 W. Seventh Street. Bloomington, IN 47404.

Ziegler, E. (2002). The physical education and sport curriculum in the 21st century: Proposed common denominators. *The Physical Educator.* Fall, 114–124.

# CHAPTER 2

# Physical Education for a Physically Active Lifestyle

## OVERVIEW

This chapter takes the position that developing a physically active lifestyle is the major goal of physical education programs and presents different perspectives on how physical education should reach that goal. The national standards were designed so that each of the standards makes a contribution to developing a physically active lifestyle. Each of the national standards is explored, with a discussion of their contribution to a physically active lifestyle and alternatives for their development.

## OUTCOMES

- Why developing a physically active lifestyle is important.
- How each of the national standards contributes to this goal.
- Curricular alternatives to accomplishing the goal

Over the past few years the idea of developing a physically active lifestyle for students has received a lot of consensus as the goal of a K–12 physical education program. The idea of a physically active lifestyle means that students will choose to be physically active over their lifespan and they will make physical activity a regular and normal part of their lives. This means that students enrolled in physical education should be leading a physically active lifestyle and when students leave school they should leave with the skills, knowledge, and dispositions to be physically active. Educating students to lead a physically active lifestyle by giving them the skills, knowledge and dispositions to lead a physically active life becomes the responsibility of physical education programs. In one sense, physical education programs can determine their success by how many students and adults actually do lead a physically active lifestyle. If we are really doing our jobs, few people should be inactive.

## Why Is Developing A Physically Active Lifestyle So Important?

Usually, support for a physically active lifestyle comes from two ideas. The first is that a physically active lifestyle is important to a high quality of life and the second idea is that a physically active lifestyle is important to our health. While all of us are most familiar with defending participation in physical activity based on health reasons, few consider how important the ability to be physically active is to our quality of life. A physically active individual enjoys a better quality of life that is not available to an individual who is not physically active. Physical activities are a large part of our culture. The ability to engage in a wide variety of physical activities gives an individual a choice of how to use leisure time. Having physical activity skills increases opportunities for participation in activities that can have a positive effect on our emotional and social well-being. Those people who cannot be active regularly are also limited in their choices of occupation as they are excluded from jobs that require physical stamina and ability.

Support for physical activity based on health reasons is more common. In 1996 the Surgeon General's Report identified lack of physical activity as a major health crisis in the United States (U.S. Department of Health and Human Services, 1997). Next to smoking, lack of physical activity was identified as a major cause of the escalating chronic disease problems including, but not limited to, increases in obesity, diabetes, heart disease, and life-threatening cancers. Not only is lack of physical activity threatening the health of children and adults, the escalating percentage of the gross national product of this country devoted to health care costs is threatening the economy.

Physical education is not solely responsible for increasing the level of physical activity. Families, communities, and other programs having responsibility for the health and well-being of the population share this responsibility (U.S. Department of Health and Human Services, 1997). However, school physical education programs are in a unique position to educate students for physically active lifestyles. Physical education programs work with young people in compulsory settings over a long period of time. These are the only programs within the school setting that have this unique responsibility.

## What Does This Mean Physical Education Must Do?

Physical education programs need to focus their attention on issues related to how to educate young people and youth to develop a physically active lifestyle. They need to design their curriculums to develop physically active lifestyles. In the past

Physical education programs have done their jobs when adults are active for a lifetime. (© *PhotoLink/Getty Images*)

we have assumed that if we taught students some motor skills and sport skills they could use to be physically active, and if we told students how important it was to be physically active, they would be physically active. We have not been successful using this approach.

**A Time for Reflection**

Sometimes the study of people who are physically active can help us identify what we have to do to help people be physically active. What do you think most effects an individual's decision to be physically active? What does this mean you must do in your physical education program?

Designing curriculums to develop a physically active lifestyle means that you have to identify the skills, knowledge, and dispositions students need to be physically active. Physical *skills* involve those psychomotor abilities that are likely to have an

## Box 2.1    Definition of a Physically Educated Person

A physically educated person:

*Has*   learned the skills necessary to perform a variety of physical activities.

*Is*   physically fit.

*Does*   participate regularly in physical activity.

*Knows*   the implications of, and, benefits from, involvement in physical activity.

*Values*   physical activity and its contribution to a healthful lifestyle.

NASPE. (1992). Outcomes of Quality Physical Education Programs. Reston: VA: National Association for Sport and Physical Education.

impact on whether a person is both willing and able to participate in physical activity. Some of those physical skills will involve skills to participate in the physical activities of both the youth and adult culture (e.g., organized sport, skate boarding, hiking, bicycling) and some of those skills will involve being a willing and able participant in skills required for a lifestyle that is physically active (e.g., choosing to mow the lawn, gardening, washing the car, and walking instead of riding).

Students who are educated for a physically active lifestyle will also need *knowledge*. They will need to know about the effects of physical activity on their body, how to develop and maintain fitness, and why it is important. They will need to know what it means to choose to be physically active and where and how they can become involved in physical activity in their own communities. They will also need to know how to perform skills correctly and how to continue to develop skills they will need to be a participant.

A person who has a *disposition* to be active is more likely to choose to be physically active. It is possible to have the skills and knowledge to be physically active and yet not choose to be physically active. Students who are taught to like and value physical activity are more likely to participate in physical activity both as youths as well as adults.

A document describing the characteristics of a physically educated person was published by the National Association for Sport and Physical Education (National Association of Sport and Physical Education [NASPE], 1992). These characteristics are described in Box 2.1. As an extension of that definition, the first set of national standards describing what a student should know and be able to do after graduating from high school were published in 1995 and revised in 2004. This set of standards reflects a professional consensus on physical education's role in developing a physically active lifestyle (see Box 1.1 in Chapter 1).

The national standards identify three large content areas traditionally seen to be the substance of physical education. These content areas are the major building blocks for a physically active lifestyle. The first content area relates to the development of motor skills essential for the development of a physically active lifestyle. The second large content area, lifestyle and fitness, is related to teaching lifestyle issues directly and developing and maintaining physical fitness. The third content area is related to what might be called the personal growth of students and is associated with student character, values, and social and emotional health. Each of these content areas will be discussed in terms of their contribution to developing a physically active lifestyle and the curriculum issues that surround them.

# The Motor Skill Content of Physical Education

No one would argue against the idea that in order to be physically active you need to be able to move and that to move you need to be somewhat skilled at moving. The big issues related to the role of motor skills in developing a physically active lifestyle revolve around questions related to how skilled you have to be and in what skills. As a physical educator you will need to decide how best to design your curriculum to help your students lead a physically active lifestyle. In order to do this you will need to commit yourself to a position on some of these issues. Some of the more common positions on developing motor skills for a physically active lifestyle are discussed below.

## Position 1: Engage Students in Enjoyable Physical Activity

Some physical educators believe that the most important thing that physical education programs can do to prepare students for a physically active lifestyle is to engage students in enjoyable physical activities. Professionals who support this position are not highly concerned with developing motor skills. Rather than choose activities that require skill to be successful participants, professionals who support this position would argue that we need to choose to teach those activities that do not require a great deal of skill. Age-appropriate fun activities that encourage all students to be active participants make up a large part of the curriculum for professionals who support this position. Many professionals who support this view feel as though students do not want to learn motor skills and that the process of learning motor skills is not an enjoyable experience and therefore should not be a major program emphasis.

From an "enjoyable physical activity" perspective, students in the younger grades are likely to be involved in what we have come to call *low organization* kinds of games, not unlike those you might see children playing on the playground (e.g., Red Light Green Light, Hop Scotch, Tag). Most of these games do not require a great deal of instruction in terms of the motor skills necessary to play them and most children (except for those who are not as good as many in the class) enjoy playing them.

For teachers who advocate engaging students in enjoyable physical activities, the curriculum for students at the middle school level is likely to involve a broad range of different activities. Some of these activities may be related to organized sport and some may be more related to activities this age group may experience outside of school (e.g., inline skating, orienteering) or more advanced low organization games (e.g., pickle ball, disk golf). Team sport activities are most often modified to reduce the skill expectations and are played in small-sided teams with little skill preparation.

High school programs that target the idea of providing "fun" activities for participation usually involve units that are short, may be modified forms of sports, and have very limited skill instruction. Students spend most of the time in the unit playing the activity or game rather than learning how to be a skillful participant.

Support for the position that advocates engaging students in fun physical activity is based upon the idea that if you engage students in enjoyable physical activity they will continue to seek to be physically active. A great deal of the support for this position as a major direction of physical education comes as a reaction against traditional physical education programs. Programs that are heavily focused on sports, and particularly team sports, require high levels of skill that may be beyond both the ability and interests of the very students who need most to be physically active. A major assumption of this perspective on curriculum is that learning to be skillful is not an enjoyable experience, and many physical education programs destroy a student's desire to be physically active because they put students in positions where they cannot be successful.

> **A Time for Reflection**
> What is your perspective on the relationship of skillfulness to a physically active lifestyle? How skilled do people have to be to be participants?

## Position 2: Develop Competence in Motor Skills

Physical educators who advocate developing competence in motor skills as a primary purpose of physical education have a similar goal to those professionals who want to engage students in physical activity—they want to develop a physically active lifestyle. Advocacy for developing motor skill competence comes primarily from a perspective that argues that people are more likely to be participants in physical activity if they are good at physical activities. Some research support for this position comes from studies that have found that youth who are most active are those who are participants in sport activities (organized sport or less structured activities). Youth who are not participants in sportlike activities are not participating in other kinds of activity. They are just inactive. Likewise, there is some support for the idea that inactive youth become inactive adults and active youth are more likely to be active adults. Additional support for this position comes from research that shows that adult participants have a level of competence in the activities they are participating in and do not participate in those activities for which they are not skilled.

Curriculums for elementary school students in a program with motor skill competence as a primary objective can take many forms, as will be discussed in Chapter 6. The major distinction will lie between those programs that organize the development of motor skill competence in terms of specific skills (overhand throw, tennis forehand, forward roll) and those programs that tend to organize skills by movement concepts or skill themes (throwing, striking, rolling). In both cases the

What motor skills do students need to be able to be a participant in playground activities?
(© *PhotoLink/Getty Images*)

argument for curriculum choices is based on the idea of teaching younger students basic skills and movement abilities that are fundamental to the development of more complex and specific motor skills. In other words, elementary teachers from this perspective want students to be skillful at basic patterns such as the overhand throw pattern, which can then be used in more specific skills such as the tennis or volleyball serve, baseball, or softball. A major assumption of this position is that these fundamental and basic patterns do positively transfer to more specific patterns. Research would support the idea that particular abilities related to these patterns do transfer, which would make learning the more specific pattern easier. However, no one is suggesting that if you can throw a ball overhand you can do a tennis serve.

Competence in motor skills for middle school students usually involves teaching the skills of a variety of basic sport and individual activities and the ability to use them in modified and less complex forms of the sport and activity. As you will see in Chapter 7, middle school level curriculum is made particularly difficult by the idea that this school level is assigned to both developing a variety of activities (breadth) and developing some level of skill in the activities.

Because the high school level program is the last formal instruction in physical activities for many students, for those who think developing motor skills are important, the focus at this level is on developing skills the student can actually use in play and activity settings as a participant outside of physical education class. Most high school curriculum professionals would advocate that

What responsibility does physical education have to developing skills in non-traditional activities?
(© *liquidlibrary/Jupiter images*)

students at this level be given choices of activities and that they be held accountable for developing enough skill in the activity to be a likely participant outside of school in that activity. Choice is important because while most high school students do enjoy physical activity, they do not enjoy the same physical activities.

The national standards published by NASPE (1995, 2004) largely support developing competence in motor skills. The first standard identifies competence in motor skills as a primary objective of programs. Because program time is limited, physical educators who support developing motor skill competence will have to decide on the skills they think are most critical to develop. In the past, most decisions relative to the selection of skills have been based on a preparation for the most popular sport activities of our culture, which tend to be team and international competitive sports. The national standards are inclusive of both traditional sports (team sport and competitive sports) and physical activities that are normally not competitive (backpacking, rock climbing, bicycling) and encourage the development of skills in a broad range of different kinds of activities.

## Position 3: Use Motor Skill Content for Different Educational Goals

Advocates of using physical activity and motor skill content for different educational goals do not begin their search for appropriate curriculum with questions on how to develop a physically active lifestyle. Rather, these educators choose to use the content of physical education to accomplish other goals. Sometimes these cross-curricular approaches take content from each subject area and integrate them. At the elementary school level it is not uncommon for teachers to develop motor content for the primary purpose of either teaching or enhancing academic content (e.g., reading, math). At all school levels some programs are focused not on developing a physically active lifestyle, but on engaging students in learning experiences that involve physical activities that primarily contribute to the personal development of students (e.g., social or emotional development) or cognitive development of students (e.g., learning how to learn).

While it is possible and even desirable to integrate these other ideas into a program that is primarily focused on developing physical activity, what a curriculum designer identifies as a major focus around which a curriculum is constructed is important. While many other goals are shared by other content areas in a school program, physical education programs have a unique responsibility for developing a physically active lifestyle. Programs that choose to use class instructional time to develop other goals and not those unique to physical education do students a disservice.

It is common and desirable for classroom teachers to use motor content to teach academic subject areas. (© *image100/PunchStock*)

# The Physically Active Lifestyle and Fitness Content of Physical Education

The third and fourth national standards identify exhibiting a physically active lifestyle and achieving and maintaining fitness as major goals of a physical education program. Although older and more traditional physical education programs have long claimed these goals as an outcome of their programs, placing them as distinct and unique standards underscores their importance and the need to address them rather specifically.

The standard that identifies *exhibits a physically active lifestyle* as a specific goal (Standard 3) emphasizes the responsibility of physical education programs to actually influence what students do outside of the physical education class. In the past, physical education professionals believed that if they gave students some skills and if they told students how important physical activity was to their well-being, that students would become physically active. It hasn't worked. The idea that programs can develop a physically active lifestyle if they give students motor skills to be physically active and talk to students about how important it is to be physically active is no longer supportable. Teachers must find ways to help students make connections between what they do in and outside of class. We cannot be exclusively concerned with the physically active lifestyle of the student. We will also need to prepare students for an adult life that is physically active.

> ### A Time for Reflection
> A major responsibility of physical education programs is to help students be physically active outside of the class setting. What can you do at the elementary, middle school, and high school levels in your program to facilitate this goal?

As a profession we do not have many identifiable and specific strategies for selecting and organizing learning experiences to impact the physical activity lifestyle issues our programs should be targeting. We will need to begin developing these strategies and determining their effectiveness as a change agent. These ideas will be further addressed in the chapters on the elementary school, middle school, and high school programs.

The fourth national standard identifies achieving and maintaining fitness as a curriculum goal for physical education programs. What our obligation is to fitness and how best to develop fitness is as complex an issue for the curriculum designer as *what motor skills we should teach.* Different perspectives on how best to place fitness in the physical education curriculum are described below.

## The Physical Activity and Physical Training Approaches to Fitness

Few would argue that being fit and staying fit should be a goal for physical education programs. Newer perspectives on being fit emphasize health-related fitness components (body composition, muscular strength and endurance, flexibility, and cardiovascular endurance) that are directly related to health, rather than sport-related physical abilities (e.g., agility, speed). There is little consensus on how best to encourage people to attain and maintain health-related fitness. A *lifestyle* orientation to developing fitness focuses on helping people to lead a physically active lifestyle. The assumption is that if people are physically active at things they like to do, then they will be fit or will become fit and will maintain that fitness over time. A second path to fitness is a *training* perspective, which encourages people to change their level of fitness by teaching them how to directly change each of the components of fitness through specific and prescriptive exercises. Having separate national standards for each of these directions would seem to lead the physical education curriculum planner to an equal responsibility for both (lifestyle and training orientations). Many students and adults resist doing exercises regardless of the health benefits. For these students and adults, finding more enjoyable physical activities will probably be a more successful path to health-related fitness. On the other hand, knowing how to develop fitness components through an exercise prescription model may be an important life skill.

> **A Time for Reflection**
> Think back on your own physical activity patterns as a child and presently. Is a lifestyle or training approach more consistent with what you do?

## Developing and/or Maintaining Fitness

While it would be desirable to think that physical education programs can both develop and maintain the fitness levels of students within the allotted class time, given the time constraints on most programs, it is probably not realistic. Many elementary school programs meet one or two times per week. Few high schools and middle schools have students for long enough periods of time to be able to support the three days a week necessary to achieve a training effect, even if they should choose to use all of their program time to do this. If training and lifestyle approaches to a physically active lifestyle are to be successful than different strategies need to be developed to achieve those goals.

**Treating Fitness as a Health Behavior.**     One orientation to developing and maintaining fitness is for school programs to begin approaching fitness and the maintenance of fitness as a health behavior. A health behavior is something we do almost exclusively to maintain health. Most of us don't brush our teeth because we enjoy it. We probably don't even look forward to it, but, we do it and for the most part do it quite regularly. Although treating fitness as a behavior like brushing your teeth (health behavior) is not limited to a training perspective, it is probably easier to talk about exercise and training programs that you do daily than it is to talk about lifestyle changes. Many lifestyle issues involve activities that we may not do regularly enough to get a training effect that can be maintained over a long period of time. Few of us do anything with the regularity of brushing our teeth.

If we were to take a health behavior perspective toward developing and maintaining fitness we would have to teach for, encourage, and/or provide time in the day for exercise. One perspective would be to provide time during the school day/ workplace for exercise. Schools that have initiated programs of this sort have chosen times at the beginning of the school day, at lunch, at the midpoint of the morning, or in the afternoon. Sometimes the programs are conducted on an all-school basis (over the PA system), and, sometimes each class has its own program. These programs are efficient. Because they are not voluntary, everyone gets a minimum amount of exercise every day.

Most of us don't like being supportive of a health behavior approach to developing fitness because most of us don't like just exercising for the health of it. This is particularly true of children and adolescents. However, because other orientations to developing fitness rely on convincing someone to make it a priority in his or her life, or to set aside time every day to be active, and a health behavior approach makes it an expectation regardless of daily schedule changes, a health behavior orientation may be more successful in getting people to exercise.

**Cognitive Knowledge and Fitness.**   Because people do in part act on what they know, it is important that students be given knowledge on why being physically active is important, the effects of physical activity on the body, and how to be physically active. Research has identified a relationship between what students know about fitness and its importance, and the actual level of student's fitness. At the present time we do not know the strength of this relationship. Recent consensus has suggested that the following areas of knowledge related to fitness be targeted by physical education programs:

- How can I both develop and maintain fitness (all the components of fitness)?
- How can I monitor the development of fitness (all components)?
- How can I develop fitness components in a variety of ways, including both an exercise and lifestyle approach?
- How does physical activity and training affect the body?

More recently it has been suggested that students who are to be fit and physically active will need a knowledge base that goes beyond training. They will also need knowledge about how to lead a physically active lifestyle, such as:

- What activities and opportunities are available in my community to be physically active?
- How do I access community opportunities?
- What abilities and knowledge do I need to be a participant in different activities?
- How are my interests in physical activity likely to change over my lifespan?

**Affective Learning in Fitness.**   Most behavior change experts support the idea that attitudes and dispositions toward a behavior are major contributors to the chances of a person doing something that may be beneficial. But knowledge alone that something is good will not have a major impact on whether a person does what is good for him or her. Professionals who support the position that the physical education curriculum should consist of enjoyable physical activities use this idea for support of their position—if a person enjoys physical activity, he or she will have a disposition to engage in physical activity. Likewise, professionals who emphasize the development of motor skills would say that it is success in motor skill activities that will increase the chances of people being physically active. Both positions on how to increase the likelihood of participation in physical activity acknowledge the role of affective learning.

Acknowledging the role of success and enjoyment in previous movement experiences are not mutually exclusive ideas. Learning to become skillful can and should be an enjoyable experience. Physical educators will have to avoid putting students in experiences that develop negative feelings toward participation.

**Fitness Testing.**   Fitness testing has long been a part of physical education programs. What should be included on a fitness test has changed with different perspectives on what it means to be fit. More recently, fitness tests that have included more sport-related components like agility and sport-specific skills have been replaced with more of an emphasis on health-related fitness (HRF) components (Fitnessgram®). Cardiovascular endurance, muscular strength, muscular endurance, flexibility, and body fat composition are the components of fitness thought to be most related to maintaining health.

The Fitnessgram® test supported by NASPE measures health-related fitness components and sets up a criterion level for each component for different age groups and genders. Some advocates of a more stringent standard for fitness would argue that the level of fitness required by the Fitnessgram® is not high enough. Students who graduate from high school just meeting the Fitnessgram® standard for HRF would not be able to pass entrance exams for physically demanding occupations like being a policeman or fireman, nor would they be able to play most sports on a regular basis. In reality, a very small percentage of today's youth actually meet the standard in all five components.

Although assessing fitness as part of physical education curriculum has been done for a long time, it hasn't always been done in the right way and for the right reasons. Many programs spend an inordinate amount of time in testing only to file the results of the tests away in a file draw never to be seen again. Testing can be made a valuable educational experience. Some of the following ideas highlight a more defensible use of fitness testing:

- Use the process of testing to talk about each of the components of HRF and their importance to health.
- Teach students how each of the components can be developed with both an exercise orientation and a lifestyle orientation.
- Give students feedback on their fitness levels, from which students can receive help to design a personal fitness program.
- Inform parents of the fitness status of their children and what they can do to help their children (and themselves) become fit.
- Identify lifestyle activities that can develop each of the components of fitness.

■ Compare physical activity that discriminates between commercial claims to improve fitness and weight control that does work and those that do not and understand why.

In addition to testing fitness, many programs have moved to assessing students' participation in physical activity. The Activitygram®, also supported by NASPE, uses a student activity log to determine the daily and long-term activity levels of students. The Activitygram® is oriented toward helping students change their lifestyles to include more physical activity. Supporters of Activitygram® would argue that if you change a student's lifestyle to increase his or her level of physical activity, you will improve fitness and perhaps have a longer-lasting effect. The reader will note that while the Fitnessgram® is more associated with a training and exercise orientation toward fitness, the Activitygram® is more associated with a lifestyle orientation toward fitness. Fitness supporters would argue that if students are more fit, they are more likely to be participants. Again, the programs should not be seen as mutually exclusive.

## The Personal Growth Content of Physical Education

When physical education became a school educational program, it adopted an educational perspective with a commitment to developing the *whole child*. Physical education became more *humanistic* in its orientation, moving away from an emphasis on the physical. A whole child perspective on education goals assumes a responsibility for the personal growth of students as well as a responsibility for teaching students the skills and knowledge of a field. The idea of personal growth usually encompasses helping students to develop emotional competency, social competency, and the values and orientations of the community. In curriculum, we usually lump all of these goals into one category called affective goals. The personal growth and social development of students is largely about developing character. Parents and teachers want students to acquire those values more generally referred to as those of a "good person" and "good citizen." You want students to be confident, honest, and caring people who have the ability to work hard to achieve personal goals and to work with others in positive ways to achieve group goals.

The national standards talk about these ideas in terms of responsible personal and social behavior, respecting both self and others. Although the national standards frame these ideas in the context of physical activity settings, the intent of most physical educators when they work with children and youth is to have these ideas transfer to situations outside of the gymnasium. You don't just want your students to respect others inside of the gym. You want them to respect others as part of their character wherever they go. You don't just want them to work hard and put forth effort in improving their fitness, you want them to learn to achieve goals through hard work as part of their life.

Participation in physical activity, particularly sports, has provided many people with a mechanism for developing these characteristics. While participation in sports has had a profound positive influence on many people, it also has great potential for just the opposite. The effect of sport participation on the development of positive character depends largely on the leadership children and youth are provided in these settings.

> **A Time for Reflection**
> Many of you have been involved in sport experiences both in and outside of school. What positive and negative effects have these experiences had on your personal development and your perspectives on participation? Why? What does this mean to you as a physical education professional?

The issues surrounding this goal orientation of physical education largely revolve around two important decisions teachers have to make. The first is whether affective goals and objectives are *the* primary orientation of your program. That is, do you teach affective kinds of behaviors as your curriculum and use other program goals such as fitness, lifetime physical activity, and movement skills to accomplish the affective goals? As you will see in upcoming chapters, some physical educators see the responsibility for the personal growth of students as the major responsibility of physical education. Educators who take this perspective will organize their physical education curriculum around affective goals, which means they will choose content that allows them to best teach these goals.

A second decision that teachers have to make in regard to affective goals is to decide on the specific affective goals that should be part of the program. What values, attitudes, and affective behaviors do you want to teach? Although there probably is more consensus than most realize, moving beyond general statements of personal responsibility and social development can sometimes be a daunting task for teachers. Helping students transfer ideas of cooperation from the gymnasium to outside the gymnasium can be even more difficult.

## Quality of Life Issues

In recent times, most of the support we have received for physical education programs has come from our contribution to the physical health of students. However, there is a broader perspective that acknowledges a quality of life contribution that is just as important. A physically active lifestyle can make a major contribution to the quality of life of students as well. Students and adults who are healthy and who have the skills, knowledge, and dispositions to lead a physically active life have a far greater potential to enjoy life and be active participants in our culture. Being a participant in physical activity creates many opportunities to participate with others and develop unique personal goals and interests.

The national standards (NASPE, 2004) acknowledge this broader contribution of physical activity to the quality of life in the sixth standard, which describes opportunities for enjoyment, challenge, self-expression, and social interaction. Participating in physical activity not only makes us healthy, it gives us the opportunity to participate in activities that are fun and bring pleasure to our lives. It provides opportunities to challenge our physical abilities and to find an outlet to express ourselves through physical movement. It gives us opportunities to participate with others in social experiences. Daryl Siedentop acknowledges this perspective when he talks about physical education as play education (Siedentop, 2007). From his perspective it is important that people play and be given the skills to play.

Over the years we have learned to understand that different people will enjoy different kinds of physical activities for very different reasons. While some people enjoy the physical contact that comes from contact sports, others enjoy the opportunity to express themselves through dance activities. For others, jogging not only contributes to their level of fitness, it also brings them pleasure. Many physical education programs have begun to look at ways to meet the very diverse needs and interests of students for participation. While team sports have dominated many programs, a large percentage of students do not enjoy team sports and will be better served by expanding curriculums to develop skills in other types of movement experiences they would be more likely to use as adults.

---

**A Time for Reflection**

Which of the reasons for participation identified in the sixth national standard motivates you to be a participant? What kinds of activities do you most enjoy and why?

---

How to meet the diverse needs and interests of students for different kinds of physical activities is likely to be one of the biggest challenges faced by physical educators in curriculum design. There are many issues you will have to resolve, including the following:

- Do I meet the present needs and interests of students or prepare them for changes in those interests as they get older?
- Do I *expose* all students to many different kinds of activities or let them choose the activities most of interest to them?
- What basic skills do students need at early ages to prepare them for diverse types of activity?
- Do all activities have to contribute to physical health?
- What role does the local culture of the community play in the activities I choose to include in my program?

All of these issues will be explored as you begin to think about designing your curriculum for different school levels. They are not easy decisions but need to be addressed.

## Focusing on Lifestyle Issues

It should come as no surprise from the previous discussions in this chapter that one of the major changes in physical education curriculum in recent times has been on finding ways to develop a physically active lifestyle for students and measuring our success by the extent to which adults lead a physically active lifestyle. We can no longer assume that if we give students the skills for participation, if we give them the knowledge they need about how to do something, and if we talk to them about how important it is to be physically active, that they will be physically active. Physical education programs must find ways to increase the chances that students will actually be participants in physical activity outside of our classes. We need to find ways to ensure that physical activity is built into the lifestyle of our students.

## Connecting Physical Education to the Community

One of the biggest changes that must take place in our programs if we are serious about lifestyle issues is to connect physical education programs in schools and physical educators with community opportunities for participation. Students need to learn about opportunities for participation, both as students as well as the opportunities available for adults. If we are serious about this goal, even units of work in sports like basketball would need to be taught so that students learn that there are many adults still playing basketball and that there are many leagues and recreational opportunities available for their own participation. Students need information on how to access those opportunities and how to safely participate in those activities. The easier the physical education teacher makes it for a student to become a participant in outside class activities, and the more the teacher makes it an expectation to be a participant outside of the physical education class, the greater the chance that the teacher will be successful in getting students to be physically active outside of class.

## Developing and Rewarding Lifestyle Changes

Although most of our discussion about a physically active lifestyle has revolved around the notion of getting students and adults to be participants in physical activities most associated with sport and play, physical educators will also want to help students choose to be physically active in the manner in which they go about their daily life. Most of our technology has been designed to make life tasks physically easier. While it may be unpopular to suggest that we choose a way to conduct our lives that is physically more difficult, it may be important for us to consider the potential of such a position.

We have participants taking the elevator to the gym and spending 10 minutes searching for the closest parking space at the tennis courts. Physical activity does not have to be formal and organized or even an activity we do just to be physically active. As adult lives become more complex, it is more and more difficult for people to take time out just to be physically active. Making students aware that they can choose to be physically active through lifestyle changes and decisions they make in daily routines, and rewarding students when they make those changes, is an important part of programs that want to affect physical activity. Throwing away all the remotes, taking the stairs rather than the elevator, deliberately parking further away from where you are going, selecting a push rather than a riding lawnmower, getting a dog that needs to be walked every night, saying yes when a parent asks you to help with a physical task, requires a paradigm change from focusing on how to make life less physically demanding to how to increase opportunities to be physically active. Like all paradigm changes it will take time to change an established mind-set.

## Check Your Understanding

1. Why is developing a physically active lifestyle important?
2. How does each of the national standards contribute to developing a physically active lifestyle?
3. What are the major curricular alternatives advocated for developing a physically active lifestyle?

## References

U.S. Department of Health and Human Services, Centers for Disease Control and Prevention. (1997). Guidelines for School and Community Programs to Promote Lifelong Physical Activity Among Young People. *Morbidity and Mortality Weekly Report, 46,* No. RR–6.

NASPE (1992). Outcomes of Quality Physical Education Programs. Reston, VA: National Association for Sport and Physical Education.

NASPE (2004). *Moving into the Future: National Standards for Physical Education.* (2nd ed.) Reston, VA: NASPE.

Siedentop, D. (2007). *Introduction to Physical Education, Fitness and Sport.* Boston: McGraw-Hill.

## Suggested Reading

Cothran, D., & Ennis, C. (2001). "Nobody Said Anything about Learning Stuff: Students, Teachers, and Curriculum Change." *Journal of Classroom Interaction, 36,*1, 1–5.

Corbin, C., Dale, D., & Pangrazzi, R. (1999). "Promoting Physically Active Lifestyles Among Youths." *JOPERD, 70,* no. 6, 26–28.

McKenzie, T. (1999). "School Health-related Physical Activity Programs: What Do the Data Say?" *JOPERD, 70,* no.1, 16–20.

U.S. Department of Health and Human Services. (2000). *Healthy People 2010: Understanding and Improving Health.* Washington, DC: Government Printing Office.

# CHAPTER 3

# The Process of Designing the Curriculum

The purpose of this chapter is to help you design curriculum by giving you a process to do so using the national standards or a set of other standards as basis for your work. In this chapter you will learn why long-range curriculum planning is important and you will be able to identify the essential parts of a curriculum guide and what needs to be included in each part.

## OUTCOMES

- Distinguish the task of curriculum planning from unit and lesson planning.
- Identify the parts of a good curriculum guide and what should be in each part.
- Explain the role of context in making curriculum decisions.
- Identify the characteristics of a good curriculum guide in terms of the relationships between the parts.

In today's educational climate, a lot of the decisions about what students should learn in a program are being guided by work at the national and state levels. These guidelines are in the form of national and state standards that describe program outcomes. It is still the responsibility of individual districts and schools to design a program to achieve those outcomes.

Good curriculums take time to plan and are collaborative efforts. (© *Ryan McVay/ Getty Images*)

Curriculum design is a process of thinking through how you want to organize what you want students to learn. Whereas lesson plans are what the teacher plans to do for the day and unit plans are what the teacher wants to do over several lessons or weeks, curriculum plans should be what the teacher wants students to learn over years. Sometimes teachers do yearly plans for a grade level that describe what students in a particular grade will learn over a year's time. These yearly plans can be separate documents from the curriculum guide or part of the curriculum guide. This relationship is described below:

| | |
| --- | --- |
| **Levels of Planning** | |
| *Curriculum:* | A plan for grades K–12, K–5, 6–8, or 9–12. |
| *Yearly Plan:* | A plan for a grade level over a year's time that describes the distribution of units over the year. |
| *Unit Plan:* | A plan for a series of lessons in the same content area. |
| *Lesson Plan:* | A plan for a lesson. |

Theoretically, teachers at all school levels should coordinate their plans to develop a K–12 perspective for their physical education curriculums, which means that there should be a coordinated district plan for a K–12 physical education program. Sometimes the district plan is broader in scope and lacks specifics, which are then left to school levels or individual schools. More often physical education curriculums are planned for a school level (elementary, middle, and high school). In most school districts that means that the elementary curriculum is planned for grades K–5, the middle school curriculum for grades 6–8 (or sometimes junior high school grades 7–9), and the high school curriculum for grades 9–12.

Planning should begin with decisions about the curriculum. All other levels of planning should then be consistent with the curriculum decisions that are made. Curriculum planning is one of the most important and perhaps most neglected responsibilities of the physical education teacher. Finding time to chart a course and struggling with big issues involved in the curriculum decision-making process is not easy. Not finding the time is the equivalency of embarking on a trip without really knowing where you are going. One reason that curriculum planning is important is because it makes yearly, lesson, and unit planning easier. The more elaborate the curriculum plan the less time we have to spend deciding what it is that we want to teach today or next month. A more important reason for curriculum planning to be done well is that it puts all those lessons and units into a perspective that makes explicit why we want students to experience particular content. In this respect it acts as a rudder, setting the direction to a larger goal.

## The Curriculum Guide

Most practitioners will be involved in a curriculum project that asks them to develop a curriculum document that is a course of study for their subject area. Often this document is called a *curriculum guide*. The curriculum guide usually includes the following:

1.  A statement of philosophy that describes the purpose of your program and the rationale for including your program in the school curriculum.
2.  The *specific goals of your program* drawn from your philosophy and your understanding of students that describe the skills, knowledge, and dispositions you want your students to have when they leave your program.
3.  A *sequence of performance indicators/objectives/outcomes* by grade level that take the learner from where they are at the beginning of your program to the specific goals you have established for the end of your program.
4.  A *content framework* that organizes your program objectives by content area into units or themes and describes what will be taught in each grade.
5.  A *yearly block plan* for a grade level that describes what content area will be taught and when throughout the school year.
6.  An assessment plan that will be used to determine if the program goals have been achieved (Chapter 9).

Education programs have an intent, which means that educational experiences are selected to accomplish specific purposes that are identified as outcomes ahead of time. A lot of the work developing a curriculum guide involves specifying program outcomes at different levels of specificity, beginning with program purposes that are broad, general statements about what a program should accomplish, and ending with specific objectives for units of instruction that are actually measurable. These levels of intent should be consistent with each other, meaning that if you have a purpose, the objectives that you select for your units of instruction should be consistent with that purpose. *Consistency* in all levels of the curriculum plan is one of the most difficult and one of the most important characteristics of a good curriculum. Physical educators often identify lofty purposes for their programs, but identify goals for their programs and write objectives for their units that would not accomplish those purposes.

Most schools are asked to use a set of national and/or state standards to plan and conduct their programs. The national and state standards provide the teacher with a set of outcomes that should be achieved at the end of a program. They also describe the outcomes or a description of the content that should be achieved at the end of selected grade levels in the curriculum. Most state standards use the national standards either exclusively or in some variation. It is important to realize that standards are not curriculum. These materials provide the teacher with a good base, describing outcomes for a program without dictating the way to get there. The curriculum guide that you develop will be a plan for how you get there. As each of the curriculum guide sections is discussed below, a special emphasis will be placed on how to use the national standards (or state standards) to develop your curriculum.

## Step 1: Developing a Philosophy Statement

**What are the purposes of my program?**

**Why do I think these purposes are worth including in the school program?**

**How are these purposes best accomplished in the context of my school with my students?**

The philosophy statement of the curriculum should describe the purposes of your program and defend those purposes in terms of their inclusion as a school program. The previous chapter introduced many diverse positions on what is most important for physical education to accomplish as a school program. The philosophy statement of the curriculum document requires that teachers designing the curriculum take a position on those issues. In this respect a planned curriculum represents a value position. The curriculum plan selects from all those potential program purposes those that are actually going to be achieved in a specific program. What should be included in a philosophy statement is described below:

---

**The Philosophy Statement**

Should include:

- What you think the purposes of your program are.

- Why you think these purposes are worth including in a school program.

- How you think these purposes are best accomplished in the context of your school with your students.

A sample statement of philosophy and program aims is described in Appendix A.

---

> **A Time for Reflection**
>
> Although you will probably modify and further develop your philosophy statement many times in your career, you should begin to think through the answers to the questions above. Write a brief philosophy statement using the statement in Appendix A as a guide. It is not important that you agree with the philosophy statement in the text. What is important is that you are clear on what you believe to be important, can defend what you say, and can designate a program that is consistent with your beliefs.

Although there is no right or wrong position in terms of these issues, where there is national or state consensus on what should be taught in a program, teachers are normally obligated to work within that framework. In today's education climate, teachers are expected to teach toward the national or state standards and accept the idea that developing a physically active lifestyle is the major goal of a good physical education program.

**The Statement of Philosophy and the National Standards.**   The purpose of physical education as described in the national standards is to *develop a physically active lifestyle* (2004). If you support this idea as the major goal of your program, you will then have to describe in your philosophy statement why you think developing a physically active lifestyle is an important goal for your school program. Rationale and support for this goal is now abundant in the literature and revolves around several factors:

■   Next to smoking, lack of physical activity is now the single most prevalent cause of chronic disease.

■   Physical education programs are the only programs in the school curriculum that have this goal as the primary goal.

■   The school physical education program is required and will reach all children over their developing years.

■   Education for a lifetime of physical activity requires the development of skills, attitudes, and knowledge.

Although the rationale described above should be sufficient to justify your program's inclusion in the school curriculum, a concern for competence in the academic areas now dominants the criteria for inclusion and support used in many schools. Teachers may want to add to their rationale:

■   Students who achieve more academically are more fit.

■   Students learn better when they are healthy.

When you accept developing a physically active lifestyle and the state or national standards as the purposes of your program, you will also have to take a position on how those purposes are best accomplished in the context of your school and your students. You will need to describe what you consider to be the best way to give students the skills, knowledge, and dispositions they need to lead a physically active lifestyle. Your perspective on how to accomplish the purposes of your program is an opportunity for you to describe your approach to the content of physical education and how to organize the content of your program to accomplish your purpose(s).

Your statement of philosophy should also describe your approach to developing a physically active lifestyle. You will want to take a position on many of the issues described in Chapter 2 on how best to develop a physically active life style, such as:

- What is the role of skill development in motor skills?
- What is your approach to fitness and lifestyle issues?
  - ☐ Physical training
  - ☐ Lifestyle approaches
  - ☐ Developing fitness
  - ☐ Maintaining fitness
  - ☐ Affective dispositions
- How much and what kind of knowledge do students need?
- What is physical education's contribution to the personal development of students?
- Is your approach to physical education a health approach or quality of life issue?
- How much responsibility do you want to take for what students do outside of the physical education class?

**Context-Specific Factors in Long-Term Planning.**   Sometimes context-specific factors are included as a separate section of your guide and sometimes they will be incorporated in the philosophy section or goals section of your guide. In this section you will include factors specific to the needs and interests of the students in your situation. You need to have a clear idea of where your students are, where you want them to be, and how best to get them there. You will want to consider students':

- Prior experiences.
- Social and cultural backgrounds.
- Ability in the content you want to teach.
- Interests.

You can obtain this information from a variety of sources, including student records; information on the school available from the state department of education; teachers who have worked with students prior to you teaching them, including teachers at other school levels; and student surveys that you do with your students.

You will also want to consider the context of your teaching situation in terms of the amount of time that you have with students in your program and what you can realistically accomplish in that amount of time. You may want to do all that the national standards say a good program should do, but realistically you do not have the time to meet these standards. One of the more difficult decisions that teachers have to make is to prioritize what they think is the most important to do given limited program time. The decision oftentimes involves having to choose between good alternatives and having to decide between doing a few things really well or many things with a limited level of achievement. Your philosophy statement should articulate these decisions and all of these issues will be important to resolve before you determine what the goals are for your program and how you intend to develop those goals in your program.

## Step 2: Developing the Goals of Your Program

**What should students know and be able to do as a result of (at the end of) my program?**

The goals for your program are what you expect students to know and be able to do as a result of your program. They are the exit outcomes of your program. They should describe the skills, knowledge, and dispositions that you want your students to have when they leave your program and outcomes that you think you can reach with *every* student. The idea of every student is important here because there is a tendency to write goals that are directional or "lofty" that perhaps only a few students in your program can accomplish. The idea of every student commits you to writing goals that you think you can get every student to reach.

The best situation would be for goals to be written for a K–12 curriculum, in which case they would describe what students should be able to do when they leave high school. If your curriculum is being written for an elementary or middle school program, the specific goals should describe what students should be able to do when they leave the fifth grade or eighth grade, or the last grade for which your school is responsible.

*Examples:*

*High School:* Students should be competent in at least two different movement activities.

*Middle School:* Students should be able to keep a ball going back and forth across the net in a net game.

*Elementary School:* Students should be able to demonstrate mature form in several throwing and striking patterns.

The level of goal specificity is sometimes problematic. While it is important to get as specific as you can, you don't want to end up with endless lists of goals that make planning difficult and lose the meaning of what you are trying to do. Most goals are not written in a form that can be measured directly. That means that you cannot measure competence in two movement activities without first knowing what those movement activities might be and defining what competence might be in that activity. You cannot measure whether a student can keep a ball going back and forth with a partner in a net activity without knowing what net activity you are referring to. Writing goals at this level of specificity has both advantages and disadvantages. The advantage is that it provides a framework for what you will do at each grade level leading up to the outcome without tying you into accomplishing the goal in a narrow way. Broader goals are useful when curriculums are written for more than one school because they allow teachers to accomplish goals in different ways. For example, a program can include lots of different movement activities in the high school curriculum but expects competence in only two. Different schools can decide what those two movement forms should be. The disadvantage of a broader level of specificity is that it puts off decisions as to exactly what content to include and how to measure those outcomes for the next level of planning.

**Developing Goals Using the National Standards.**    When you are using the national standards for a K–12 program, your specific goals are the national standards. These are the outcomes of your program.

> *Standard 1:* Demonstrates *competency* in motor skills and movement patterns to perform a variety of physical activities.
>
> *Standard 2:* Demonstrates understanding of movement concepts, principles, strategies, and tactics as they apply to the learning and performance of physical activities.
>
> *Standard 3:* Participates regularly in physical activity.
>
> *Standard 4:* Achieves and maintains a health-enhancing level of physical fitness.
>
> *Standard 5:* Exhibits responsible personal and social behavior that respects self and others in physical activity settings.
>
> *Standard 6:* Values physical activity for health, enjoyment, challenge, self-expression, and/or social interaction.

You will want to decide on:

- The most important goals to achieve in physical education.
- Whether or not you want to add any additional goals.
- Whether or not these goals are achievable for your program.
- Whether you think these goals need to be modified to meet the unique needs of your students.

The national standards are exit goals for a high school program. If you are writing your curriculum for the middle school or elementary school level, you would have to decide how far you think you can get in your program at your level toward the accomplishment of these goals. The material written in the standards text for each grade level will help you make these decisions. The exit goals for a K–5 elementary program would be those appropriate for the end of the fifth grade. The exit goals for a 6–8 middle school program would be those appropriate for the end of the eighth grade.

## Step 3: Selecting and Sequencing Objectives/Outcomes for Grade Levels

**What objectives should students meet at the end of each grade level that will take me to my goals?**

Once you have decided on the goals for your program, which are exit outcomes for the end of your program, you will have to sequence objectives that will take you to those outcomes. For instance, if you want fifth graders to be able to strike a ball back and forth with a racket and a partner over a low net without losing control, what does that mean students in your kindergarten should be doing? The following sequence of objectives is one perspective on what a progression of goals over K–5 grades might look like for the outcome: *With a partner, continuously strike a small ball back and forth with a racket over a low net without losing control.*

> *Kindergarten:* Strike a balloon to keep it up in the air without it hitting the ground.
> *First Grade:* Strike a large light ball against the wall with the hand continuously in control.
> *Second Grade:* Strike a balloon with a paddle to keep it up in the air without it hitting the ground.
> *Third Grade:* Tap a small ball up in the air and down continuously with a racket without losing control.
> *Fourth Grade:* Tap a small ball continuously against the wall with a racket without losing control.
> *Fifth Grade:* With a partner, continuously strike a small ball back and forth with a racket over a low net without losing control.

A high school goal might be that students should participate in physical activity on a regular basis by the time they graduate from high school. If you were planning a K–12 program, what do you think a good outcome for kindergarten should be in relation to this goal? If you were planning just the high school program, what should the ninth graders be able to do in respect to this outcome?

At this level of planning you are asked to describe the outcomes by grade level that will take you to your goals. If you are working with a K–12 program and you want students to be competent at movement activities, then you might think about these ideas as outcomes for different grade levels that would lead you to students being competent at movement activities. The following examples for a few grade levels illustrate the point:

*Kindergarten:* Use fundamental locomotor patterns in open ways by changing the direction, level, force, pathway, and body/space relationships of the pattern.

*Fourth Grade:* Demonstrate mature form in a variety of receiving and sending actions used in both team and individual sport activities.

*Seventh Grade:* Demonstrate competence in the specific patterns of movement activities and sports in modified situations.

If at the high school level you wanted students to be able to design a personal fitness program, you might think about these ideas as appropriate objectives for grade levels that precede the high school.

*First Grade:* Identify a variety of sport and lifestyle activities that make your heart beat faster.

*Third Grade:* Identify at least one exercise or activity that can be used to develop each of the fitness components.

*Seventh Grade:* Interpret a personal level of fitness based on fitness scores and logs of physical activity kept over a period of time.

In each of these examples you are asked to identify what you think students need to know and be able to do through each grade level in order for students to reach your goal at the end of the curriculum. In this sense, the sequence of objectives represents a sequence of objectives for a year for a grade level for a particular goal. When you have finished you should be able to see a plan for accomplishing your goal that is sequenced across grade levels. (See Box 3.1.)

Sometimes this section of the curriculum document is called a *scope and sequence* of content. When it is done appropriately it should result in a chart that describes the objectives for how to achieve each goal across the top (columns) and all of the objectives for a grade level going down (rows). When the scope and sequence of objectives is done well, the objectives across the grade levels are progressive, achievable, and developmentally appropriate for the students at each grade level.

**Sequencing Your Outcomes by Grade Level Using the National Standards.**   If you are using the national standards as your source for grade level objectives, the grade level objectives will be either:

■  The emphases and sample benchmarks for each grade level as described in the 1995 version of the standards;

■  The sample outcomes as described in the 2004 version of the standards;

■  The performance indicators as described in the assessment materials designed for the national standards; or

■  What you think is the most important for students to learn in this grade consistent with the standards you have adopted or adapted.

## Box 3.1  Planning Objectives for a Goal Across Grade Levels

# Goal: Participate Regularly in Physical Activity

**Kindergarten Objectives:**

Identify the effects of vigorous activity on the speed of your heart and breathing.

Identify activities that make your heart beat faster.

Do something after school that makes your heart beat faster.

Do something at recess that makes your heart beat faster.

**First-Grade Objectives:**

Identify muscular strength as a component of being healthy.

Identify the activities that make you strong.

Identify activities you like to do that are physically active.

Identify lifestyle activities that you like to do that are physically active.

Participate in physical activity at recess and after school.

**Second-Grade Objectives:**

Identify the components of fitness and why they are important to being physically active.

Identify activities you like to do that are physically active.

Identify lifestyle activities that you like to do that are physically active.

Participate in physical activity at recess and after school.

Identify someone you know who is not physically active and do something physically active with them.

Select a skill to improve and do it on a regular basis to get better.

**Third-Grade Objectives:**

Describe the health benefits of being physically active.

Explore and select a community activity that involves physical activity.

Identify at least one physical activity associated with each component of fitness.

Identify the physical activities that are most enjoyable.

Participate in physical activity at recess and after school.

Change one lifestyle pattern to improve physical activity.

**Fourth-Grade Objectives:**

Identify several exercises and lifestyle activities associated with each component of fitness.

Match each item on a fitness test to a fitness component.

Participate in a physical activity outside of school on a regular basis.

Change one lifestyle pattern to improve physical activity.

**Fifth-Grade Objectives:**

Use personal fitness data to determine a personal level of fitness.

Identify several ways (exercise as well as other physical activities) that can be used to develop a component of fitness.

Identify a physical activity or sport to get better at.

Participate in a physical activity outside of school on a regular basis.

Change one lifestyle pattern to improve physical activity.

**Sixth-Grade Objectives:**

Identify opportunities in the school and community for physical activity.

Select a fitness component for improvement and develop a plan to improve that component.

Keep a personal log of activity patterns for a week.

Participate in an organized activity that is physically active.

*(continued on next page)*

*(continued from previous page)*

**Seventh-Grade Objectives:**

Select a fitness component for improvement and develop a plan to improve that component.

Keep a personal log of activity patterns for a week and evaluate personal physical activity participation.

Participate in an organized activity that is physically active.

Determine personal interests in physical activity.

**Eighth-Grade Objectives:**

Identify long-term benefits of physical activity.

Set personal fitness goals with the help of the teacher and determine a plan to achieve those goals using both exercise and lifestyle activities.

Participate in an organized activity that is physically active.

**High School Objectives:**

Know how and where to access opportunities for participation in physical activity in the community.

Demonstrate the etiquette of participation in a variety of activities.

Be able to select equipment and know how to participate safely in a variety of physical activities.

Independently assess personal fitness, set personal fitness goals, and develop a plan to achieve those goals.

Identify the physical components (fitness) necessary for participation in a variety of activities.

Participate in an organized activity that is physically active.

Identify one lifestyle change that has been made to increase physical activity.

Examples of grade level objectives for Standard 1 and Standard 3, indicating the level of specificity needed to describe outcomes by one grade level and two standards, are described below:

**Examples of Grade Level Objectives for Standard 1 and Standard 3**

*Standard 1: Demonstrates competency in motor skills and movement patterns to perform a variety of physical activities.*

**Second-Grade Objectives:**

Demonstrate mature form in skipping, hopping, galloping, and sliding.
Combine locomotor patterns in time with music.
Combine traveling, balancing, and rolling into a smooth sequence.
Toss and catch a small ball.
Strike a ball into the air consecutively with a paddle.

*Standard 3: Participates regularly in physical activity.*

**Eighth-Grade Objectives:**

Identify personal goals for participation in physical activity.
Participate regularly in some kind of physical activity.
Participate in one new activity outside of physical education class.

Establishing objectives related to your program goals (standards) for each grade level is a very critical step in curriculum design. When you have finished you should have a set of objectives under each one of your goals for each grade level. This set of objectives is what you hope to accomplish in a year's program. If you have done

## Box 3.2   Second-Grade Program Objectives

**Standard One:**

Demonstrate mature form in locomotor skills.

Demonstrate smooth transitions between combinations of movements (locomotor skills and manipulative patterns).

Use movement concepts to vary patterns.

**Standard Two:**

Use feedback to improve performance.

Identify the critical elements of basic movement patterns.

Apply movement concepts to a variety of basic skills.

**Standard Three:**

Experience and express pleasure in physical activity.

**Standard Four:**

Engage in sustained physical activity that causes an increased heart rate and heavy breathing

Recognize the physiological signs of moderate to heavy physical activity.

**Standard Five:**

Work cooperatively with another to complete an assigned task.

Apply rules, procedures, and safe practices with little or no reinforcement.

Play and cooperate with others regardless of personal differences.

**Standard Six:**

Try new activities.

---

your work carefully, this set of objectives should represent a *developmental plan* for accomplishing each standard across the grades in your program. When you have finished, the product should be developmentally sound, which means that the outcomes should be appropriate outcomes for a grade level, and the process of achieving those outcomes from one year to the next should lead to achievement of your goals/standards. An example of a set of objectives across standards is provided in Box 3.2.

### Step 4: Selecting an Organizing Framework for Your Content

**How can I best conceptually organize the content of my program?**

Once you have determined what you want students at each grade level to do in relation to your goals, you will want to select an organizing framework that you think best facilitates the delivery of that content. An *organizing framework,* sometimes called a content framework, is a conceptual scheme to organize the objectives that you have for your program by content area into units or themes. In this step of designing your curriculum, you will place your grade level objectives into the content framework used for a grade level. Different programs will be comfortable with different content frameworks for organizing their curriculums.

In one sense the organizing framework is a way to help you describe what you will name your units of instruction. Often the content of physical education is organized into a framework at two levels. The first level is broader and describes the *kinds* of units that will be included. The second level describes the units or themes that will be taught under each larger heading. The following examples in Box 3.3 describe frameworks that utilize two levels of specificity for the elementary, middle, and high school level. For example, the first level at the high school

## Box 3.3 Organizing Frameworks for Curriculum—Sample Units*

| High School Framework | Middle School Framework | Elementary School Framework |
|---|---|---|
| **Team Sports**<br>■ Basketball<br>■ Volleyball<br>■ Soccer<br>■ Lacrosse<br>**Individual Sports**<br>■ Tennis<br>■ Golf<br>■ Bowling<br>■ Archery<br>**Individual Activities**<br>■ Rock climbing<br>■ Canoeing<br>■ Tai Chi<br>**Aquatics**<br>■ Intermediate swimming<br>**Fitness**<br>■ Weight training<br>■ Aerobic dance<br>**Dance**<br>■ Line dance<br>■ Social dance | **Net Activities**<br>■ Pickle ball<br>■ Tennis<br>■ Volleyball<br>**Invasion Games**<br>■ Ultimate Frisbee<br>■ Basketball<br>■ Soccer<br>**Individual Activities**<br>■ Project Adventure<br>**Individual Sports**<br>■ Archery<br>■ Golf<br>**Dance**<br>**Aquatics**<br>**Fitness** | **Locomotion**<br>■ Traveling on the feet<br>■ Combining patterns<br>■ Using locomotor patterns with other skills<br>**Educational Games**<br>■ Tossing and catching<br>■ Striking with a paddle<br>■ Soccer<br>**Educational Dance**<br>■ Locomotor patterns to different rhythms<br>■ Contrasting quick and slow movement<br>■ Folk dance<br>**Educational Gymnastics**<br>■ Traveling on different body parts<br>■ Balancing in different ways<br>■ Rolling<br>■ Combining traveling, balancing, and rolling<br>**Fitness and Physical Activity**<br>■ Identifying components of fitness<br>■ Awareness of personal preferences |

*The units identified under each broad content area are not meant to be inclusive, but rather samples of units that might be taught under a particular heading.

level would be team sports and the second level basketball. The first level at the elementary level would be locomotion and the second level traveling on the feet.

Most high school curriculums and many middle school curriculums use some variation of an activity framework to organize their content. At these school levels the teacher decides which content units will be taught at which grade levels. There is far more variation in the type of framework used at the elementary level. Because of the great variation in the needs of kindergarten students and fifth-grade students, the framework may change for different grade levels. For instance, in the example above it would not be appropriate to include locomotion as a content area for fifth graders but it might be appropriate to begin to teach skills for specific sports such as basketball. Later chapters in this text will help you sort out the options that you have for selecting a framework for different school levels.

## Box 3.4   Content Framework for Second Grade

**Locomotion**

Develop mature patterns and combinations of patterns in all locomotor skills.

**Educational Gymnastics**

Combine balancing and traveling actions.

Change the dynamics of rolling (speed/direction/body shape, etc.).

Move onto and off of small apparatus using different parts of the body.

**Educational Dance**

Contrast quick and slow movements.

Use a variety of body parts to link movements.

Use changes of body shape in sequences.

Create short sequences of action words with a partner.

Perform simple group dances with a partner.

**Educational Games**

Throw a ball for distance using a mature pattern.

Toss and catch with a partner.

Strike a ball with a paddle/bat/club for control.

Kick a stationary ball for a distance.

---

The content framework for a grade level should reflect the content framework that you will use for your entire program. The content framework for a year's program will actually represent the units that you teach in that year for a grade level. Box 3.4 describes a content framework for second grade. You will notice that the teacher has decided to teach 13 units during this school year represented in four different content areas.

## Step 5: Developing a Yearly Block Plan

**How long will it take me to accomplish the objectives I have for this unit?**

**When in the school year is the best time to teach this unit?**

Once you have decided on the units that you will teach and have placed your objectives in your units, you will need to decide when you will teach these units over the school year and for how long you will teach each unit. This decision should be made relative to the questions:

- How long will it take me to accomplish the objectives I have for this unit?
- When in the school year is the best time to teach this unit?
  - ☐ How can this unit be scheduled with other units other teachers in the program might be teaching?
  - ☐ Where should this unit be placed relative to other units in the yearly program?

The *yearly block plan* describes the units you will teach at what times during the school year for a particular grade. You will need to look at the objectives that have been drawn directly from program goals as well as any additional and more specific objectives you may have for a unit and decide how much time it will take for all students to learn these objectives. You will also have to decide where to best place this unit in the school year.

**How Much Time Do You Need?**    One of the more difficult decisions to make in designing a yearly program is to make a decision about how much time it takes for students to really learn the content we want them to learn. There is more and more evidence from research both in the academic areas as well as in physical education that we are simply underestimating how long it takes for us to get all students to meet the objectives that we have for them. Learning is produced with repetition and overlearning. Consider for example how many times a student has to throw and catch a ball before he or she can be considered competent at throwing and catching a ball. Learning is a relatively permanent change in behavior. Seeing students do something once does not mean that they have really learned what we want them to learn even though their performance at that time may be considered acceptable. If you come back after some time has passed and students still can exhibit the behavior you want them to learn, then you can be better assured that they have learned it. Building repetition and overlearning opportunities into your units adds time to the length of those units. Elementary programs may consider recycling units or revisiting units so that students may experience skills such as throwing or catching several times during the school year.

When students don't learn because you have not planned enough time to learn, you either have to change your objectives for your unit or change the amount of time you are willing to devote to that content. If, for instance, you planned on taking your eighth-grade middle school students to a level where they can *use a zone defense in a three-on-three basketball game* and you don't have time in your unit to get to that objective, then you may have to revise your unit objectives. What you can accomplish in your eighth-grade unit also has great implications for the ninth-grade program that may be anticipating receiving students with particular skills. If you find yourself increasing the amount of time you need in your units, you may have to go back to your curriculum framework and eliminate some units and objectives from your program.

**Where to Place a Unit in the School Year.**    The yearly block plan also requires you to decide where in the school year you will place your unit. Many factors are considered in placing a unit, including those related to the seasons and weather in a particular area, the availability of equipment and facilities, holidays, community and school events, and school schedules.

*Seasonal and Weather Conditions.*    Many units like soccer or Project Adventure will need to be taught outside. In more northern parts of the country, the time you can go outside in the school year is reserved for the fall and spring. In some southern states the time you can go outside and participate hard in physical activity is reserved for the winter because it is too hot at other times of year. Some geographical locations have a rainy season. All of these factors need to be considered when you teach a unit.

*Availability of Equipment and Facilities.*    Some school districts share large equipment between schools. For instance, gymnastics equipment may only be available for a particular time in the school year, making the choice of when to teach that unit limited. Teachers who work in a department with other teachers will have to work out a schedule for who will teach an activity and where it will be taught. Indoor teaching stations are often at a premium, particularly in large schools and middle schools. Making the best use of the teaching stations that you do have requires some long-term planning and organization so that the indoor stations don't sit empty for parts of the year and are overcrowded during other parts of the year. Some activities require very specialized space and others have more flexible requirements.

***Holidays and Community Events.***   Holidays affect students in school. The week before winter vacation, Halloween, or Valentine's Day are particularly difficult times for teachers to get the full attention of elementary students. Many teachers plan accordingly by doing special units that use these events to their advantage, for example: doing creative dance with monsters and scary creatures during Halloween week or doing chasing and fleeing games that revolve around a Valentine theme for Valentine's Day.

Teachers may not have the gym for a week if voting takes place in a school on election day or if school pictures are going to be held in the gym. In some areas students take off from school when the state fair is in town. All of these factors should be considered when planning when your units will be taught so that you are prepared ahead of time and can use the program time that you do have to its greatest advantage.

***School Schedules.***   All schools have a published schedule. Most divide the school year into quarters. In some high schools, or middle schools, students may only take physical education for a quarter or semester (two quarters in a row). At the end of each quarter teachers would be expected to give students a grade for physical education or do some kind of report to parents on the status of a student in physical education. Organizing your units so that you are culminating what you are teaching at the time grades are due would be important in these situations.

***Relationship to Other Units in Your Curriculum.***   Another factor to consider relative to where to place a unit relative to the school year is the relationship of a unit to other units in the curriculum. If you want to teach students how to use

Some activities need to be planned as "seasonal activities." (© *liquidlibrary/ Dynamic Graphics/Jupiterimages*)

## Box 3.5   Elementary School and High School Yearly Block Plan

**ELEMENTARY SCHOOL: FIFTH GRADE**

| Week | # of Lessons | Unit Content Area |
|------|--------------|-------------------|
| 1, 2, 3 | 6 | Educational games: Soccer |
| 3, 4, 5 | 6 | Educational dance: Using effort actions with a theme |
| 6, 7, 8, 9 | 8 | Educational gymnastics: Developing a partner routine using body shape concepts |
| 9, 10, 11 | 6 | Educational games: Paddle and racket skills |
| 12, 13, 14 | 6 | Educational dance: Line and folk dance |
| 15, 16, 17, 18 | 8 | Educational games: Basketball |
| 19, 20 | 4 | Educational games: Inline skating |
| 21, 22, 23 | 6 | Fitness concepts and lifestyle issues (bicycle) |
| 24, 25, 26, | 6 | Educational games: Volleyball |
| 27, 28, 29 | 6 | Educational gymnastics: Apparatus routines |
| 30, 31, 32 | 6 | Educational games: Softball/baseball |

**HIGH SCHOOL YEARLY PLAN**

| Week | # of lessons | Unit Content Area |
|------|--------------|-------------------|
| 1 | 2 | Orientation |
| 1 | 3 | Pre-test—fitness |
| 2–18 | 48 (M–W–Fr) | Student selection of activity (#1) |
| 2–18 | 32 (Tu–Th) | Fitness concepts |
| 19–28 | 45 | Student selection of activity (#2) |
| 29–35 | 30 | Student choice of activity (#3) |
| 35 | 3 | Post-testing and closure—fitness |
| 36 | 2 | Lockers and closure |

**Student Activity Choices (Students must have at least two different movement forms for the year)**

| Block 1 | Block 2 | Block 3 |
|---------|---------|---------|
| Soccer | Basketball | Gymnastics |
| Tennis | Volleyball | Baseball |
| Golf | Badminton | Football |
| Lacrosse | Bowling | Swimming |
| Backpacking | Aerobic dance | Line dance |
| Weight training | Weight training | Kayaking |

offensive and defensive concepts for invasion types of games, you may want to teach units like soccer and basketball following each other so that the connection between them is more easily made by students. If you want to teach cardiorespiratory endurance in your fitness unit you may want to teach an activity that utilizes cardiorespiratory endurance at the same time. A sample yearly block plan is described in Box 3.5 for elementary and high school grade levels.

## Step 6: Placing Objectives in Units

### Where in the block plan will the objectives be taught?

The teacher uses a framework to determine the units that will be taught. Once the units are identified, the teacher then places the objectives of the program under each unit. The yearly plan and placing objectives in units often occur simultaneously in the planning process for obvious reasons. Teachers need to know what will go into a unit if they are to determine where and how much time the unit will take.

In the example using the goal *participate regularly in physical activity,* the logical place to put most of these objectives would seem to be the fitness units identified in each of the frameworks. However, it would be far more effective to consider this goal a continuous responsibility for all the units in the curriculum and to place many of the objectives encouraging outside class participation, fitness development, and an awareness of personal preferences for physical activity in other units as well. The unit objectives related to *participating regularly in physical activity* for a basketball unit might be:

1. Identify the location of opportunities to play basketball both as an informal recreational activity as well as on a team.
2. Describe how to select shoes and balls for participation in basketball.
3. Describe a strategy for conditioning for basketball.
4. Describe the benefits of participation in basketball.

In placing your objectives into a content framework, you will want to identify in what unit you will teach all of your objectives for the year. You will also want to consider that some objectives are best taught over several units in your program. Box 3.6 pulls out the locomotion unit of this framework from Box 3.4 and illustrates how the objectives are inserted into the unit. You will notice that the teacher has described the program objectives in rather specific terms. Describing what objectives go into what unit at this level of specificity will make unit planning much easier. In Box 3.6, critical learning experiences are also described to give the reader a good understanding of how the objectives would actually be delivered to the learners.

# What Should Be and What Can Be—The Role of Context in Curriculum Planning

National and state standards are usually designed as "best case scenarios," which means they are designed for programs that meet students, often and have good working conditions, including adequate equipment and facilities, lots of time with students, and small classes. Many teachers do not have these conditions. More often teachers at the elementary school level meet their students once or twice a week. Teachers at the middle school level meet their students every other day and teachers at the high school level have their students for one or two years.

# Box 3.6    Placing Objectives into a Unit—Three-Week Unit on Locomotion

**Week One:**

Demonstrate mature form in each locomotor pattern.

Use lcomotor patterns in combination with one another in general space.

Vary the pattern using space and effort movement concepts.

Identify critical elements of locomotor patterns.

Engage in sustained activity that causes heavy breathing.

Sample critical learning experiences:

1. Use a check sheet of process characteristics to do peer assessment of locomotor patterns.
2. Engage in sustained activity (five minutes) varying the speed, direction, type, and pathway of a locomotor pattern with smooth transitions.

**Week Two:**

Develop routines using locomotor patterns with small equipment.

Demonstrate smooth transitions between sequential motor tasks.

Work cooperatively with another to complete an assigned task.

Use feedback to improve performance.

Sample critical learning experiences:

1. Develop a sequence of three different locomotor patterns using hoops and hurdles that is the very best that you can do.

2. Teach your routine to a partner who is in some way different from yourself, demonstrating your ability to work together.
3. With your partner, provide feedback to another set of partners demonstrating your ability to both give good feedback to others and use feedback from others to improve your performance.

**Week Three:**

Use locomotor patterns effectively in gamelike conditions.

Recognize the physiological signs of increased activity.

Apply rules, procedures, and safe practices with little or no reinforcement.

Experience and express pleasure in physical activity.

Sample critical learning experiences:

1. Participate in chasing- and fleeing-type games. Check physiological characteristics of activity both before and after.
2. Invent a game that uses locomotor skills. Self-assessment of ability to follow the rules once they have been established.
3. At close of the unit, the teacher asks students to identify the activities they most enjoyed by putting a smiley face on the activity.

Although there is great similarity in the needs of students wherever they may be in the country, there are also some differences. Geographic region influences the types of physical activities that are important to a culture. Programs in Maine may need to consider more of an emphasis on winter activities while students in Florida focus on summer water sports. Students in rural areas may not have access to the activities available to students in urban areas. Community culture and student interest and access will play a role in the activities you choose to emphasize.

The most important factor affecting what you can accomplish in your program is going to be the amount of time that you have with students. The national standards were designed primarily for programs that meet with their students every day. If you do not meet your students every day, you will want to modify the objectives you select for each grade level and perhaps your goals so that they reflect what you can achieve with all your students in the time that you do have with them. In today's educational climate, the emphasis is on outcomes, what students learn. It is more important that students learn what you intend them to learn than it is for you to cover material. There are many things we think students should learn as part of a good physical education program. Making decisions about what they can learn in the time you have with them means that you will have to make some hard choices between good objectives. Curriculums that are effective in producing student learning have targeted accurately what they think students can learn in the time allotted.

## What Characterizes a Good Curriculum Guide?

After you have finished all of the parts of a curriculum guide, it is useful to look at the guide and determine if the parts make sense as a whole. There are several characteristics that make up a good guide. One of the most important is to determine if the parts are *aligned* with each other. Are the purposes, goals, objectives, units, and assessment consistent with each other? Do they go together? For example, if you say your purpose is to develop a physically active lifestyle, can the goals and objectives of your program actually do this? Do you assess whether students are leading a physically active lifestyle? Do you address physically active lifestyles in any of your units?

For those programs that use the national standards or their state standards as their purpose and goals, the curriculum must not only be aligned in terms of all of its parts, but it must also be *aligned* with the standards. The sequence you use to get there should be progressive and developmentally appropriate, as the standards are developed from early grade levels to later grade levels. Programs are also more effective if many of the standards are *integrated* into all or most units. Content should be specific enough so that units can be easily designed from the objectives. Some guides also spell out specific learning experiences that are part of each unit.

The assessment of the curriculum will be discussed in Chapter 11. It is important to realize at this point that you will have to provide a way to assess your goals and objectives. Good guides not only suggest alternatives, they provide the assessment material the teacher will use to do the assessment.
In summary:

- Are the parts of the guide aligned with each other?
- Is the content aligned with the standards?
- Is the content specific enough to provide direct help for unit planning?
- Is the sequence progressive and developmentally appropriate over the years?
- Are assessment materials provided that assess the goals and objectives of the curriculum?

## Box 3.7   Decisions to Be Made in Developing a Curriculum Guide

**Step 1: Statement of Philosophy**

- What are the purposes of my program?
- Why do I think these purposes are worth including in a school program?
- How are these purposes best accomplished in the context of my school with my students?.

**Step 2: Specific Goals of Your Program**

- What should students know and be able to do as a result of (at the end of) my program?

**Step 3: Sequence of Objectives/Outcomes**

- What objectives should students accomplish at each grade level that will take me to my goals?

**Step 4: Content Framework**

- How can I best conceptually organize the objectives I have for my program into content areas?

**Step 5: Yearly Block Plan**

- How long will it take me to accomplish the objectives I have for this unit?
- When in the school year is the best time to teach this unit?
  - How can this unit be scheduled with other units other teachers in the program might be teaching?
  - Where should this unit be placed relative to other units in the yearly program?

**Step 6: Placing the Objectives into Units**

- Where in the curriculum can I best teach an objective?

**Step 7: Assessing the Curriculum**

- How can I determine that the goals and objectives I have for my curriculum have been achieved (Chapter 9)?

## The Decisions Involved in Developing the Curriculum Guide

Each of the parts of the curriculum guide has been explored in this chapter in terms of the decisions that the curriculum designer must make in order to plan an educational program to accomplish particular goals. This process is summarized in Box 3.7. Although the process appears to be a linear one, which means that it goes smoothly from step 1 to step 7, in practice it is not. For example, the process of developing objectives often makes program purpose clear. The process of doing a yearly plan often requires revisions in objectives or the framework we have chosen. Curriculum guide developers often find themselves moving back and forth from one section of the plan to another as they try to develop a consistent document that is a useful guide for developing an effective educational program.

## Check Your Understanding

1. Why is long-term planning important and what are the consequences of not having a long-term plan?
2. What are the six parts of a curriculum guide?
3. What should be in a philosophy statement that begins the curriculum guide?
4. What questions should you ask to identify the goals of your program?

5.  What is the relationship between goals and objectives?
6.  What is meant by the idea of scope and sequence of content?
7.  What is an organizing framework for curriculum? Give an example of a potential elementary school, middle school, and high school organizing framework.
8.  What factors have to be considered in order to do a yearly plan for a grade level?
9.  What contextual factors from a particular situation might influence what you do in your curriculum?

## Suggested Reading

Wiggins, G., & McTighe, J. (2005). *Understanding by Design* (expanded 2nd ed.). Alexandria, VA: ASCD.

Sowell, E. (2004). *Curriculum: An Integrative Approach*. Englewood Cliffs, NJ: Merrill.

# CHAPTER 4

# Designing Units in Physical Education

## OVERVIEW

This chapter will teach you how to plan a unit of instruction. You will learn the parts of a unit plan in physical education, how to design a unit plan, and the criteria by which you judge a good unit plan.

## OUTCOMES

- Identify the parts of a good unit plan.
- Write unit objectives consistent with curriculum goals and objectives.
- Develop a scope and sequence for content.
- Develop a block plan for a unit that recognizes the critical factors involved in decisions relative to beginning the unit, developing the middle of the unit, and ending the unit.

The unit plan is the stage of planning between your curriculum and your lesson plan. Unit plans describe a sequence of learning experiences to be delivered over more than one lesson that are designed to accomplish objectives in a single content area. For example, teachers might have unit plans for a basketball unit, a fitness unit, or a unit devoted to a skill theme like jumping and landing. Once you have planned your yearly program, you will be ready to plan your units. Your *yearly* program should have:

- ■ Listed each unit you will teach for the year.
- ■ Indicated the length of time you will devote to each unit.

■   Listed the performance indicators/ benchmarks/objectives from the national standards that the unit will incorporate. (In most cases the performance indictors should be drawn from more than one standard.)

If you begin your unit planning after thinking through the above steps, unit planning will be a lot easier. Although units should be planned to meet the specific needs of a group of learners, if you take the time to plan good units, you will usually be able to use or adopt the unit to a class you want to teach in the future. Developing good units takes time but will save you time in the long run because you will not have to start each lesson totally fresh and you will be able to use the work you have done in the future. A sample unit plan for high school basketball is provided in Appendix B. Each of the important ideas related to unit planning are highlighted in this sample unit. Sample lesson guides are provided at the end of the unit so that you can see how what you put in the block plan of a unit might translate into an actual lesson.

Unit plans can be written very sparsely or in great detail depending upon the usefulness of the ideas to the teacher. Minimally, your unit plan will include the following:

■   Heading material

■   Clearly stated objectives in the three domains of learning for the unit

■   An outline of the content (scope and sequence/developmental analysis of the content of the unit)

■   A block plan for the unit that sequences the major learning experiences and content over the unit

■   Assessment and evaluation materials and procedures

■   The resources and references you have used for your unit

Each of the above will be described in this chapter.

## Heading Material

The heading material needs to include:

■   Your name

■   Date

■   Title of the unit

■   The class or grade for which the unit is appropriate

■   The space/facilities required to teach the unit

■   Equipment and supplies required to teach the unit

An additional heading item you might include is the anticipated set of skills that you expect the students to have before you teach the content of the unit. Each of these items are straightforward but can be problematic if you come back to the written unit at another time and want to use it again.

# Clearly Stated Unit Objectives

Planning at all levels involves specifying learning outcomes that describe what students are expected to know and be able to do as a result of your program. Curriculum outcomes tend to be described in broader terms than unit outcomes. It is at the unit level that the teacher should describe exactly what the student should be able to do in measurable terms. When you think in terms of writing objectives for your unit you will have to think about how to link your unit to the curriculum you have planned. In order to do this you will want to have objectives that are not only consistent with the curriculum goals that you have set but also that contribute to them. In the previous chapter we talked about doing a yearly block plan that specified what units were to be taught and what performance indicators from the standards were assigned to that unit. At the unit level you will need to plan on designing learning experiences that actually accomplish the performance indicators you have assigned that unit.

## Matching Unit Objectives to Curriculum Goals and Objectives

There are many people who design curriculum in physical education who have very good ideas about what students should know and be able to do at the curriculum level. For instance, we all want students to be able to maintain fitness or to be able to respect the rights of others, or to be able to identify the critical cues of basic movement patterns. Somehow those lofty goals never get translated into actual learning experiences for students. One of the reasons why they do not is that teachers fail to write unit objectives related to those goals that actually contribute to the development of those goals. The unit objective should describe how students will demonstrate that they have maintained fitness and for what skills you expect students to identify the critical cues. The following examples of unit objectives developed from curriculum objectives illustrate how the two levels support each other:

> *Fourth-grade curriculum objective:* The student will be able to balance and roll in a variety of ways.
>
> *Fourth-grade unit objectives:* The student will be able to perform a gymnastics sequence using a variety of traveling, rolling, and balancing actions with the criteria identified for a good sequence.
>
> *Ninth-grade curriculum objective:* The student will be able to use offensive and defensive tactics in a modified invasion game.
>
> *Ninth-grade unit objective:* The student will be able to move a basketball down the court against an active defense with two other players by using quick and accurate lead passes and opening up the passing lane.

In each of these cases the curriculum objective or performance indicator was broader and was translated to a unit objective. Sometimes a unit will be able to directly address a curriculum objective, as is the case with a curriculum objective for the fifth grade that may require students to be able to throw a ball overhand with a mature pattern. In some cases the yearly plan may focus on the same curriculum objective in more than one unit, as might be the case with the curriculum objective related to working productively with others.

## Integrating the Standards In Unit Objectives

As part of developing a curriculum, in the previous chapter you outlined your yearly plan and made a decision where to include the grade level objectives/performance indicators you identified from the standards. When you did this you had to make a decision about where the performance indicators for all of the standards would be taught. If, for instance, you assigned your soccer unit the performance indicator *Identifies opportunities in the community for participation in physical activity,* then one of your unit objectives would have to be, for example:

> The student will be able to identify two opportunities to play soccer in the community for his or her age group.

If you identified *Uses feedback to improve performance,* then one of your unit objectives would have to be, for example:

> The student will be able to use peer feedback to improve dribbling skills moving in general space.

You will notice that these performance indicators technically could be taught in any or many units. If you have done a good job with your curriculum planning, you have identified where you think they are best taught. You will then need to write a unit objective that is related to that performance indicator. When you are planning your unit and deciding what you are going to teach each day of the unit, you will need to incorporate these objectives into the learning experiences that you design. You will also be asked to assess these objectives at the end of your unit.

## Writing Unit Objectives in the Three Learning Domains

Unit objectives should be written in the three domains of learning. Remember that these are cognitive, affective, and psychomotor. The performance indicators that accompany this text are inclusive of the three domains. You should be able to go to the file of performance indicators for a grade level and identify those that have affective, cognitive, and psychomotor outcomes. There is a tendency for physical educators to do a good job writing curriculum outcomes in the affective and cognitive domain, but not include these outcomes in their unit planning. For example, teachers want students to be *able to work cooperatively in competitive and cooperative settings,* but they fail to plan *how* and *where* they are going to actually teach to these outcomes.

Teachers often assume that affective and cognitive outcomes like the one described above are *implicit* in the unit. Often we presume that if students are working in team sport units, that cooperation and teamwork will automatically occur. In reality, affective and cognitive objectives need to be taught *explicitly*. This means that teachers need to identify the specific unit(s) that will be used to teach affective and cognitive outcomes and to actually design learning experiences that teach to those unit objectives. You cannot assume that because you ask students to work as a team, that they will know what it means to be able to work as a team or be able to exhibit those behaviors. If I have assigned the performance indicator *work cooperatively in competitive and cooperative settings* to a sport education ultimate Frisbee unit, I still have to decide what my unit objective is going to be and how I am going to teach it. For instance I might write a unit objective such as:

> *The student will be able to identify three personal instances of cooperative behavior within his/her team as well as with the other team during the tournament week of the unit.*

I would have to decide where in the unit to teach this and how I am going to teach students what it means to work cooperatively, which would make the teaching toward this outcome explicit.

Student participation in community activities during a soccer unit would be an appropriate objective. (© *image100/Punch-Stock*)

## Box 4.1  Scope and Sequence for Middle School Volleyball Unit

1. Underhand Serve
   a. Against a wall from a short distance
   b. Against a wall from a larger distance
   c. To a partner over a net a short distance
   d. To a partner in a serve and set pattern
   e. To a partner over a net from a regulation distance
   f. Into broad target areas on the court
   g. In a modified 4-on-4 game

2. Forearm Pass
   a. From a partner toss short distance
   b. From a partner toss into a target area
   c. Continuously against the wall
   d. From a short underhand serve
   e. Continuously with a partner
   f. From a toss with a change in direction

3. Overhead Set
   a. From a partner toss short distance
   b. From a partner toss into a target area
   c. From a forearm pass
   d. Continuously with a partner
   e. From a toss with a change in direction
   f. From a forearm pass with a change in direction

4. Game Play
   a. Working with another person
      i. Up and back
      ii. Side by side
   b. Offensive tactics
      i. 2 vs. 2 place the ball into an open space/ use 3 contacts
      ii. 4 vs. 4 place the ball into an open space/ use 3 contacts
   c. Defensive tactics
      i. Maintain ready position
      ii. Go back to home base after every play

5. Rules and Etiquette
   a. How to rotate
   b. What is a legal hit
   c. Out of bounds
   d. How to score

6. Integration of Other Standards
   a. Volleyball as a coed Olympic sport
   b. Volleyball as a community activity
   c. Cooperation in a competitive activity
   d. Producing and reducing force in the three skills
   e. The effect of practice on learning

## An Outline of the Content

Before you make any decisions about what you are going to teach on what day, you need to outline the content of the unit. There are several ways to do this. One is to do a scope and sequence of the content and the other is to do a developmental analysis of the content of the unit. In both cases the emphasis is on developing a conceptual framework of the content that you are going to teach.

### Scope and Sequence of Content

A scope and sequence of unit content describes what you are going to teach. If, for instance, for a volleyball unit I listed: underhand serve, forearm pass, and overhead pass, I would be saying that these are the skills I am going to teach. What this also means is that I am not going to teach other kinds of serves, the spike, and other more advanced skills. Box 4.1 describes a scope and sequence for a middle school volleyball unit.

There are no real rules for how to outline the content. What is important is that the scope and sequence provides an outline of the content that can get you to your objectives. If, for example, I wanted students to be able to play 6 vs. 6 volleyball on a regulation court, the scope and sequence outline in Box 4.1 would not get me there.

## Developmental Analysis of the Content

Like the scope and sequence of content, a developmental analysis of the content describes what is going to be taught in the unit, but it does it in a way that provides some guidance as to how the content will be developed in instruction (Rink, 2006). An example of part of a developmental analysis is provided in Box 4.2. You will notice that there are three columns. Each of the columns is described below:

**The Extension Column.**  The first column of the developmental analysis is the extension column that provides a progression of tasks for a skill/skills. The extension column creates a sequence similar to the scope and sequence by manipulating the factors that make skills more complex and/or difficult. These factors are described by Rink (2006) and are reproduced in Box 4.3.

**The Refinement Column.**  The refinement column of the developmental analysis provides information on how to do each of the tasks/experiences in your sequence well. For many motor skills this description will most often be the cues that you want to focus students on. The cues should change as the task progression gets more difficult and students need different information on how to adapt their movement to the new conditions. It is not enough to say that a basketball dribble involves the use of the finger pads, a forward stride position, and a relaxed pushing action. These cues may be good for learning how to dribble in a stationery position but would not be appropriate for dribbling on the move, changing direction at a fast speed, or against a defender. For each of these conditions the basic dribbling pattern changes, and the teacher should identify how the student has to adapt the dribble to these conditions.

The refinement column helps teachers to identify the information they want to communicate. It also provides the teacher with criteria for observing students as they do a task, and information that can be used to provide students with feedback on their performance.

From an instructional standpoint, when a teacher does not see good performance using the information provided in the refinement column, the teacher has several choices:

- Correct the problem individually.
- Stop the whole class and give a refining task that refocuses students on what you want to see.
- Change the task to make it less difficult.

**The Application/Assessment Column.**  The application/assessment column of the developmental analysis should describe experiences that will help the students apply the task/or test their ability with the task. Oftentimes these experiences are

## Box 4.2 Example of a Developmental Analysis

**Striking with Paddles (Third Grade)**
**Initial Task: Strike the ball down continuously with your paddle in your own space.**

| Extension | Refinement | Application/Assessment |
|---|---|---|
| Strike the ball up continuously with your paddle. | Keep the paddle level.<br>Try to get the ball to go up so that it comes down right in front of you.<br>Get under the ball—bend your knees. | How many times can you keep the ball going in the air without losing control. |
| Alternate striking the ball up and down with your paddle in your own space. If you have trouble with control, add an extra bounce in between or do three of each before you make the switch. | Use the same side of your paddle and flip your wrist to make the change. | Try to get five in a row without moving out of your own space.<br>Partner observation of:<br>■ Flat paddle<br>■ Getting under the ball<br>■ Control of the ball |
| When you can do the above task at least five times in a row, you can begin this task: Strike the ball against the wall from about 8 feet using a tapping motion and make it come back to you so you can keep it going. | Use a forehand grip.<br>Tap the ball with a high (tosslike) trajectory (by getting under the ball) with just enough force to make it come to where you are. | See who can keep it going the longest without missing. |
| When you can keep the ball going against the wall for 8 times in a row you may begin this task: Move back to about 15 feet and see if you can still keep the ball going.<br>Strike the ball with a partner against the wall. | Use a side orientation.<br>Transfer the weight to your forward foot.<br>Keep the ball above a 4-foot line on the wall to create a bounce that makes the ball come back to you.<br>Send the ball so that it comes back to your partner with a playable ball.<br>After you make the hit, move out of the way to let your partner return the ball. | See who can keep it going the longest without missing.<br><br>See how many you can do and then try and beat your own record. |

self-testing (individual or group), competitive, or a "test" or assessment of ability. The application/assessment column should apply/use the task at the same level of ability as the extension task in the first column. Application/assessment tasks are a powerful focus for student work. When students have acquired a reasonable amount of competence in the task that you have taught, application/assessment tasks will serve to focus their efforts.

## Box 4.3 Factors that Can Be Manipulated to Make Skills More Complex and Difficult

Break down skill into parts.

Modify equipment.

Make the space larger/smaller.

Change the conditions of performance.

Change the goal (intent) of practice.

Increase or decrease the number of people.

Change the rules.

Combine several skills or do the same skill more than one time in a row.

Produce more than one correct response for tasks with divergent responses.

Lesson planning is much easier for teachers who have done a developmental analysis of the content because they not only have identified a scope and sequence of content, they have identified what they are looking for in terms of performance in that content. They have also identified ways in which that content can be applied and assessed.

## The Unit Block Plan

One of the most important parts of the unit plan is the block plan describing in broad terms student-learning experiences for each day of the unit. In one sense the block plan depicts what you are going to do on what day of the unit. This doesn't mean that you cannot change what is on a block plan, and often teachers will need to do this. What it does mean is that you now have a map to chart your way through the unit.

A sample block plan for a high school basketball unit is provided in the sample unit in Appendix B. When you do a scope and sequence/developmental analysis of the unit plan, you focus primarily on the content of the unit and sequencing the content. You will use this information in designing your block plan but will now need to consider how you are going to translate and develop that content over the course of the unit in a way that will get you to your unit objectives. A unit has an integrity of its own, which means that it is more than a collection of different lessons. It has a beginning and an end and each of the lessons are related in some way to each other. For example, a single lesson using station teaching might be a great learning experience for students. If however, too many other lessons in the unit use station teaching, then that single lesson would go differently. Some of the things you will need to consider when writing your block plan are described below in terms of suggestions for how to begin a unit, how to develop the body of the unit, and how to end the unit.

## Beginning the Unit

What you choose to do at the beginning of a unit can set the stage for the entire unit and determine student motivation to be engaged in the content of the unit. The beginning of the unit should first orient students to the content. What is the content?

How is the content meaningful for the students? What expectations does the teacher have for students both during and at the end of the unit?

## Orienting and Motivating Students

Oftentimes, physical education teachers begin units by teaching isolated skills in a content area for which the students have no context. There are many students practicing a forehand pass in volleyball who have never seen a volleyball game and therefore cannot relate the practice to other skills in the game or anything meaningful for them. The beginning of a unit should give the student context and motivate students to want to be participants in a way that makes them look forward to the unit. Some ideas for motivating students at the beginning of units follow.

**Show a Short Film/Tape/DVD on the Activity or Sport.**   The idea of using media is not to spend a class period watching the performance of others, but to let students see how the activity/sport is played. If commercial products that do this aren't available for an activity, teachers might consider recording participants in the community or recording short clips from TV. Teachers might also use tapes of previous students who are older or who have completed the unit. If the participants can be the same age as the students and different genders, it will make identifying with the models easier for students. You don't want to send the message that a sport is either a male or female sport.

**Dress the Part of the Participant.**   A good attention-getter for a unit is to dress the part of the participant of that sport, particularly when the dress is very special- ized, such as in gymnastics, or folk dance, tennis, or field hockey.

**Give Students the Opportunity to "Try It."**   If safety is not an issue, students can be motivated to want to learn if they first have a chance to try an activity or to be a participant in an activity for which they already have experience. After they have participated, they would be more willing to set goals and work to get better. Often we think that every tennis unit needs to start with how to hold the racket and every basketball unit with dribbling. Sixth graders who play tennis/pickle ball on the first day of the unit and then are helped to assess where they are and set goals for improvement will probably be more motivated to want to go back and work on becoming more skillful.

**Bring in Guest Participants.**   Special guests in your class can be good motiva- tors. Guests can be from the community, from the high school or a college athletic team, or just a parent who has an interest in an activity who might be willing to demonstrate the activity and talk to students about why they are par- ticipants.

**Assign/Suggest/Require Students to Attend an Event Related to That Activity.** A good way to give students context for a unit is to have them see people par- ticipating in that activity "live." Sometime during the school year, even if it is before the unit starts, students can attend a game or performance or even visit a place where people are participating in the activity of the unit.

Asking students to attend a community event is a good motivator for a unit. (© *PhotoLink/ Getty Images*)

## Pre-testing

In order to best know where to begin your unit in terms of the skill level that is appropriate, you have to have some idea what your students can already do. Units that assume students can't do anything and bore them with material they have already mastered are just as inappropriate as units that assume students can do more than they really can. If you had your students in the activity from previous years, you already know what they can do. If you haven't had a group of students in that activity then you need to find a way to determine what the students can already do. If you allow the students to participate in the activity you can take notes on where they are and perhaps even have students do self- or peer assessment. Some teachers will want to give more formal skill tests that they will use to track student progress throughout and at the end of the unit and have students track their own progress.

## Developing the Body of the Unit

Planning a good unit takes time. A teacher cannot just lift the content from the scope and sequence or developmental analysis and plug it into a calendar. The following characteristics of a good unit should be considered when you develop your block plan.

### Material Moves from Simple to Complex

Content throughout the unit should be developed from simple to complex. If you have done a good job with your scope and sequence or developmental analysis, then it will be easier for you to develop your material in this manner.

### Repetition and Review Is Built into the Unit

How many times do you think that the math problem 2 + 1 appears on a worksheet for first graders throughout the year? If you answered many times throughout the whole year you would be correct. Many physical educators observe a student performing a skill or responding correctly to a verbal question and assume that the student has learned that skill or cognitive material and he or she immediately moves on. Unfortunately, learning does not take place that way. By definition, learning is a permanent change in behavior. If a student has learned something you should not have to come back and reteach it the next time you have a unit in that content area.

A lot of the learning that takes place in physical education takes place through repetition and review. For motor skills it is engaged practice over time that will produce more effective movement patterns. Teachers can facilitate student learning by building review and repetition, into their unit plans, not only of psychomotor skills, but objectives in all of the domains. Repetition and review should be planned and should be explicit on the block plan for a unit. You should be able to point to the part of the block plan where each of the objectives will be explicitly addressed. How many times do students have to work with the components of fitness before they can identify them? How many times do students need to work with ideas related to acceptable competitive interaction with opponents before they understand what it means to be a good participant and competitor?

### Game Play and Skill Practice Is Integrated Throughout the Sport Unit

Related to the idea of repetition and review discussed above is the idea that good units in individual and team sports integrate both skill practice and game play throughout the unit. Currently, too many units are organized with skill practice at the beginning of the unit and game play exclusively at the end of the unit. Typically, the student must "live through" several days of skills practice that they have little interest in before they get to play the game. When they get to the *play the game* part of the unit, they never get a chance to go back and practice the skills of the game.

Units that integrate both skill practice and game play throughout the unit have a better chance of producing skillful game players. This does not mean that students who are not ready to play THE game should be put in that position. What it means is that students can use the skills of the game in some form of game play throughout the unit. Self-testing activities and cooperative-competitive activities that emphasize control of the skill, as well as modified and small-sided games, can all be spaced throughout the unit so that you may never have a skill-focused lesson without some game play and you never have a game play lesson without some skill practice.

### A Variety of Teaching Strategies Are Used

Motivation to learn is increased when students experience a variety of teaching strategies and when they cannot always predict what is going to happen in a lesson. Using a variety of teaching strategies is important because it doesn't make every lesson predictable. Although some level of routine and predictability is necessary to maintain order, there is a point when routine begins to negatively affect student attention and motivation. Using different teaching strategies is also important because different students learn in different ways and because different teaching strategies are more appropriate for different content.

Different approaches to teaching include ideas such as station teaching, interactive teaching, peer teaching, cooperative learning, cognitive orientations toward learning motor skills, and team teaching. In many of these strategies the role of the learner and the teacher differs. For example, a teacher working on the overhand throw pattern might:

- Have students throw the ball in some different ways and identify which way they think is best for throwing the ball the furthest (cognitive problem solving).
- Demonstrate and explain how to do the overhand throw pattern (direct teaching).
- Give the students group assignment to use written or Internet resources to identify how best to do an overhand throw pattern (group project).

Variability in teaching strategies should be evident in the block plan of the unit. Matching the teaching strategy to the objectives in a particular lesson is challenging. A fun exercise is to see if you can take the same content, and plan on teaching it using different teaching strategies. Then you must decide which one is better for that particular content and that particular set of objectives and students.

## Students Experience Variety in Types of Learning Experiences

A teaching strategy assigns different roles to the student and therefore gives students a variety of learning experiences. A change of teaching strategy is not the only way to manipulate the learning experiences that students encounter over the course of a unit. The teacher can also design different learning experiences by changing the organization and management of lessons, like whom students work with and how you select whom they work with. There are lots of ways to practice skills or to learn cognitive material. Listed below are several ways in which the overhead set can be practiced without changing the relative difficulty of the skill:

*Overhead Set*
> Continuous to self
> Continuous to the wall
> From a partner toss
> Over a rope into a target area
> Into a basketball goal

Because students often need repetition and practice of the same skill without changing the difficulty of the skill, teachers must be able to design practices of the same skill in very different ways. Doing a comprehensive block plan allows you to think through how you can engage students at a high level in practice without making the skill more difficult.

## The Transition to Outside of School Is Addressed

Most physical education programs will identify a physically active lifestyle as a major program goal. If so, then helping students to make the transition from what they do in class to participation outside of class is important, not only for the fitness unit, but for all units. It is no longer acceptable to say that a teacher's responsibility for what students do outside of class ends with giving students the skills to be participants. Unless teachers are willing to help students make that transition to participating outside of class, in most cases participation will end with the physical education class.

Good units in physical education take the time to help students begin to make these transitions. The teacher may do nothing more than talk about youth sport leagues in the area and provide application forms. Older students might visit community facilities for a variety of activities. Community sponsors, both government sponsored as well as private enterprises, are most willing to help with your efforts to get students to participate in the activities they sponsor.

## Formative and Summative Assessment Is Built into the Unit

Formative assessment is usually considered that which takes place during instruction and summative assessment that which takes place at the end of instruction (e.g., final written or skill test). For physical education, summative assessment usually takes place at the end of the unit of instruction on that content. Both types of assessment are essential to a good unit and both can be either of a formal nature (e.g., published test or scoring rubric administered with careful attention to protocols) or informal (e.g., student self-testing activity for which they record their own scores).

**Formative Assessment.**    Formative assessment is part of the instructional process. It is used to collect information on student performance that can be used by the student and/or teacher to improve performance. Formative assessment can motivate students and give the teacher information needed to plan and improve the instructional process. When formative assessment is used as part of the instructional process, it becomes a learning experience that is part of the learning process. For example, students who have to use a set of criteria to assess their performance or the performance of other students are more likely to remember and use those criteria in their performance. Teachers who involve students in self-assessment, peer assessment, self-testing activities, and more formal opportunities to gather information on student performance are not taking time "out of instruction," they are including an essential part of the instructional process.

**Summative Assessment.**    Summative assessment is used at the end of the unit to determine the extent to which students achieved the objectives of the unit. Summative assessment can be used for grading purposes, for student feedback, or to determine the effectiveness of instruction. Summative assessment is usually more formal than formative assessment and needs to be if the data is going to be used for grading purposes. Assessments need to be valid and reliable indications of student performance. Written tests, skill tests, and formal observations with established scoring rubrics are some examples of tools that can be used for summative assessment. The criteria used to assess students should be shared with them throughout the unit so that the expectations are clear.

## Individual Differences Are Addressed

Students are not at the same level of ability coming into a unit and will not be as they progress through a unit. The teacher needs to acknowledge and plan ways to accommodate those differences. Teachers can accommodate differences in a variety of ways, including having students set personal goals, provide choices of tasks, or find ways for students to practice tasks under different conditions (equipment, space, number of people, etc.). Indicating how you are going to do this on the block plan gives you time to think through how you might make these accommodations ahead of time so that you do not get in the middle of instruction and realize that what you are doing is inappropriate for some of the students.

## Students Are Given Opportunity for Responsible Decision Making

Throughout educational literature in almost any content area you will find a commitment to helping students be responsible decision makers. This is one of those educational goals that permeate all of education. Translating this goal into program objectives and learning experiences takes thoughtful planning that gradually gives students more and more responsibility for making decisions in curriculum and in the instructional process. The unit plan should indicate what decisions are going to be given to students and when they will occur in the unit. Ideas such as self-analysis and goal setting, choosing a skill that needs practice, deciding on the level of play you want to be a participant in, and choosing between different ways to practice are just some of the decisions that can be built into units as learning experiences. When teachers prepare students so that they make good decisions and when they evaluate the decisions students make afterward, they make student decision making an explicit objective in the unit and lesson.

# Ending the Unit

Successful units have a culminating experience. A culminating experience usually gives students the opportunity to use and perhaps even "showcase" what they have learned in the unit. Culminating experiences for competitive sport units are often a tournament of some sort. Many individual activities like dance and gymnastics lend themselves to a culminating performance in which students perform for each other or invited guests. Culminating experiences can also include events such as a backpacking trip or visit to a "real" golf class in a golf unit. Culminating experiences give students something to work toward and add a sense of completion to a unit for both the teacher and the student.

## Box 4.4 Assessing Objectives in the Three Domains

| Cognitive | Psychomotor | Affective |
|---|---|---|
| Written test | Skills test | Written test |
| Observation of performance—real or contrived | Observation of performance—real or contrived | Observation of performance—real or contrived |
| Verbal response | | Verbal response |

### Unit Assessment

Often there is not time in a single lesson to accomplish significant objectives. It simply takes longer than the single lesson to develop many motor skills and other important behaviors to a level where you can actually document change. That is why planned formative and summative assessment in a unit are important.

Unit assessment answers the question, "To what extent have students reached the objectives for the unit?" Each objective in the unit needs to be assessed. Learning objectives for a unit will be written clearer if the method of assessment is identified at the same time the objective is written. In the basketball unit provided in Appendix B, assessment materials are provided for each unit objective.

Box 4.4 describes common tools and techniques that can be used to assess learning objectives in the different domains. With the current emphasis on performance-based assessment, a lot of the traditional skills and written tests have been replaced with alternative assessment tools. Much of what we do in physical education cannot be measured with paper and pencil tests or other written types of assessment. We don't want to know if students know how to do something, we want to know if they can do it. We don't want to know if they can identify appropriate behavior, we want to know if they behave appropriately. Objectives that are performance based are usually measured with observational tools. For summative assessment, particularly assessment that is going to be used to grade students or teachers, the teacher needs to make sure that the observational tool actually measures the objectives for the unit and that the observational tool can be used reliably by the teacher.

### Check Your Understanding

1. Identify five parts to a good unit plan.
2. What should go in the heading of a unit plan?
3. How do you match the objectives of your unit to the curriculum goals and objectives you have established?
4. Describe what a scope and sequence of content is likely to look like for a unit.
5. What are some potential ways to start a unit that could potentially set the stage for the unit and motivate learners to want to participate?

6.  What are the characteristics of a good unit of instruction?
7.  What are some potential good ways to culminate a unit?
8.  Why is assessment of unit objectives at the end of the unit important?

## Reference

Rink, J. (2006). *Teaching Physical Education for Learning.* Boston: McGraw-Hill.

## Suggested Reading

Posner, G., & Rudinitsky, A. (2005). *Course Design: A Guide to Curriculum Development for Teachers.* Boston: Addison-Wesley.

Kelly, L., & Melograno, V. (2004). *Developing the Physical Education Curriculum: An Achievement Based Approach.* Champaign, IL: Human Kinetics.

# CHAPTER 5

# Foundations of the Elementary School Curriculum

## OVERVIEW

Elementary school children should not be thought of as a miniature adults. They are different and have very unique needs in terms of an appropriate physical education program. This chapter will help you understand the needs of the elementary school student within the physical education curriculum. Guidelines and program outcomes based on the national standards are specified, followed by a discussion of the issues surrounding choosing an appropriate curriculum.

## OUTCOMES

- Identify the physical, cognitive, and social characteristics of the elementary-school-age child.
- Identify the characteristics of a good physical education program for children.
- Identify appropriate outcomes for the physical education curriculum.
- Describe and take a position on the issues involved in the elementary school physical education curriculum.

One of the reasons so many physical education teachers enjoy teaching elementary school physical education is that for many elementary school students, physical education is their favorite subject. They enjoy moving and spend a good part of their day in active play when given the opportunity. Because the experiences that children have in physical activity and sport at early ages can have a profound influence on the physical activity patterns of the child for the rest of their life, what a child experiences in physical education at this age is critical.

Physical play is a large part of a child's life. Children grow socially, cognitively, and physically through these opportunities for play. Because physical activity and physical skills are such a large part of the child's everyday life, children who have not developed these skills are often denied opportunities to participate. They are not invited to play and when they are, they are put in experiences that often have negative consequences for them.

While it is true that most children will choose to be active, they do not always have the opportunity to be active. For a variety of reasons, many children cannot just go outside and "play" in today's world and for those who do, it is not true that they will *automatically* develop the motor skills, attitudes, and knowledge they will need for a lifetime of physical activity. A sound foundation of basic skills obtained in a developmentally appropriate physical education program is necessary to the development of the more specialized activity and sport skills that will come later. Children should not leave the elementary school without having developed these skills.

## The Elementary School Child

Perhaps one of the most important ideas related to children is to understand that children are not just miniature adults. They are different. The children that you will teach in a K–5 elementary school program will be approximately 5 to 11 years of age. Developmentally, this age group is experiencing childhood. The difference between the 5-year-old kindergarten student and the 11-year-old fifth grader is significant, which means that somewhere in those years a great deal of physical, social, and emotional development is taking place. The kindergarten child who hasn't fully developed the locomotor skills to use all of them in isolation will be expected to do the footwork necessary to defend a player with the ball in basketball.

### Physical Development

Although children grow at a very rapid pace up to the age of 5, growth after that point to adolescent is slow but steady. For most of the time in the elementary school girls and boys will have equal stature. Girls begin puberty earlier than boys, for some as early as 10 years of age. With puberty comes a rapid growth spurt, which means that many girls who have reached puberty will be bigger than boys of the same age, perhaps the only time that girls will have the physical advantage over boys.

The more important issue is the variance in physical maturity levels between children. Most experts would say that in any one class of children you will have, there can be a difference of five years in physical maturity between the least mature and most mature student of the same age. Physical maturity determines a lot of the student's readiness to learn, which means it is unfair to expect the same physical ability from one child that you do for another.

Elementary children come in many sizes and shapes with very different needs. (© *Comstock/PunchStock*)

Children tire more easily and recover faster than adults. They do not dissipate heat in the body as efficiently, which means that teacher needs to be careful in hot weather not to "push" children beyond what is healthy. They also need to offer frequent periods of aerobic activity that is at a low or medium level, rather than expecting students to sustain high levels of activity for long periods of time.

## Cognitive Development

Many children coming into school will still be at a stage of cognitive development Piaget referred to as preoperational. This means that they are just beginning to master the use of symbols and that they do not reason in the same way adults do. Rather, they attribute cause and effect relationships to events that occur simultaneously whether they are related or not. They are also likely to be egocentric, meaning they can only view the world from their own narrow perspective and not the perspective of others. Box 5.1 describes the experience of an elementary physical education teacher with an egocentric child. Children at this stage have difficulty dealing with more than one aspect of a problem at a time.

A major transition occurs somewhere in the K–2 grade levels, moving the child into a concrete operations stage, which is also a limitation in that abstract reasoning is still a major problem for a child at this stage. While they can deal with what is concrete and in front of them, they still cannot deal with hypothetical situations or abstract ideas. Many children in the upper elementary grades enter the stage of formal operations characteristic of adults.

Young children need help with perceptual motor skills, particularly the awareness of space, time, and direction. Initially, they have difficulty understanding external space and relate all positions in space to themselves. Because letters like *b* and *d*

## Box 5.1   The Egocentric Elementary School Child

An elementary school physical education teacher was teaching a kindergarten class how to move in general space. The teacher had students look for empty spaces and talked about the need to be aware of where other people were moving. One child kept pushing others out of his way rather than moving into empty spaces. The teacher went up to the child and asked, Why are you pushing others instead of looking for empty spaces? The child remarked, "Because they were in my way."

are differentiated only by their position in space, many children entering school see no difference. They have difficulty determining the speed of objects, which makes timing in skills like catching and striking problematic. They are likely to not have an awareness of their bodies, both in terms of its parts and where those parts are in space when they cannot see them.

The implications of the cognitive development of children are many for physical education. First, because children are at early stages in their cognitive development, movement experiences are critical to their development. The active manipulation of their bodies and their bodies in relation to objects facilitates cognitive development. Understanding where children are cognitively can help teachers communicate better with students and design learning experiences that are more appropriate for their stage of development.

### Affective Development and Social Development

Play, particularly physical play, is pleasurable for children. They will spin, run, and skip just because it feels good to do so. The child's ability to do physical skills in play becomes a critical part of his or her willingness to be a participant in the play activities of childhood, affecting all aspects of their development. The child entering school participates mostly in what is called associative play with others characterized by the lack of a group goal and lack of real cooperation between the participants. A good example of the lack of cooperation between students can be seen in the way first and second graders play "catch." It is not uncommon for a student to throw a ball that is not "catchable" and blame the catcher rather than see his or her responsibility for the success of the catcher. Throughout childhood, the number of participants in the play group gradually increases from partners to small groups to larger groups.

Children in the early primary grades have difficulty verbalizing their self-worth, which is related to their feelings about themselves, probably because of limited cognitive development. They are in the process of being "socialized" into both going-to-school behaviors and appropriate behaviors in their interactions with others. It is the job of adults to help children acquire the skills to be both successful in school and in their relationships with others.

# What Is a Good Elementary Physical Education Program?

The National Association for Sport and Physical Education has published guidelines for what the field thinks is an appropriate physical education program for children (2000). Among the key points identified in this literature are the following descriptors. A good program:

- Is based on the national standards.
- Is designed to enhance psychomotor, cognitive, and affective development of all children.
- Provides frequent practice opportunities.
- Integrates opportunities for cognitive development in other subject areas.
- Supports cultural diversity.
- Intentionally designs experiences to promote affective development.
- Takes an activity-based approach to fitness rather than an exercise approach.
- Uses fitness testing as an educational experience.
- Teaches children how to exercise in the correct manner.
- Uses assessment to collect information to improve their programs.
- Is designed to meet every child's need for active participation.
- Provides rhythmical, expressive, and creative dance opportunities.
- Provides body management skills (jumping, landing, rolling, balancing, and transferring weight).
- Teaches games skills and uses them in modified situations.

The full guidelines are available on the NASPE Web site (www.aahperd.org/naspe) and take the form of describing what is and is not appropriate. Many of the guidelines will be recognized by experienced teachers as a reaction to "poor practice," which means the authors selected criteria they felt needed correcting in many programs. From this list you should begin to identify what the authors feel is the appropriate content and conduct of an elementary program.

Good elementary physical education programs will take much more of a holistic approach to the development of children than other school levels. Teachers need to be concerned about the children's emotional, social, and cognitive development and not just their physical skills and physical development. You will also notice that the guidelines recommend the integration of content with other content areas. While this will be a discussion point later in the chapter, there are many opportunities for teachers to use content from other subjects in the school curriculum while teaching the content of physical education. The more specific content of the program for this school level is identified in the national content standards that follow.

# What Is Appropriate Content for the Elementary School?

The national standards are in fact exit outcomes for a K–12 program. Teachers, however, must understand more specifically what those outcomes look like for different school levels and grade levels. There is a great deal of development over the elementary program, which makes it really important for the teacher to understand the expectations for student learning at all grade levels. The current national standards group the grade levels in the elementary school K–2 and 3–5. Box 5.2 describes the emphases for the standards by K–2, 3–4, and 5–6. The grade levels were further broken down because many schools still have sixth grade at the elementary level, and because the third- and fourth-grade programs are unique and sometimes get lost in a 3–5 division.

# Understanding the Intent of the Standards for the Elementary School Level

## Standard 1: Demonstrates Competency in Motor Skills and Movement Patterns Needed to Perform a Variety of Physical Activities

The intent of Standard 1 is to give students the motor skills they will need for a lifetime of physical activity under the assumption that people who participate in physical activity on a regular basis do so because it is enjoyable and enjoyment comes to a large degree from things you are good at. The major focus of the elementary school program is the development of fundamental and basic skills that are essential to the play activities of the child, as well as a foundation for learning more complex motor skills.

### Kindergarten–Second Grade

*Emphases:*

- Demonstrate mature form in all locomotor patterns and the ability to vary and combine locomotor patterns with a smooth transition.
- Demonstrate a clear body shape in weight-bearing and balance activities.
- Perform basic manipulative activities on the move (e.g., dribbling [collecting], catching, throwing, and striking).
- Adapt basic manipulative patterns to a partner.
- Demonstrate control in traveling and balance activities on a variety of body parts.
- Create expressive movement sequences with and without a defined rhythm.

Most schools have kindergartens but not all kindergarten students have physical education. That is unfortunate because kindergarten students can make tremendous progress in their motor skills with some help. Managing the body and the development of both static and dynamic balance is a major focus for this age group. The

## Box 5.2  Elementary School Content Emphases for Each of the National Standards

**Standard 1: Demonstrates competency in motor skills and movement patterns to perform a variety of physical activities.**

**Kindergarten–Second Grade:**

- Demonstrate mature form in all locomotor patterns and the ability to vary and combine locomotor patterns with a smooth transition.
- Demonstrate a clear body shape in weight-bearing and balance activities.
- Perform basic manipulative activities on the move (e.g., dribbling, catching, and throwing).
- Adapt basic manipulative patterns to a partner.
- Demonstrate control in traveling and balance activities on a variety of body parts.
- Create expressive movement sequences with and without a defined rhythm.

**Third and Fourth Grade:**

- Demonstrate mature form in selected manipulative patterns.
- Adapt a skill to dynamic and unpredictable environments.
- Acquire a few specialized sport skills.
- Combine movement skills in applied settings.

**Fifth and Sixth Grade:**

- Demonstrate mature form in throwing, catching, and striking patterns.
- Combine manipulative patterns of specialized sport skills.
- Demonstrate basic strategies for net and invasion games.
- Acquire the specialized pattern of one individualized and one lifetime activity.

**Standard 2: Demonstrates understanding of movement concepts, principles, strategies, and tactics as they apply to the learning and performance of physical activities (cognitive domain).**

**Kindergarten–Second Grade:**

- Identify the critical elements of basic movement patterns.
- Use feedback to improve performance.
- Apply movement concepts to a variety of basic skills.
- Understand why people perform at different abilities and attribute those differences to practice and experience.

**Third and Fourth Grade:**

- Use critical elements of a skill to improve performance and provide feedback to others.
- Apply simple learning and biomechanical principles in learning.

**Fifth and Sixth Grade:**

- Identify and apply principles of practice and conditioning to improve performance.
- Use basic offense and defense tactics of invasion and net activities in noncomplex settings.

**Standard 3: Participates regularly in physical activity (motor, cognitive, and affective domain).**

**Kindergarten–Second Grade:**

- Engage in moderate to vigorous activity outside of physical education class on a daily basis.
- Willingly participate in new activities.

**Third and Fourth Grade:**

- Participate in organized activity and sport programs provided by the school and community.
- Identify an activity associated with each of the components of fitness.
- Monitor participation in physical activity for a period of time.
- Identify several vigorous activities that provide pleasure.

**Fifth and Sixth Grade:**

- Identify community resources for participation in physical activity.

*(continued from page 83)*

■ Participate regularly in physical activity outside of the school.

■ Monitor participation in physical activity and set reasonable goals for improvement.

### Standard 4: Achieves and maintains a health-enhancing level of physical fitness (motor, cognitive, and affective domain).

**Kindergarten–Second Grade:**

■ Recognize the physiological indicators of moderate to vigorous physical activity.

■ Sustain a level of moderate to vigorous physical activity for at least five minutes.

**Third and Fourth Grade:**

■ Identify the components of health-related fitness and one activity related to the development of each of the components.

■ Meet the health-related fitness standard as defined by Fitnessgram.

■ Identify the benefits of participation in physical activity on a regular basis.

**Fifth and Sixth Grade:**

■ Meet the health-related fitness standard as defined by Fitnessgram.

■ Identify personal strengths and weaknesses and fitness.

■ Identify what can be done to improve each of the fitness components in terms of physical activities as well as exercises.

### Standards 5: Exhibits responsible personal and social behavior in physical activity settings (affective domain).

**Kindergarten–Second Grade:**

■ Apply rules, procedures, and safe practices with little or no reinforcement.

■ Follow directions.

■ Support and work cooperatively with another on a task.

■ Demonstrate consideration for others.

**Third and Fourth Grade:**

■ Work independently on a task without reinforcement.

■ Work cooperatively and productively with a partner or small group.

■ Willingly participate with others who may be different from themselves.

**Fifth and Sixth Grade:**

■ Work cooperatively and productively in competitive and cooperative settings.

■ Utilize time productively to complete assigned tasks.

■ Identify rules, procedures, and safe practices for a variety of activity settings.

■ Work cooperatively with more and less skilled participants.

■ Demonstrate support for others in practice and applied settings.

■ Identify what they need to practice and practice it independently.

### Standard 6: Values physical activity for health, enjoyment, challenge, self-expression, and/or social interaction (affective domain).

**Kindergarten–Second Grade:**

■ Willingly try new activities.

■ Indicate they enjoy an activity.

■ Feel good about participation in physical activity.

■ Use physical activity as a means of self-expression.

**Third and Fourth Grade:**

■ Choose a challenging activity and get better at it.

■ Identify the activities that are personally most enjoyable.

■ Identify the relationship between success at an activity and enjoyment.

■ Use physical activity as a means of self-expression.

**Fifth and Sixth Grade:**

■ Identify different benefits from different activities.

■ Identify the activities that are personally most enjoyable.

■ Seek challenges in physical activity.

■ Use physical activity as a means of self-expression.

development of locomotor skills and body management skills such as transferring weight and balancing and rolling are all affected by the child's balance limitations. Work at the kindergarten level establishes a movement vocabulary that will be further developed at other grade levels (e.g., general space, personal space, directions, pathways). You will notice that you don't see a lot of manipulative skills identified for the kindergarten level. Children of this age can throw, strike, and kick to generate a lot of force and need these experiences. However, they can't be expected to control the direction of these objects and can't be expected to receive what they can throw, strike, and kick. Catching and receiving skills of any sort are difficult for most children who cannot visually track a ball, making it imperative that equipment be modified and expectations are limited.

The first and second grader is increasingly gaining control of his/her own body and objects. Many fundamental and basic skills need to be accomplished at these early ages in the areas of body management, locomotor patterns, and manipulative patterns. These basic and foundational skills are critical to being a participant in both structured and nonstructured opportunities for physical activity. Good programs will make every effort to ensure that all students are competent in these skills.

## Third and Fourth Grade

*Emphases:*

- Demonstrate mature form in selected manipulative patterns.
- Adapt a skill to dynamic and unpredictable environments.
- Acquire a few specialized sport skills.
- Combine movement skills in applied settings.

Two characteristics differentiate the third- and fourth-grade program from what the first and second graders should be doing. First, the third and fourth graders should be working to refine *all* basic and fundamental skills. Developmentally, this student will be motivated to refine and develop these skills if given the opportunity to do so. Second, the student is being introduced to sport-specific skills. Throwing now becomes passing in basketball or throwing in baseball/softball and striking now becomes floor hockey, softball/baseball, golf, or tennis. They work on sport-specific skills to develop control over the objects and not to use these skills in competitive situations. Students at this age who have a racket in their hands think they are playing tennis. Students at this age who are dribbling and passing a basketball think they are playing basketball. When children get to third and fourth grade, all basic and fundamental skills should be developed at a level of competence in those skills.

## Fifth and Sixth Grade

*Emphases:*

- Demonstrate mature form in throwing, catching, and striking patterns.
- Combine manipulative patterns of specialized sport skills (e.g., dribble and shoot, dribble and pass, receive and pass).

Roller blading would be appropriate content for upper elementary students. (© *image100/PunchStock*)

■ Demonstrate basic strategies for net and invasion games.
■ Acquire the specialized patterns of one individualized and one lifetime activity.

Fifth and sixth graders are making the transition from childhood to preadolescence. In terms of their motor skills, they are doing likewise. While some students in this age group will still need to spend time on the refinement of basic skills, most will be making the transition to using basic skills and sport-specific skills in simple conditions. Teachers should not be in a hurry to use skills in too complex conditions. Rather, they need to concentrate on helping these students master the fundamentals of sport activities and lifetime physical activities. While any one program cannot give students experiences in all appropriate sports and activities, the long-term picture of a K–12 program in terms of the sports and activities that will be further developed at the secondary level should guide what is chosen to be taught in the elementary school.

## Standard 2: Demonstrates Understanding of Movement Concepts, Principles, Strategies, and Tactics as They Apply to the Learning and Performance of Physical Activities (Cognitive Domain)

The intent of this standard is to provide the knowledge students need to perform motor skills and participate in motor skill activities. While it is not the intent of this standard to make cognitive learning the major focus of physical education classes, it is the intent to provide students with basic information from all the disciplines as well as knowledge of how to perform a variety of motor activities.

### Kindergarten–Second Grade

*Emphases:*

- Identify the critical elements of basic movement patterns (locomotor and manipulative skills).
- Use feedback to improve performance.
- Apply movement concepts to a variety of basic skills.
- Understand why people perform at different abilities and attribute those differences to practice and experience.

The intent of this standard for kindergarten is to begin to establish a movement vocabulary that can be used throughout the student's physical education experiences and to begin to give students information they can use about how to do movement that they can use to enhance performance. For the kindergartener, the primary emphasis will be on establishing a vocabulary primarily from the BSER (Body/Space/Effort/Relationship) framework of Laban, that the teacher can use in the design of future learning experiences. Awareness of the body and its parts, awareness of the spatial qualities of movement (e.g., pathways, directions, general space, personal space), contrasting effort qualities (e.g., speed, force, flow), and relationships with objects in relation to themselves (e.g., under, over, on top of) are critical concepts to be identified and applied to their movement experiences.

The motor skill standard of the first- and second-grade curriculum focuses heavily on basic and fundamental skills. As students refine those skills, the cognitive emphasis of the program for these students should focus on identifying the critical elements, of good performance for these skills (the cues). They should not only be able to identify these critical elements but also be able to use them to provide feedback to others. They will have to be able to use the BSER concepts they learned at the kindergarten level to modify their movements and be able to understand how best to produce and reduce force and maintain balance.

### Third and Fourth Grade

*Emphases:*

- Use critical elements of a skill to improve performance and provide feedback to others.
- Apply simple learning and biomechanical principles in learning motor skills.

Third and fourth graders are naturally inquisitive. They want to understand principles and rules that govern their bodies and movement, making this age a perfect time to introduce them to many concepts that can help them learn and perform motor skills. Students can learn concepts on how to produce and reduce force in their skills and ideas related to balance and ready positions for different skills.

### Fifth and Sixth Grade

*Emphases:*

- Identify and apply principles of practice and conditioning to improve performance.
- Use basic offense and defensive tactics of invasion and net activities in non-complex settings.

Many fifth and sixth graders are participating in competitive youth sport programs and/or are interested in being members of a team. Some are beginning to develop interests in recreational activities that require them to be able to use complex movement patterns such as skate boarding. At the same time they are just developing the specialized skills to be competent in those activities. They are entering adolescence or are preadolescent, giving them a natural curiosity about their bodies and more independence and control over what they do. Giving them knowledge that will help them make better decisions should be part of a good physical education program.

## Standard 3: Participates Regularly in Physical Activity (Motor, Cognitive, and Affective Domain)

Although all of the standards are designed to develop a physically active lifestyle, Standard 3 specifically addresses this standard as an outcome of a good program and identifies grade level expectations that will help a student develop a physically active lifestyle as a child and later as an adult.

The national association has developed guidelines for children for participation in physical activity, which appear in Box 5.3 on page 89. These guidelines can be shared with school administrators and parents. Although they are meant to help the adults who control the child's life, there is no reason why students should not be aware of them.

### Kindergarten–Second Grade

*Emphases:*

- Engage in moderate to vigorous activity outside of physical education class on a daily basis.
- Willingly participate in new activities.

### Third and Fourth Grade

*Emphases:*

- Participate in organized activity and sport programs provided by the school and community.
- Identify an activity associated with each of the components of fitness.

## Box 5.3   Guidelines for Physical Activity for Children*

*Guideline 1*   Children should accumulate at least 60 minutes, and up to several hours, of age-appropriate physical activity on all, or most, days of the week. This daily accumulation should include moderate and vigorous physical activity, with the majority of the time spent in activity that is intermittent in nature.

*Guideline 2*   Children should participate in several bouts of physical activity lasting 15 minutes or more each day.

*Guideline 3*   Children should participate each day in a variety of age-appropriate physical activities designed to achieve optimal health, wellness, fitness, and performance benefits.

*Guideline 4*   Extended periods (periods of two hours or more) of inactivity are discouraged for children, especially during the daytime hours.

*NASPE, 2001.

- Monitor participation in physical activity for a period of time.
- Identify several vigorous activities that provide pleasure.

At the third- and fourth-grade levels, the intent is to help students make good decisions regarding what they do outside of physical education class.

### Fifth and Sixth Grade

*Emphases:*

- Identify community resources for participation in physical activity.
- Participate regularly in physical activity outside of the school.
- Monitor participation in physical activity and set reasonable goals for improvement.

Fifth and sixth graders will have many opportunities to participate in community activities. More formal attention and efforts to change behavior in terms of their participation in physical activity on a daily basis are reflected in the expectations for this grade level.

## Standard 4: Achieves and Maintains a Health-Enhancing Level of Physical Fitness (Motor, Cognitive, and Affective Domain)

Standard four is the "fitness" outcome of physical education programs. Developmentally, the concept of fitness, and skills related to the development of fitness, progress through the curriculum, from creating an awareness of the indicators of more vigorous activity to identifying the components and knowing how to develop fitness. Fitness testing is not recommended until the fourth grade.

### Kindergarten–Second Grade

*Emphases:*

- Recognize the physiological indicators of moderate to vigorous physical activity.
- Sustain a level of moderate to vigorous physical activity for at least five minutes.

Because of their physiological characteristics, students at the kindergarten age should be able to sustain vigorous activity for only short amounts of time. They will go all out but then will need frequent but short rests. Cognitively they should be aware of what happens to their body (increases in heart rate, breathing hard, and sweating) as they increase their levels of physical activity and know that it is good to do so. Students are introduced to the benefits of being fit in the first and second grade. They should be increasing their ability to sustain vigorous activity.

### Third and Fourth Grade

*Emphases:*

- Identify the components of health-related fitness and one activity related to the development of each of the components.
- Meet the health-related fitness standard as defined by Fitnessgram.
- Identify the benefits of participation in physical activity on a regular basis.

Students are introduced to the components of fitness in the third and fourth grades and to the activities associated with them. It is at this age when fitness testing and learning experiences built around fitness testing can begin to give students more knowledge of their personal status in regard to fitness and help them begin to improve that status.

### Fifth and Sixth Grade

*Emphases:*

- Meet the health-related fitness standard as defined by Fitnessgram.
- Identify personal strengths and weaknesses and fitness.
- Identify what can be done to improve each of the fitness components in terms of physical activities as well as exercises.

Students at the fifth and sixth grade should have the knowledge and skills to work on developing their personal fitness goals with the help of the teacher.

## Standard 5: Exhibits Responsible Personal and Social Behavior in Physical Activity Settings (Affective Domain)

The intent of Standard 5 is to develop responsibility for both self and others. The development of reflective thought and a sense of others beyond the self are developmental. At the kindergarten level children are learning the rules of "going to school" as well as the rules of the gym. At the fifth- and sixth-grade level students should be learning to act independently in a responsible way and to acquire a value system they can apply to their participation. This standard also includes personal behaviors such as those that relate to how students feel about themselves and their participation in physical activity.

## Kindergarten–Second Grade

### *Emphases:*

- Apply rules, procedures, and safe practices with little or no reinforcement.
- Follow directions.
- Support and work cooperatively with another on a task.
- Demonstrate consideration for others.

For the kindergarten student the focus of this standard is on following rules and playing well with others. Teachers must have specific goals for this standard and an intent to teach these ideas directly and reinforce them often. The first- and second-grade student begins to focus on working productively with others rather than just not interfering with the rights of others. Working with others at this level usually means with another student. At this level an awareness of differences between people begins to develop and must be channeled positively.

## Third and Fourth Grade

### *Emphases:*

- Work independently on a task without reinforcement.
- Work cooperatively and productively with a partner or small group.
- Willingly participate with others who may be different from themselves.

While the third and fourth grader are becoming very capable of independent behavior from adults, they will need to be taught how to be independent in responsible ways. They are beginning to be concerned with peer alignments and competitive behaviors and attitudes with others. Again, channeling their feelings productively becomes a major concern of this standard for this age group.

## Fifth and Sixth Grade

### *Emphases:*

- Work cooperatively and productively in competitive and cooperative settings.
- Utilize time productively to complete assigned tasks.
- Identify rules, procedures, and safe practices for a variety of activity settings.
- Work cooperatively with more and less skilled participants.
- Demonstrate support for others in practice and applied settings.
- Identify what they need to practice and practice it independently.

Appropriate competitive and cooperative behaviors are a major focus of this age group. The oftentimes inappropriate behavior of sport models and lack of tolerance for others must be counteracted. Likewise, these students are capable of independent and productive learning and need to focus in that direction.

## Standard 6: Values Physical Activity for Health, Enjoyment, Challenge, Self-Expression, and/or Social Interaction (Affective Domain)

Standard 6 focuses on the idea that most people do not participate in physical activity only for the health of it. Rather they participate in physical activity because they enjoy it, and people enjoy participation in different activities for different reasons. Standard 6 should develop an interest in different kinds of activities both within and outside of school. It should also develop a personal awareness of preferences for physical activity.

### Kindergarten–Second Grade

*Emphases:*

- Willingly try new activities.
- Indicate they enjoy an activity.
- Feel good about participation in physical activity.
- Use physical activity as a means of self-expression.

Almost everything will be new to kindergarten students and most will be willing to try new things. Encouraging them to "try" and helping them to understand that it is not only okay to be a beginner at something but that it is desirable, is important learning. They may not be able to identify why they like or do not like an activity, but they will be able to acknowledge feelings associated with participation in different activities.

The first and second graders' world is expanding beyond the home. Teachers can take advantage of this by helping them to understand the world of physical activity in the community. They should be encouraged to identify what they enjoy and be willing to participate in those activities they may not initially enjoy as well to express their ideas and feelings through expressive movement.

### Third and Fourth Grade

*Emphases:*

- Choose a challenging activity and get better at it.
- Identify the activities that are personally most enjoyable.
- Identify the relationship between success at an activity and enjoyment.
- Use physical activity as a means of self-expression.

Third and fourth graders can identify different activities as they become more aware of the "sport world." They should also begin to identify the relationship between what they enjoy and what they are good at while they are learning how to "get good."

### Fifth and Sixth Grade

*Emphases:*

- Identify different benefits from different activities.
- Identify the activities that are personally most enjoyable.

- Seek challenges in physical activity.
- Use physical activity as a means of self-expression.

The fifth- and sixth-grade student should be able to associate the characteristics of an activity for enjoyment with the activity. As they become comfortable with different activities they may not be willing to try new ones. Students of this age can also begin to recognize good performance and value it.

## Issues in the Elementary School

A teacher must come to a decision on many issues surrounding the development of curriculum in the elementary school. Primary among these are issues surrounding the best preparation for the development of skills needed for physical activity, what kinds of activity the student should be prepared for, the role of the physical education teacher in integrating academic content, the role of the teacher and program in meeting the physical activity needs of the student, and whether the development of fitness should be an activity or an exercise approach.

### Developing Skills Needed for Physical Activity

There is no consensus in the field regarding how best to give students the skills they need for a lifetime of physical activity. There are many valid approaches to reaching the outcomes presented in the beginning section of this chapter, each with its advantages and disadvantages. As you read through the discussion below, think about the kinds of experiences you had as a child in your own physical education experiences and what the advantages and disadvantages of the approach were to you.

**A Physical Activity Approach Versus Instructional Skill Approach.**  Currently there is a debate about whether students will be more active as both children and adults if the program they participate in emphasizes skill development or whether they are likely to be more active if the approach taken is one of engaging students in fun physical activity. While the division between these may not always be clear, the decision you make on this issue will have strong consequences for how you design your curriculum.

Advocates of a physical activity approach think that if students are engaged in fun physical activities and we do not demand too much from students in terms of more complex skills, that they are more likely to be engaged throughout their lifetime. Advocates of a more-skill-instruction orientation to the program counter that argument with the idea that students are more likely to be participants if they are good at something and have the skills to participate. You do not learn skills by participating in games, particularly those that do not demand any skill.

While the jury is still out on the long-term effects of both approaches, the national standards clearly define outcomes in terms of skills students should have as a result of their physical education program.

**Low-Organization Games.**    Closely related to an activity approach to the curriculum is a low-organization games approach (e.g., Red Rover, Steel the Bacon, Call Ball, Kick Ball). The curriculum is designed around game forms that increase in complexity and utilize different motor skills in less-complex organizational formats than most sports. Many professionals are opposed to the inclusion of these activities and a program built around these activities because many of the games and activities are elimination-type games, few students get to actually be active at one time, and many of the skills that are used are very unrelated to the skills students would need in physical activities they would later want to participate in. Many professionals support the inclusion of low-organization games as a preparation for childhood play. Children can use these activities at home. The argument for the inclusion of these activities rests heavily on how much fun they are for children, at least those children who do well in them. The argument against them is that children don't learn skills under these conditions.

Some professionals are not supportive of instructional programs and believe that if you provide children with physical activity they enjoy, they will be active for a life time. (© *image100/ PunchStock*)

**A Sport-Oriented Skill Orientation.**   Many skill-oriented programs are designed to begin with specialized sport skills regardless of the fact that most young children are not yet ready for the complexity involved in those skills. Advocates of a *begin sport skills early* approach support this orientation with the idea that the development of skill is specific and that there is no such thing as general motor ability. They would say that if you want to produce a tennis player, teach them tennis and not striking with the hand or a paddle. First graders would learn to hit a ball with a tennis racket and set a volleyball. Many youth sport programs for young children take this approach. The curriculum using this orientation would select specialized sport skills to begin at an early age and develop them in increasingly more complex forms. To some extent the notion of skill specificity is accurate. The problem lies in the issue of whether we want to produce tennis players.

**A Movement Education Orientation.**   Professionals who support a movement education orientation to physical education build their programs around the content areas of educational dance, games, and gymnastics and the body/space/effort/relationship concepts of Rudolf Laban. The term *educational* in front of the content areas signifies that these content areas are not the same as formal gymnastics, sport instruction, or performance-oriented dance. What is different about them is that for the most part the focus is on developing larger concepts (a bigger chunk of the content) than the specific skills of these activities. Students learn to roll, catch, strike, and take weight on their hands in a manner that can be used for all kinds of rolling, catching, striking, and weight bearing.

Several variations of movement education have emerged over the years. The more purist form of movement education uses the themes of the body, space, effort, and relationships as the major organizer of the content (see Chapter 6). In this orientation the content is these concepts. Students learn about using the body in space, with different effort actions, and in relationships with others and equipment. The more popular version of movement education divides the content into skill themes, with body actions being the organizer, such as jumping and landing, traveling on different body parts, and striking. The skill themes are then developed using the movement concepts.

What is critical to understand about movement education is that the student is working with general patterns such as sending, striking, and jumping (elevation), and not the specialized sport skills that emerge from these patterns. Advocates believe that if competence in these skill themes is developed very broadly, then learning more specialized patterns will come easier as the child gets older.

When students make the transition from the more general skill themes to actually working on pitching and passing rather than just throwing varies from program to program. Somewhere in the third or fourth grade most programs begin to make the transition in most skills from skill themes like striking with different body parts to a volleyball set, serve, and pass, and soccer skills.

**Fundamental and Basic Skill Orientation.**   A fundamental and basic skill orientation to the elementary program focuses on the development of basic locomotor (hop, skip, jump, etc.) and manipulative skills (throwing catching, striking, etc.)

without the broad development and variations of these skills common in movement education programs described above. Students will learn to skip but not necessarily to skip in different directions, pathways, with a partner, etc. They will learn to throw without the emphasis on throwing different objects with different trajectories, for example. The assumption is that if students really learn the basic pattern well, they will be able to vary it when needed. A program with a fundamental skill orientation will usually make the transition to more specialized sport skills by the third or fourth grade.

## What Kinds of Activity Should Students Be Prepared For?

As you can tell from the discussion above, most elementary programs are oriented to the development of some form of basic and fundamental skill development under the assumption that learning more specialized skills for participation will come later. One of the issues the profession is dealing with today is the nature of the specialized skills students will need to maintain their levels of physical activity. Although the fundamental and basic skills for the primary level should provide a sound foundation for many different activities, when the students get to the upper elementary grades, decisions will need to be made about the specialized skills of the program. One of the issues is related to the dichotomy between a preparation for participation in sport and a preparation for more lifetime activities. Lifetime activities can include those of childhood like bicycle riding, inline skating, or climbing walls, or those to be used later by adults such as golf, archery, tennis, or backpacking. Most children who are active on a regular basis are participants in sport, but not all have the ability or interest to be participants in sport forms that use complex motor skills. The *deskilling* of the program to include some activities easily mastered by the majority of students has the potential to be more inclusive, whether the skills to be included are those used by the students in the present or those that are a preparation for adolescence or adulthood.

## The Integration of Academic Content into the Physical Education Curriculum

There are elementary schools that specialize in math, science, the arts, or just about any content area in the school curriculum. In many of these schools it is the job of every teacher to integrate that special subject into the physical education curriculum. Because children learn better when subject matter is integrated, the call for integration in the elementary school is a strong one.

Because movement is an active medium for learning, just about anything can be taught through movement. What is sometimes a problem with the idea of integration is that the objectives of the lesson no longer are the objectives appropriate for physical education. Third graders can walk through the blood vessels to the heart to understand the workings of the heart. Walking, however, is hardly an appropriate third-grade physical education objective. Having both the academic objectives and the physical education objectives as appropriate goals for a lesson integration can be a powerful tool.

Physical educators can do much to integrate what young children are learning into their lessons. Math and language arts skills in the primary school (e.g., counting, spelling, reading, writing, colors) are easy for physical education teachers to integrate into their lessons. Social studies and science tend to be a little more difficult to do without spending a lot of time that is taken away from physical education content.

## An Activity or Exercise Approach to Fitness

The national guidelines that describe a good physical education program clearly indicate that an activity orientation to fitness is most appropriate for the elementary school level. An activity approach stresses the attainment of fitness through activity rather than exercise, implying that it is not appropriate for children to spend their time in exercises to meet fitness requirements, but rather in fun-type activities. At the same time there are knowledges and skills related to an exercise approach to fitness that the student needs as a preparation for understanding fitness. Most of the performance indicators related to these knowledges and skills appear in the upper elementary grades (e.g., identifying the components of fitness, checking heart rate). The childhood obesity problem in this country has caused legislators and educators to find ways to implement the guidelines for elementary children 30 minutes a day of physical activity. For most schools this means a combination of both time spent in physical education and time spent in other school programs designed to promote physical activity. School programs that focus on encouraging students to participate in physical activity rather than exercises are likely to be more successful with the long-term goals of a physically active lifestyle.

## The Role of the Physical Education Teacher as Physical Activity Director

Children need at least 30 minutes of moderate to vigorous physical activity a day and most recommendations suggest an hour. Many students do not get it and few schools can give it to them in a daily physical education class. As a response to the increasing levels of obesity in children, many states have introduced the idea that it is the school's responsibility to provide at least 30 minutes of physical activity a day for students, but not necessarily in physical education. Because it is the physical education teacher who is most qualified to administer these programs, it is the physical education teacher who is most often called upon to direct these programs.

Students can be provided with opportunities to be active in the school outside the physical education class in a variety of ways. The physical education teacher can have the classroom teacher follow up on physical education lessons, or have the classroom teacher encourage walking, jogging, or active game programs during recess. Parents can be brought in to help supervise before- and after-school programs that are not high-risk activities. All faculty in a school can be involved in helping run special events that involve students in marathons and other community events, walk-your-child to school programs, parent and child activity nights, etc. The important idea here is that although the physical education teacher is expected to direct these programs, they are not expected to run all of the events. The physical activity model for the school makes physical activity the responsibility of the entire school.

## Check Your Understanding

1. Describe the major cognitive affective and psychomotor characteristics of young children.
2. Why is the elementary school program so critical to developing a physically active lifestyle?
3. What does the national association say is a good physical education program in the elementary school?
4. What skills should children at different ages in the elementary school be able to do?
5. For each of the national standards, describe at least two outcomes for each grade level.
6. What curriculum orientation do you think is most appropriate for the elementary school and why do you think so?

## References

National Association for Sport and Physical Education (NASPE). (2000). *Appropriate Practices for Elementary School Physical Education*. Reston, VA: NASPE.

National Association for Sport and Physical Education (NASPE). (2004). *Moving Into the Future: National Content Standards for Physical Education*. Reston, VA: NASPE.

Mohnsen, B. (Ed.). (2003). *Concepts and Principles of Physical Education: What Every Student Needs to Know*. Reston, VA: National Association for Sport and Physical Education (NASPE).

## Suggested Reading

Allison, P., & Barrett, K. (2000). *Constructing Children's Physical Education Experiences*. Boston: Allyn and Bacon.

Cone, T., Werner, P., Cone, S., & Woods, A. (1998). *Interdisciplinary Teaching Through Physical Education*. Champaign, IL: Human Kinetics.

Gallahue, D., (2002). *Developing Physical Education for Today's Children*. Champaign, IL: Human Kinetics.

Graham, G., Holt-Hale, S., & Parker, M. (2001). *Children Moving: A Reflective Approach to Teaching Physical Education*. Boston: McGraw-Hill.

# CHAPTER 6

# Designing the Elementary School Program

## OVERVIEW

In Chapter 5 you learned to describe what a good elementary physical education program should be and some of the issues involved in planning one. In Chapter 3 you learned the steps involved in planning a curriculum. In this chapter you will integrate your knowledge from both chapters to actually plan an elementary school curriculum. The chapter takes you through the steps of planning an elementary curriculum one step at a time.

## OUTCOMES

- Describe the issues that should be part of the philosophy statement for an elementary school curriculum.
- List appropriate objectives for the elementary school consistent with each of the national standards.
- Sequence objectives for the elementary school program.
- Describe several content frameworks that might be appropriate for the elementary school.
- Place program objectives into a content framework for an elementary school program.
- Describe alternative assessment plans for program evaluation in the elementary school.

The process of designing a curriculum was outlined in Chapter 3 of this text. A full curriculum should include:

1. A statement of philosophy that describes the purpose of your program and the rationale for including your program in the school curriculum.
2. The specific goals of your program drawn from your philosophy and your understanding of your students that describe the skills, knowledge, and dispositions you want your students to have when they leave your program.
3. A sequence of objectives/outcomes by grade level that take learners from where they are at the beginning of your program to the specific goals you have established for the end of your program.
4. A content framework that organizes your program objectives by content area into units or themes and describes what will be taught in each grade.
5. A yearly block plan for a grade level that describes what content area will be taught over which lessons.
6. An assessment plan that will be used to determine if the goals of the program have been achieved (Chapter 9).

## Step 1: A Statement of Philosophy

A statement of philosophy for the elementary school level should include your perspective on the kinds of experiences elementary school children need in order to develop and maintain a physically active lifestyle both as children and as adults. Because school programs are increasingly dealing with the idea of physical activity in terms of both the physical education program as well as other opportunities in the school day to be physically active, your statement of philosophy can be inclusive of the entire school program. Chapter 5 described some of the issues that you need to consider when planning the elementary program, including:

■ How best to prepare children with the motor skills they will need to be a participant in physical activity?
■ For what kinds of activity should the student be prepared?
■ What is the role of the physical education program in integrating academic content?
■ Should the approach to fitness be an activity or an exercise approach?

Your statement of philosophy should address these issues. Box 6.1 is a sample of one school's statement of philosophy.

## Step 2: The Specific Goals of Your Program

The specific goals of the elementary school program are the exit outcomes for the end of the elementary program. In Chapter 5 we listed emphases for each grade level. While you can use the emphases as goals, the specific goals of the

## Box 6.1 Sample Elementary School Statement of Philosophy: K–5

The student in the elementary school program needs at least 30 minutes a day of physical activity. This should be provided in three days a week of instructional physical education experiences and two days a week of structured school physical activity experiences. School activities will include walking clubs, structured play, and game activities during recess planned by the elementary physical education teacher and conducted by the classroom teacher, and after-school clubs and intramurals for the upper grades. The physical education instructor will also play a major role in introducing students to, and facilitating student participation in, community activities.

The purpose of the physical education program is to develop the skills, knowledge, and disposition students will need to be physically active as children and later as adolescents and adults. The elementary school program is part of a comprehensive K–12 program preparing students to be skillful in a variety of team and individual sports as well as lifetime activities that can be used as adolescents and adults. Students in our geographic area have many opportunities to participate in individual sports such as golf and tennis. These activities will be stressed throughout the whole K–12 program. Students in the K–12 program will also be knowledgeable about fitness and will know how to develop and maintain fitness through both an exercise and activity approach.

In order to best meet the needs of students with a wide range of ability, the program will use a movement education approach and will focus on skill themes that allow students to perform at their own level and advance at their own rate, including educational games, education gymnastics, and dance (e.g., creative, folk, and rhythm activities) at all grade levels. A gradual transition to specialized sport skills will begin in the third grade with the introduction of racket skills, basketball, and soccer skills. Each level will include as part of the program physical activities that students can do as part of normal play outside of school (e.g., jumping rope, inline skating, four square).

The physical education program will map out academic content that is being taught in the classroom for each month and grade level and will make every effort to reinforce the knowledge and skills being developed there.

program are more useful for planning if you make them more specific to your own program. Box 6.2 describes the goals of one program that are more specific than the emphases.

## Step 3: A Sequence of Objectives/Outcomes by Grade Level

After you have decided on the goals of your program, which are exit outcomes for your school level, the next step in planning your program is to take the exit outcomes for the end of your program and describe what the outcomes/objectives should be for each grade level. In one sense what you are describing is how to get to those exit outcomes. Box 6.3 on page 104 describes a sample of what one school has designated as their grade level outcomes/objectives that is pretty consistent with "best practice," meaning that a lot of professionals would agree that these outcomes should be achieved at these grade levels.

Many times teachers will say that they cannot reach the defined outcomes for a grade level with students in one or two years of physical education. You are not expected to. The scope and sequence of objectives represent outcomes at the end of the designated grade levels. It does not mean that you cannot or should not be

## Box 6.2   Sample Elementary School Program Goals: K–5

**Standard 1: Demonstrates competency in motor skills and movement patterns needed to perform a variety of physical activities (psychomotor domain).**

■ Demonstrate competency in all locomotor movements alone and in combination with each other.

■ Demonstrate competency and mature form in the following manipulative skills:

  □ Overhand throwing pattern.

  □ Underhand throwing pattern.

  □ Catching a small ball thrown from 30 feet—fly and grounders.

■ Demonstrate mature form under simple conditions with the following sport skills:

  □ Golf swing.

  □ Volleyball set and forearm pass.

  □ Forehand striking pattern with a racket continuously against the wall.

  □ Soccer dribble and pass to a partner.

  □ Basketball dribble and pass to a partner.

■ Demonstrate competency in the following body management skills:

  □ Maintain weight on hands in a vertical position for at least three seconds.

  □ Sequence rolling, inverted balances, and traveling actions with good form.

■ Demonstrate competency in the following dance skills:

  □ Perform an age-appropriate folk or line dance accurately with the beat of the music.

  □ With a partner dribble/throw/and catch a ball with the music in a self-designed rhythmic routine.

  □ Create an expressive dance contrasting either the speed or effort characteristic of movement.

■ Skate 50 feet at a moderate speed, turn and skate back to a stop without losing balance.

**Standard 2: Demonstrates understanding of movement concepts, principles, strategies, and tactics as they apply to the learning and performance of physical activities (cognitive domain).**

■ Identify the critical elements of the fundamental manipulative patterns and basic skills of the sports of the program.

■ Identify the components of fitness, how they may be tested, and at least one activity and one exercise that can be used in their development.

---

working on those outcomes in earlier grades. In fact to achieve those outcomes you will need to build work on those outcomes into previous grades. The scope and sequence below illustrates that point for both the K–2 program and 3–6 program. The grade level objective is identified and then the potential learning experiences in earlier grades that would help develop that grade level outcome are identified.

### Second-grade Objective: Demonstrate a Mature Form of Skipping

*Kindergarten experience:* Travel in different ways using your feet in general space and stop in control when you here the signal.

*First grade experience:* Choose either a skip or a gallop to the music.

*Second grade experience:* Show me what a good skip looks like.

- Describe how people get better at motor skills and why some people perform better than others.
- Use and provide accurate and supportive feedback to others.
- Describe the basic offensive and defensive tactics of a one-on-one situation in two different invasion sports and a net activity.
- Describe how to increase and decrease for production in the following skills: throwing for distance, striking with a racket or club, jumping for distance.

**Standard 3: Participates regularly in physical activity (motor, cognitive, and affective domain).**
- Identify the opportunities in and out of school for regular participation in physical activity.
- Participate daily in some form of physical activity.
- Identify lifestyle changes that can be made to increase physical activity.

**Standard 4: Achieves and maintains a health-enhancing level of physical fitness.**
- Meet the health-related fitness standard as described in Fitnessgram.
- List and define each component of fitness and how it might be developed both through exercise and physical activity.

**Standards 5: Exhibits responsible personal and social behavior in physical activity settings (affective domain).**
- Describe what it means to play safely in high-risk activities.
- Work productively with others in cooperative and competitive settings.
- Describe how to accommodate individual differences in physical activity settings.

**Standard 6: Values physical activity for health, enjoyment, challenge, self-expression, and/or social interaction (affective domain).**
- List two activities that you really enjoy enough to do on a regular basis.
- Demonstrate an appreciation of the performance of others.
- Demonstrate tolerance toward others who are different than you.
- Identify those activities that are more associated with challenge, self expression, and social interaction.

## Sixth-grade Objective: Maintain a Personal Record of Participation in Physical Activity over a Period of One Month

*Kindergarten experience:* Raise your hand if you were active at recess today.

*First and second grade:* Do at least one thing that is really physically active after school today. Check the box on your physical activity homework and have your parents initial it.

*Third and fourth grade:* Write down all the things you did after school yesterday and check those things that are physically active.

*Fifth and sixth grade:* Maintain a personal record of participation in physical activity over a period of one month.

# Box 6.3   Sample Elementary School Outcomes/Objectives by Grade Level

**Kindergarten: Standard 1**

**Grade Level Objectives/Outcomes**

- Run, hop, jump, gallop, and slide.
- Maintain stillness while supported on a variety of body parts.
- Travel in straight, curved, and zigzag pathways.
- Transfer weight from the feet to the hands and come down softly.
- Travel to the beat of even and uneven rhythms.
- Contrast quick (fast) and slow (sustained) movements.
- Drop and catch an object with one bounce.
- Demonstrate controlled traveling actions using a variety of body parts.
- Throw an object using opposition.
- Catch a softly tossed beanbag or yarn ball.
- Strike, throw, and kick an object forcefully.

**First and Second Grade: Standard 1**

**Grade Level Objectives/Outcomes**

- Combine walking with hopping, jumping, galloping, skipping, and sliding with smooth transitions.
- Demonstrate a mature form of hopping, skipping, sliding, and jumping.
- Combine balancing, weight transfer, and rolling movements into a repeatable sequence with a clear beginning and ending.
- Dribble an object from a stationary position.
- Catch a softly tossed ball from a partner 15 feet away.
- Throw a hand-sized ball with a side orientation, opposition, and rotation for a distance of 30 feet.
- Perform dance sequences to music.
- Create expressive movement sequences.
- Jump and land in various combinations (one to same foot, one to the other foot, one to two feet, two to two feet, two to one foot).
- Use fundamental manipulative and nonmanipulative skills in self-testing and cooperative activities.

- Toss an object to a partner so that it can be caught.
- Momentarily support weight on hands and come down softly.
- Maintain stillness in a variety of balances for at least three seconds.
- Balance, travel, and roll using small apparatus.

**Third and Fourth Grade: Standard 1**

**Grade Level Objectives/Outcomes**

- Demonstrate mature form in all basic manipulative patterns.
- Dribble and kick an object while moving.
- Throw a ball overhand and underhand with mature form.
- Catch a thrown ball from at least 30 feet.
- Continuously strike an object with a paddle.
- Demonstrate strategies for chasing, fleeing, and dodging.
- Perform simple dances to music (creative, folk, line, rhythmic).
- Combine traveling, balancing, and rolling actions with a change in level, direction, or speed.
- Jump a single rope continuously.
- Demonstrate competence in the specialized sport skills of at least one invasion game (soccer, floor hockey, basketball); net game (volleyball, badminton, and pickle ball); striking/fielding game (baseball, softball, Whiffle ball); and target game (bowling, golf).
- Apply movement concepts (body, space, effort, and relationships) to gymnastics actions and sequences.
- Use a wide variety of manipulative patterns in self-testing and low-organization gamelike activities.

**Fifth and Sixth Grade: Standard 1**

**Grade Level Objectives/Outcomes**

- Strike an object continuously with a paddle/racquet using a mature forearm pattern.

- Receive and pass an object with a partner against a defender.
- Travel and maintain control of an object in a two-on-one situation.
- Perform the given steps and sequences in rhythm to the music for an age-appropriate dance (e.g., line, square, folk, step, and social).
- Perform a gymnastics/movement sequence with a partner using a variety of body management skills with variations in movement concepts.
- Demonstrate competency in an individual non-competitive activity.
- Use the basic skills and tactics of invasion and net activities in a small-sided modified game.
- Demonstrate the basic pattern of a target activity.

## Kindergarten: Standard 2

### Grade Level Objectives/Outcomes

- Recognize a run, hop, jump, gallop, and slide.
- Recognize basic movement concepts of space (direction, pathway, level).
- Identify in, out, over, under, and through relationships with objects relative to movement experiences.
- Identify a dominant hand and foot for throwing and striking patterns.
- Identify what you have to do to land softly from a jump.
- Identify general and personal space.

## First and Second Grade: Standard 2

### Grade Level Objectives/Outcomes

- Identify the critical elements of a run, hop, jump, gallop, skip, and slide.
- Identify the critical elements of throwing, striking, and kicking patterns.
- Use the concepts related to space (direction, pathway, size), effort (strong, light) and time (quick, sustained) to intentionally modify basic locomotor patterns and nonlocomotor movements.
- Use specific feedback to improve performance.

- Understand that good practice is what makes you better at motor skills.
- Identify the difference between symmetrical and nonsymmetrical balances.
- Identify dodging skills as a strategy in taglike games.
- Identify principles related to how to improve balance.
- Identify the principles related to how to increase and decrease force.
- Understand that it is okay to make mistakes.

## Third and Fourth Grade: Standard 2

### Grade Level Objectives/Outcomes

- Identify three critical cues for the dribble, kick, catch, throw, and strike.
- Use critical elements to provide feedback to others.
- Understand that high amounts of appropriate practice improve performance.
- Describe basic offensive and defensive tactics in an invasion type of game (basketball, soccer, floor hockey).
  - Identify the characteristics of good practice.
  - Explain why some people are better than others at motor skills.
  - Understand the importance of safety in all activities but particularly those that are high risk.
  - Identify the characteristics of skilled performance.
  - Identify the importance of warm-up and cool down.
  - Know how to lift and pull a heavy object safely.
  - Distinguish between the symmetrical and asymmetrical patterns of the body

## Fifth and Sixth Grade: Standard 2

### Grade Level Objectives/Outcomes

- Identify skills/sports that use similar patterns/concepts.

*(continued on next page)*

*(continued from previous page)*

- Identify how to increase or decrease force in a variety of manipulative and nonmanipulative patterns.
- Identify principles of practice and conditioning that enhance performance.
- Identify basic offensive and defensive tactics for modified invasion and net activities.
- Identify the cues for good performance for a variety of specialized sport skills.
- Identify the relationship between body size and performance for a variety of different activities.
- Identify what makes good team work for a variety of competitive and noncompetitive activities.
- Identify the required equipment and appropriate attire for a variety of sport and other physical activities.

### Kindergarten: Standard 3

**Grade Level Objectives/Outcomes**

- Demonstrate involvement in physical activity during recess.
- Demonstrate involvement in physical activity outside of school.
- Identify likes and dislikes connected with participation in physical activity.
- Recognize that physical activity is good for you.

### First and Second Grade: Standard 3

**Grade Level Objectives/Outcomes**

- Demonstrate involvement in physical activity during recess and outside of school.
- Identify appropriate physical activities for recess and outside of school.
- Distinguish between those activities that are aerobic and those that are not.
- Identify the health benefits of physical activity.
- Set physical activity goals and meet them.

### Third and Fourth Grade: Standard 3

**Grade Level Objectives/Outcomes**

- Identify moderate and vigorous physical activities that can be done outside of school.

- Demonstrate regular participation in at least one physical activity (moderate or vigorous) outside of school.
- Identify lifestyle changes that can be made to increase the level of physical activity.
- Invite others to participate in physical activity with them (parents, friends, siblings).

### Fifth and Sixth Grade: Standard 3

**Grade Level Objectives/Outcomes**

- Identify opportunities in the school and community for regular participation in physical activity.
- Participate daily in some form of moderate to vigorous physical activity.
- Identify lifestyle changes that can be made to increase the level of personal physical activity.
- Maintain a personal record of participation in physical activity over a period of one month.
- Identify at least one organized community activity for personal participation and inquire as to how to become a participant in that activity.
- Describe how opportunities for participation change over the seasons.
- Identify moderate and vigorous physical activities that can be done outside of school.
- Demonstrate regular participation in at least one physical activity (moderate or vigorous) outside of school.
- Identify lifestyle changes that can be made to increase the level of physical activity.
- Invite others to participate in physical activity with them (parents, friends, siblings).

### Kindergarten: Standard 4

**Grade Level Objectives/Outcomes**

- Identify the physiological signs of physical activity (e.g., increased heart rate, faster breathing).
- Sustain moderate to vigorous physical activity for short periods of time.

### First and Second Grade: Standard 4

**Grade Level Objectives/Outcomes**

- Explain the cardiovascular benefits of regular participation in physical activity.

■ Sustain moderate to vigorous physical activity for a period not less than five minutes.

## Third and Fourth Grade: Standard 4

### Grade Level Objectives/Outcomes

■ Meet the health-related fitness standards defined in programs such as Fitnessgram.

■ Identify at least two activities that can develop each of the components of fitness.

■ Match physical fitness assessment items to the appropriate fitness component.

■ Identify the health benefits of physical activity.

■ Identify characteristics of activity needed to maintain health-related cardiovascular fitness.

■ Measure heart rate before and after activity.

## Fifth and Sixth Grade: Standard 4

### Grade Level Objectives/Outcomes

■ Meet the health-related fitness standards defined in programs such as Fitnessgram.

■ List and define each of the health-related fitness components and one activity that can be used to develop each of the components.

■ Understand the basic principles of training (frequency, intensity, and time).

■ Explain the physiological differences between fit and unfit individuals.

■ Participate daily in at least 60 minutes of moderate to vigorous physical activity.

■ Identify fitness components from the Fitnessgram that needed/or want to be improved and describe the types of activities needed to improve these components.

■ Identify personal fitness goals and develop a strategy to meet them.

## Kindergarten: Standard 5

### Grade Level Objectives/Outcomes

■ Apply established class rules, procedures, and safe practices with minimal teacher reinforcement.

■ Understand what it is to respect the rights of others in physical activity settings.

■ Share space and equipment with others.

■ Treat others with respect during play regardless of personal differences, including gender, skill level, or ethnicity.

■ Know the rules for participation in the gym or on the playground.

■ Respond to teacher signals for attentions.

■ Handle equipment safely and put it away when asked.

## First and Second Grade: Standard 5

### Grade Level Objectives/Outcomes

■ Apply established class rules, procedures, and safe practices.

■ Work cooperatively with another to complete a task.

■ Accurately report the results of work.

■ Practice specific skills as assigned until the teacher signals the end of practice.

■ Demonstrate respectful behavior toward others in physical activity settings.

■ Resolve conflicts in acceptable ways.

■ Practice a skill without being told.

■ Understand the value of contributions of different people to a group.

■ Respond positively to those more limited than themselves.

## Third and Fourth Grade: Standard 5

### Grade Level Objectives/Outcomes

■ Apply established class rules, procedures, and safe practices.

■ Work cooperatively with another or others to complete a task.

■ Accurately report the results of work.

■ Practice specific skills as assigned until the teacher signals the end of practice.

■ Demonstrate respectful behavior toward others in physical activity settings.

■ Resolve conflicts in acceptable ways.

■ Practice a skill without being told.

■ Understand the value of contributions of different people to a group.

■ Respond positively to those more limited than themselves.

*(continued on next page)*

*(continued from previous page)*

### Fifth and Sixth Grade: Standard 5

**Grade Level Objectives/Outcomes**

- Identify and apply conflict resolution strategies for competitive and cooperative activities that are age appropriate.
- Work productively in cooperative and competitive settings.
- Describe how to accommodate individual differences in physical activity settings.
- Recognize the role of game, sport, and dance in other cultures.
- Identify cultural factors that influence gender participation in physical activities.
- Identify the relationships between cooperative and competitive skills in a sport.
- Describe what teamwork means in a team activity.
- Describe what it means to play safely in high-risk activities and those that are not high risk.
- Identify appropriate participants and observe behavior for community sponsored sport leagues and other community sponsored settings for physical activity.

### Kindergarten: Standard 6

**Grade Level Objectives/Outcomes**

- Attempt new movement activities and skills.
- Identify feelings resulting from participation in physical activity.

### First and Second Grade: Standard 6

**Grade Level Objectives/Outcomes**

- Identify physical activity preferences.

- Express positive feelings about participation in a variety of class activities.
- Participate in an activity they may feel they might not enjoy.
- Identify physical activities available for their age group in the community.
- Effectively express ideas/feelings through physical activity.

### Third and Fourth Grade: Standard 6

**Grade Level Objectives/Outcomes**

- Identify physical activities that bring personal enjoyment.
- Describe the relationship between skill competence and enjoyment.
- Effectively express ideas through physical activity.

### Fifth and Sixth Grade: Standard 6

**Grade Level Objectives/Outcomes**

- Identify the characteristics of physical activities that bring personal enjoyment.
- Willingly participate in new activities or those not identified as a favorite.
- Appreciate the good performance of others.
- Identify the potential of various physical activities for challenge, self-expression, and social interaction.

The sequence of objectives by grade level represents the scope and sequence of your curriculum. Box 6.3 organizes that scope and sequence by standard and grade level. A scope and sequence is really a grid with grade level down the vertical axis and content standard along the horizontal axis.

In each of these examples there were experiences that would contribute to the development of the grade level objective in previous grade levels. In the first example the intent is that students be able to use a mature skip by the second grade. Kindergarten students are not asked to skip because there will be some who will not be able to skip. They are asked to travel on their feet in different ways. From this experience hopping and galloping responses almost always emerge, which will be a good preparation for actually skipping. In the first grade students are given a choice to respond with a skip or a gallop to an uneven rhythm. Although almost all students will be able to skip at the first grade, there will be some who are not yet ready. Giving them a choice enables them to respond with an appropriate response and prepares them for the day that the skip will emerge.

In the second example students are prepared to look at their levels of participation in physical activity with increasing formality and responsibility. Young children are just learning to read and write, and the teacher must make sure that any written material used with these age groups is appropriate.

## Step 4: The Content Framework of the Curriculum

Choosing a content framework for your curriculum is perhaps the most difficult part of the curriculum planning process. A content framework gives structure to the curriculum. In one sense teachers could take all of the outcomes that have been designed for each grade level, design learning experiences to achieve each one, and decide what days those learning experiences would be taught. You could do this, but it would be very unwieldy and not a meaningful way to think about or organize your content. Think about the idea of taking all the skills used in three different sports, shuffling them, and then teaching them in the order in which they were shuffled. The first thing you would want to do is to organize those skills by the sport that used them. The content framework helps you organize learning experiences by larger, more meaningful units. Most of you will be familiar with the most common content framework used at the high school level, which is to organize the content by sports or activities. Teachers at this level have units in basketball,

Skill in jumping rope is an appropriate second grade objective. (© *Comstock/ PunchStock*)

fitness, weight training, tennis, etc. This framework is the one we are most familiar with in physical education, it but is not appropriate for the content of the elementary program.

Most school content frameworks in physical education are organized around concepts taken from the motor skill standard (standard 1), which is in the psychomotor domain. There are content frameworks used in physical education, particularly at the elementary school level that are organized around other themes from the physical education standards (e.g., exhibits responsible personal and social behavior in physical activity settings) or from more general goals shared by all teachers in the elementary school (e.g., critical thinking, creativity, social responsibility), but most teachers think about and plan what they teach in physical education in terms of psychomotor content. Content frameworks for the elementary school begin with some description of the "whole," meaning the areas of content that are important to teach children. Box 6.4 describes several content frameworks for the total elementary curriculum.

A *movement education* framework sees the content of physical education in terms of four broad areas: educational games, educational gymnastics, and educational dance, as well as physical activity and fitness. The term *educational* is meant to imply a program that primarily focuses on the concepts involved in these content areas. In most movement education programs, the movement analysis framework of Rudolf Laban is used to develop the content. The second framework attempts to focus on the developmental nature of the transition from fundamental to specialized to sport skills. The third framework is most common in the work of Graham, Holt-Hale, & Parker (2006). Many of the skill themes listed are those that would emerge from educational games, dance, and gymnastics. Because some form of movement education is used in most elementary frameworks, movement education is more fully discussed in the sections that follow.

### Educational Games

There are many conceptual schemes that are useful for thinking about the games program for the elementary school and organizing the content. Consider for example the chart of manipulative skills described in Box 6.5 and the description of

## Box 6.4  Sample Content Frameworks for Elementary School

| Movement Education | Eclectic | Skill Themes |
| --- | --- | --- |
| Educational games | Personal health skills | Traveling |
| Educational gymnastics | Fundamental motor skills | Chasing and fleeing |
| Educational dance | Specialized motor skills | Throwing and catching |
| Physical activity and fitness | Sport skills | Jumping and landing |
| | | Volleying and dribbling |
| | | Striking with paddles and rackets |

## Box 6.5    Framework for Manipulative Skills

Sending Skills
    Tossing
    Throwing
    Striking
        With different body parts
        With hands only
        With feet only
        With implements
            Bats
            Rackets
            Clubs

Receiving skills
    Catching
    Collecting
Dodging skills
    People
    Objects
Propelling (Dribbling)
    With body parts
    With implements

types of games in Box 6.6. Together, both of these constitute a framework for teaching a games/sport program in the elementary school. The manipulative patterns would be developed as fundamental skills and then transitioned into specialized sport skills used in each of the types of games/sports.

## Educational Gymnastics

Most programs in the elementary school opt to teach gymnastics as body management skills rather than formal gymnastics skills. The goal of a body management program is for students to be able to control and manage their body weight in traveling, balancing, and weight transference actions rather than the development of isolated gymnastics skills. Again, there are many ways of conceptualizing this content. Box 6.7 illustrates one conceptual scheme for an educational gymnastics program that looks at the actions of gymnastics and translates those actions into a set of developmental themes. In this case the teacher might teach a unit to kindergarten on locomotion and stillness with the feet only or teach fourth graders the jumping actions.

## Box 6.6    Framework for Games

Invasion games
Net games
Target games/sports
Individual activities

## Box 6.7   Conceptual Scheme for An Educational Gymnastics Program

| Gymnastics Actions | Gymnastics Themes |
|---|---|
| Traveling actions | **I.** Locomotion and stillness—feet only |
|   Stepping and wheeling actions | **II.** Locomotion—traveling with different parts of the |
|   Rolling |   body |
|   Sliding | **III.** Locomotion—rocking and rolling |
|   Gripping and releasing | **IV.** Weight bearing |
| Stillness—weight bearing and balance | **V.** Locomotion—hanging and swinging |
| Weight transference | **VI.** Locomotion—the jumping actions |
|   Rocking and rolling | **VII.** Balance |
|   Sliding |   ■ Achieving balance |
|   Steplike actions |   ■ Moving into and out of balance |
|   Flight | **VIII.** Transferring weight—twisting, turning, spinning |

### Educational Dance

Oftentimes the elementary dance program is divided into several different orientations to dance as described below:

*Elementary Dance Orientations*

> Creative/expressive dance
>
> Moving to a rhythm (rhythmics)
>
> Structured dance (folk/line)

The creative/expressive dance is most often taught in two ways. The first is a more pure use of the dance themes of Rudolf Laban:

   **I:** Body awareness

  **II:** Awareness of weight and time

 **III:** Awareness of space

  **IV:** Awareness of the flow and space quality of movement

   **V:** Relating movement to another

  **VI:** The use of the body

 **VII:** The awareness of the basic effort actions

Each of these themes is developed as a major theme and unit of work, the intent being that the order is developmental. Students would work directly with the content such as creating dances contrasting quick and slow movements or combining different levels and pathways. A second way creative dance is often taught is to bring out the movement qualities with ideas that may have more

Educational gymnastics is part of a movement education curriculum framework. (© *image100 Ltd.*)

meaning to students such as dancing to a poem or studying the movement qualities of a falling leaf.

Rhythmic experiences are exactly what they sound like. Students move to basic rhythms, bounce balls, jump rope, etc., to different rhythms that are either self-created or musical. Although probably any kind of structured dance would be appropriate for the elementary dance program, folk or line dance is what is usually done. Children enjoy these dances, they offer an opportunity to share cultural experiences, and they use the locomotor patterns that children should be developing.

## Step 5: Creating a Yearly Block Plan of Units

From your content framework you will develop units of work for each grade level and then place these units in a yearly block plan. The yearly block plan describes what you will do each week of the school year. Most school years are 36 weeks.

From this yearly block plan (Box 6.8) you will insert the grade level objectives that you developed from your goals and from the standards—all of the standards and not just the psychomotor standard from Box 6.3 for the fourth grade. When you do this each grade level objective must be in at least one of your units. They may be in more than one. You may teach other skills besides

## Box 6.8   Sample Yearly Block Plan—Fourth Grade

| Week | Unit | Week | Unit |
|------|------|------|------|
| 1. | Soccer | 20. | Traveling and balancing using equipment with a partner |
| 2. | Soccer | | |
| 3. | Soccer | 21. | Basketball |
| 4. | Soccer | 22. | Basketball |
| 5. | Throwing and catching | 23. | Basketball |
| 6. | Throwing and catching | 24. | Fitness and physical activity |
| 7. | Bowling | 25. | Creative dance |
| 8. | Bowling | 26. | Creative dance |
| 9. | Bowling | 27. | Golf |
| 10. | Folk Dance | 28. | Golf |
| 11. | Folk Dance | 29. | Golf |
| 12. | *Thanksgiving holiday* | 30. | *Spring break* |
| 13. | Striking with a paddle | 31. | In-line skating |
| 14. | Striking with a paddle | 32. | In-line skating |
| 15. | Striking with a paddle | 33. | Softball |
| 16. | *Winter holiday* | 34. | Softball |
| 17. | *Winter holiday* | 35. | Softball |
| 18. | Traveling and balancing | 36. | Softball |
| 19. | Traveling and balancing | | |

the grade level objectives in each of your units. The important thing is that each objective is specifically planned for within the unit and taught for student competence. Often, objectives other than those in Standard 1 get lost because they are not specifically planned for. Placing the objectives with the content framework before you plan the unit ensures that you will remember to address those objectives as you plan. Box 6.9 illustrates the grade level objectives placed in several of the units from the block plan in Box 6.8.

## Step 6: Developing an Assessment Plan for the Elementary Program

The assessment plan for your program determines the degree to which students in your program reach the goals that you have identified for them. There are 24 program goals that were identified in Step 2 of the curriculum development process (See page 102). Not only would you not want to take the time out with your sixth graders to measure each of the 24 outcomes, several of them are probably not measurable in their current form. A better strategy is to identify critical objectives sometimes called performance indicators and to assess some classes in each grade

## Box 6.9　Placing the Grade Level Objectives in the Units from the Block Plan

### Soccer

- Dribble and kick an object while moving.
- Identify three critical cues for the dribble, kick, catch, throw, and strike.
- Use critical elements to provide feedback to others.
- Describe basic offensive and defensive tactics in an invasion type of game (basketball, soccer, floor hockey).
- Identify the importance of warm-up and cool down.
- Identify moderate and vigorous physical activities that can be done outside of school.
- Apply established class rules, procedures, and safe practices.

### Fitness and physical activity

- Identify at least two activities that can develop each of the components of fitness.
- Match physical fitness assessment items to the appropriate fitness component.
- Identify the health benefits of physical activity.
- Identify characteristics of activity needed to maintain health-related cardiovascular fitness.
- Measure heart rate before and after activity.

### Bowling

- Demonstrate mature form in all basic manipulative patterns.
- Throw a ball overhand and underhand with mature form.
- Use critical elements to provide feedback to others.
- Demonstrate regular participation in at least one physical activity (moderate or vigorous) outside of school.
- Accurately report the results of work.
- Describe the relationship between skill competence and enjoyment.

### Traveling and balancing

- Apply movement concepts (body, space, effort, and relationships) to gymnastics actions and sequences.
- Combine traveling, balancing, and rolling actions with a change in level, direction, or speed.
- Understand the importance of safety in all activities but particularly those that are high risk.
- Identify the characteristics of skilled performance.
- Apply established class rules, procedures, and safe practices.

### Creative dance

- Perform simple dances to music (creative, folk, line, rhythmic).
- Work cooperatively with another or others to complete a task.
- Identify physical activities that bring personal enjoyment.

### Basketball

- Demonstrate respectful behavior toward others in physical activity settings.
- Resolve conflicts in acceptable ways.
- Practice a skill without being told.
- Understand the value of contributions of different people to a group.
- Demonstrate competence in the specialized sport skills of at least one invasion game (soccer, floor hockey, basketball); net game (volleyball, badminton, and pickle ball); striking/fielding game (baseball, softball, Whiffle ball); and target game (bowling, golf).
- Use a wide variety of manipulative patterns in self-testing and low-organization gamelike activities.
- Describe basic offensive and defensive tactics in an invasion type of game (basketball, soccer, floor hockey).

level on the performance indicators. For example, a critical set of performance indicators for the sixth grade might be:

- Strike an object continuously with a paddle/racquet using a mature forearm pattern.
- Receive and pass an object with a partner against a defender.
- Travel and maintain control of an object in a two-on-one situation.
- Perform the given steps and sequences in rhythm to the music for an age-appropriate dance (e.g., line, square, folk, step, and social).
- Perform a gymnastics/movement sequence with a partner using a variety of body management skills with variations in movement concepts.
- Demonstrate competency in an individual noncompetitive activity.
- Use the basic skills and tactics of invasion and net activities in a small-sided modified game.
- Demonstrate the basic pattern of a target activity.

Box 6.10 describes the psychomotor goals for the elementary program and an assessment strategy that organizes an assessment plan around sampling classes.

## Box 6.10   Developing an Assessment Plan

| Program Goal | Assessment Strategy |
|---|---|
| ■ Strike an object continuously with a paddle/racket using a mature forearm pattern. | Assess in fifth grade—one class. |
| ■ Receive and pass an object with a partner against a defender. | Assess one class in basketball. |
| ■ Travel and maintain control of an object in a two-on-one situation. | Assess one class in soccer. |
| ■ Perform the given steps and sequences in rhythm to the music for an age-appropriate dance (e.g., line, square, folk, step, and social). | Assess one third-grade class. |
| ■ Perform a gymnastics/movement sequence with a partner using a variety of body management skills with variations in movement concepts. | Assess one fifth-grade class. |
| ■ Demonstrate competency in an individual non-competitive activity. | Assess bowling—one fourth-grade class. |
| ■ Use the basic skills and tactics of invasion and net activities in a small-sided modified game. | Assess pickle ball in sixth grade—one class. Assess 2 vs. 1 in soccer. |
| ■ Demonstrate the basic pattern of a target activity. | Assess golf in fifth grade. |

# Check Your Understanding

1. What issues should be addressed in a statement of philosophy for an elementary school program?
2. How should elementary school objectives be related to the national standards?
3. List two objectives for the elementary school that might fall under each of the national standards.
4. Choose a third-grade objective and show what that objective might look like in the first and fifth grade.
5. Describe three different content frameworks that might be used in elementary school physical education.
6. What factors need to be considered in developing an assessment plan for a middle school curriculum?

# Reference

National Association for Sport and Physical Education (NASPE). (2004). *Moving Into the Future: National Content Standards for Physical Education.* Reston, VA: NASPE.

# Suggested Reading

Graham, G. (2001). *Teaching Children Physical Education.* Champaign, IL: Human Kinetics.

Graham, G., Holt-Hale, S., & Parker, M. (2006). *Children Moving.* Boston: McGraw-Hill.

Mohnsen, B. (Ed.). (2003). *Concepts and Principles of Physical Education: What Every Student Needs to Know.* Reston, VA: NASPE.

Worrell, V., & Napper-Owen, G. (1995). "Combine Fitness and Skills." *Strategies, 8,* 9–11.

# CHAPTER 7

# Foundations of the Middle School Curriculum

## OVERVIEW

The middle school child has unique needs in a K–12 physical education program. This chapter provides the foundation for developing a middle school curriculum that addresses those needs. Characteristics of the middle school child that need to be specifically considered in planning curriculum are discussed. The chapter explores guidelines for the development of middle school curriculum established by the National Physical Education Association and looks at appropriate content under each of the national standards. It concludes with a discussion of the issues that must be considered when planning a curriculum for this age level.

## OUTCOMES

- Identify the physical, cognitive, social, and emotional characteristics of the middle school child.
- Identify the generic and unique characteristics of a good middle school physical education program as described in the guidelines established by the national professional organization.
- Identify appropriate middle school content and emphases for each national standard.
- Describe and take a position on the issues involved in middle school curriculum.

Middle school physical education programs play a significant role in developing patterns of lifetime physical activity. Most children enjoy being physically active through the elementary school years. It is at the middle school level where patterns of inactivity in physical education class begin to emerge in girls particularly, but in some boys as well. How much of this trend can be attributed to inappropriate content and poorly conducted programs is not known, but certainly, good physical education programs can impact not only what middle school children do in their physical education class and outside of school, but what they are likely to do as high school students and as adults in terms of participation.

As children enter puberty their needs change and the programs and teachers who work with them need to acknowledge that change. Establishing appropriate programs for the middle school has been a challenge, not only for physical educators but also for educators in all content areas. The Carnegie Council on Adolescent Development (2000) has set forth several goals for middle school education, including academic achievement, social equitability, and developmental responsiveness in recognition of this special period in a child's life. Nowhere in the school program is it more critical for educators in physical education to see themselves as members of a team of adults whose responsibility it is to guide these students through what can be a particularly unstable period of growth physically, socially, and emotionally.

## The Middle School Child

Any parent or teacher of a middle school child will tell you that the middle school age group is a transition time of development. It is usually labeled early adolescence and is characterized by a period of rapid physical, social, and emotional development. It can be a challenge for the child as well as the adults who work with him or her to adjust to this rapid change. This makes it very important for teachers to understand the transition and the role they are expected to play in helping children of this age group negotiate this period in a way that makes the transition to adulthood physically, socially, and emotionally growth producing.

### Physical Development

Most middle school students become sexually mature during this period accompanied by a rapid period of physical growth and other physical changes such as:

- Rapid swings in metabolism, making them lethargic at some times and hyperactive at others.
- Increases in height and weight.
- Lack of coordination due to uneven bone growth and accompanying muscular and neural development.
- Sexual gender characteristics such as voice changes for boys and breasts for girls.
- Hormonal changes that often trigger wide emotional swings.

Gather any group of middle school students together and the first thing you will notice is the great diversity in physical development. Middle school students do not experience their growth period at the same time. Although some girls are likely to begin this rapid period of development as early as the fifth grade or younger, for most girls, and especially most boys, the growth period is likely to take place sometime during the middle school years. A sixth-grade or seventh-grade class in particular is likely to have some students who have reached puberty and literally tower over other students who have not. Many girls will be considerably taller than boys. It will not be until 12 or 13 years of age that boys will begin to surpass girls in terms of physical stature.

## Cognitive Development

Middle school students have many cognitive abilities that elementary school children do not. They are establishing the potential capabilities of adults. They are capable of abstract thought, which allows them to deal with concepts such as propositions, reasoning, analysis, and hypothesis generating. They are questioning and beginning to understand complex relationships of a cause and effect nature. By nature they are curious but are unlikely to be engaged unless they find it personally meaningful.

## Social and Emotional Development

To truly understand the middle school student you need to understand the social and emotional development that is taking place during this period. Adults who seemed to have a great deal of control over a child's life find themselves in the position of no longer having unquestioned authority over what the child does. The middle school child is seeking independence from the adult world. The road to independence is for many a rocky road accompanied by:

- Periods of what would seem like very mature behavior followed by extremely immature behavior (e.g., they want to be an adult but will retreat to childlike behavior).
- Loyalty to a social group, dramatic conflicts within these groups, negative behavior to those outside the group, and an overdependence on group thought rather than independent thought.
- A desire for adult independence that may lead to confrontations with adults and a conflict in values.
- Moody, sensitive, and inconsistent behavior.
- Self-consciousness.
- Overly concerned with being different and a perspective that sees their problems as being "unique."
- A quest to establish appropriate relationships with the other gender.

From the brief list above it is obvious that independence from adults and a reliance on being accepted by peers drives a lot of behavior for this age group. How to

Peer group approval is very important to the middle school student. (© *Comstock/ PunchStock*)

meet these needs and how to move the middle school child closer to adulthood and independent behavior is one of the challenges of all education as well as physical education. While it is the role of the adult to *understand* the behavior of the middle school student, it is also the role of the adult to draw clear lines regarding what is *acceptable* and *unacceptable* behavior.

## What Is a Good Middle School Physical Education Program?

The national physical education association (NASPE) in 2001 published, *Appropriate Practices for Middle School Physical Education*. In this position statement the association describes many characteristics of a good physical education program that should exemplify good physical education at all levels, such as:

- Promoting a physically active lifestyle.
- Sequential instruction.
- High expectations for achievement.

- Maximum participation.
- Content planned and selected to develop identified learning objectives.
- Specific instructional feedback on what is to be learned.
- A psychologically safe climate for all students.
- Varying teaching styles.
- Support for cognitive learning.
- Integration with other subject areas when the content of the physical education program is not compromised.
- Regular assessment and reporting of student progress.
- Lifestyle changes to promote physical activity.

What is perhaps unique to the middle school in this document is the attention paid to:

- Individualized instruction.
- Cooperative learning experiences.
- A broad range of activities that include all of the movement forms and fitness.
- Longer units that allow for the development of complex skills.
- Attention to "grouping" of students for both social reasons and physical reasons.
- Focus on developing self-awareness, leadership, caring for self and respect for others.
- Fitness testing and development.
- Encouraging the use of community resources.

Each of the characteristics of a good program represents a focus of the particular needs of the middle school student. If you take the developmental characteristics that were identified at the beginning of this chapter, you can attach them to the recommendations for the unique needs of this group. You can then recognize what is meant by the idea of a program based on the developmental needs of the students you are working with. These ideas are discussed in the section that follows in respect to choosing appropriate content for the middle school program.

## What Is Appropriate Content for the Middle School?

There was a time when middle school and junior high programs looked very much like high school programs. Fortunately, educators have come to realize that appropriate middle school programs are not elementary programs but they are not high school programs either. They are transitional programs with very unique characteristics. Appropriate content in physical education for the middle school program is best understood in terms of the national standards. The major emphases of the middle school program for each of the standards are illustrated in Box 7.1.

## Box 7.1 Middle School Content Emphases for Each of the National Standards

**Standard 1: Demonstrates *competency* in motor skills and movement patterns to perform a variety of physical activities.**

- Achieve mature forms of basic skills.
- Participate with skill and achieve competence in the basic skills of a variety of sport, dance, gymnastics, and outdoor activities.
- Use skills and tactics successfully in modified games or activities of increasing complexity.

**Standard 2: Demonstrates understanding of movement concepts, principles, strategies, and tactics as they apply to the learning and performance of physical activities.**

- Identify the critical elements of sport-specific games and activities that characterize good performance.
- Identify the basic tactics of both invasion and net activities and how to use them effectively in modified game situations.
- Know the basic principles of conditioning for a sport or activity.
- Identify principles of good practice.
- Use information from the disciplines as well as feedback from others to improve performance.

**Standard 3: Participates regularly in physical activity.**

- Understand the importance of being physically active on a daily basis.
- Be a participant in physical activity on a daily basis.
- Understand personal interests and abilities in terms of physical activity.
- Make lifestyle choices to be physically active.

**Standard 4: Achieves and maintains a health-enhancing level of physical fitness.**

- Set personal goals and assess the extent to which they have achieved those personal goals.
- Have the skills to assess their own cardiovascular endurance.
- Meet the standard for fitness identified for their age group.
- Identify the relationship between regular participation in physical activity and fitness.
- Identify the health-related benefits of physical activity and fitness.

**Standard 5: Exhibits responsible personal and social behavior that respects self and others in physical activity settings.**

- Interact with others in a positive way regardless of skill level, gender, or status within the group.
- Accept responsibility for conducting himself/herself in a safe and productive manner in class.
- Work independently.
- Demonstrate respect for self and others.

**Standard 6: Values physical activity for health, enjoyment, challenge, self-expression, and/or social interaction.**

- Value physical activity for positive personal effects of that activity.
- Identify different positive effects of participation in different kinds of physical activity.
- Use movement to express feeling.
- Identify personal likes and dislikes of physical activity in terms of their personal affects and in terms of the kinds of activities that are personally attracting.

## Standard 1: Demonstrates Competency in Motor Skills and Movement Patterns to Perform a Variety of Physical Activities

Standard 1 describes the psychomotor content of the middle school program. Students at the end of the middle school should:

- Achieve mature forms of basic skills.
- Participate with skill and achieve competence in the basic skills of a variety of sport, dance, gymnastics, and outdoor activities.
- Use skills and tactics successfully in modified games or activities of increasing complexity.

Standard 1 does not identify the specific movement forms that should be included in a program. That is, it does not say that every program needs to teach basketball or pickle ball, or have a climbing wall. While there is great flexibility in the specific activity, the standard does describe a framework that can be used to identify the type of activities and the nature of appropriate middle school content within those activities. All programs will want to take Standard 1 and identify the specific activities they will include in their programs and the expected level of competence in those activities. What follows is a discussion of appropriate middle school content relative to Standard 1 and the psychomotor content of the middle school program.

### Transition from Fundamental to Specialized Sport and Activity Skills

The psychomotor content of the middle school program should build on the fundamental skills established in the elementary program and prepare the student to develop competence in a variety of activities and sports. The transition from fundamental skills and patterns (underhand throwing to bowling; jumping to a layup) is beginning to be made at the end of the elementary school grades. Although some middle school programs will want to use the sixth grade to continue to work on fundamental patterns before moving on to more specialized sport skills, the middle school can begin to focus on the basic and specialized skills of a variety of activities.

## What Is Competence?

The notion of competence in a skill varies with the type of skill you are referring to. In a sport skill like a badminton clear, competence for this level usually means that students should be able to consistently get the shuttlecock to the back line in modified game situations and to do it with what would be considered acceptable technique or form. If you are talking about a golf swing, competence would entail addressing the ball appropriately, a good grip, consistency in contacting the ball, and a swing that is characterized by the fundamental critical cues of a golf swing. Competence usually involves being able to demonstrate both good form and consistency in the use of that form. The next question should be, "Consistency of good form under what conditions?" The middle school student will begin learning skills in very simplified and uncomplex conditions and gradually add complexity to the conditions of practice. They are not expected to demonstrate competency in full game situations. It is not easy to develop this level of skill, but is important that the middle school program develop the basic skills of an activity to a level of competence. If you would ask any high school teacher what he or she would hope middle school students came to them prepared to do, they would tell you that they want the basic skills of a sport or activity well developed. They will add the complex conditions.

What makes the idea of introducing specialized skills for middle school children difficult is that they will not only need to develop enough skill with the individual skills, they will need to combine them and be able to use them in simple gamelike conditions. While developing competence in a skill is meaningful for most elementary school students, skill practice without also applying the skills will not be meaningful for this age level. This means that teachers have to find fun ways for students to practice and use basic skills of an activity in order to keep middle school students motivated to learn.

## A Variety of Movement Forms

The program for the middle school student should include a variety of movement forms and not rely only on team sports. The national standards define different movement forms as aquatics, team sports, dual sports, individual sports, outdoor pursuits, self-defense, dance, and gymnastics. Many middle school students enjoy being physically active, but they do not necessarily enjoy playing team sports for a variety of reasons. Programs will need to offer some opportunities for students in each of these movement forms. Pickle ball, golf, archery, tennis, and increasingly, leisure time and fitness pursuits such as bowling, aerobic dance, and bicycle touring are appropriate ways to meet the needs for competence in physical activity of a diverse group of young adolescents.

## Combining Specialized Skills

By the end of the middle school years students should be combining skills of a sport or activity with control. Gymnastics and dance work should culminate in routines and performances. Sport skills should focus not only on the set but on using the set and pass in volleyball together and pass, dribble, and shoot combinations in invasion activities. One of the best ways to have middle school students practice combinations of skills is to use them in cooperative settings where the goal is to obtain control of the skills with others rather than against them. Net activities such as tennis, volleyball, and badminton are good examples where students can work together to keep an object going using a variety of skills. Drills or practice situations where students are trying to combine dribbling and passing with others are all good examples of helping the student to gain control of the object with a variety of skills.

## Modified Gamelike Situations and Tactics

By the end of middle school, students should be using skills in increasingly modified gamelike conditions. Basketball may be only 3 versus 3 and soccer only 7 versus 7. It is not only the number of players that makes a game modified. Teachers need to change the playing space to accommodate smaller numbers and change the rules to facilitate both teamwork and the development of skill. Teachers need to consider modifying game play to maintain the "ongoingness" of play, eliminating rules that stop play on a continuous basis because students don't have the skill to avoid problems like out-of-bounds and rules infractions. By the end of middle school students should know and be able to execute the basic tactics of both invasion (e.g., basketball, soccer, lacrosse) and net activities (e.g., badminton, volleyball, tennis). The tactics need to be taught as concepts that can be transferred from one of these types of activities to another.

Modified versions of specialized sports are appropriate content for the middle school student. (© *Doug Menuez/ Getty Images*)

### Standard 2: Demonstrates Understanding of Movement Concepts, Principles, Strategies and Tactics as They Apply to the Learning and Performance of Physical Activities

The middle school students' increased cognitive abilities, experience, and inherently inquisitive nature make them ideally suited for targeted objectives in the cognitive domain. They are expected to understand basic concepts of the disciplines and to begin to transfer them appropriately to their movement experiences. Many of the cognitive expectations for this age group revolve around several expectations:

- Identification of critical elements of sport-specific games and activities that characterize good performance.
- Identification of basic tactics of both invasion and net activities and how to use them effectively in modified game situations.
- Know the basic principles of conditioning for a sport or activity.
- Identify principles of good practice.
- Use information from the disciplines as well as feedback from others to improve performance.

The text *Concepts and Principles of Physical Education: What Every Student Needs to Know* (Mohnsen, 2003) identifies basic concepts and cognitive principles that students should know in physical education from all the disciplines supporting physical education. Sample major concepts identified for the middle school are identified in Box 7.2. Additional concepts are available in the material accompanying this text.

Concepts should be integrated into lessons. The teaching of a concept is not meant to be sit down and listen experience. The teacher should be able to take each of the concepts that are to be taught in a grade level and insert them into a unit where it makes most sense to teach a concept. Table 7.1 describes a teacher's efforts to place the cognitive concepts identified for the seventh grade into the year's units.

**Table 7.1 |** Cognitive concepts placed into a yearly plan: East Lake Middle School— eighth grade

| Yearly block plan | Cognitive concepts to be taught |
|---|---|
| Creative Dance | People understand the expressive qualities of movement experience through their kinesthetic sense. |
| | Physical abilities contribute to one's potential in motor abilities and level of participation. |
| | Muscles with a large cross-sectional area can produce more force than smaller muscles. |
| Golf | Consistent use of short-term goals and self-evaluation when learning a new skill makes it easier for people to recognize and appreciate the things they are doing well. |
| | Hold stretches for major muscle groups for 30–60 seconds. |
| | Motor skills that are learned well enough to be kept in long-term memory are kept for a long period of time. |

## Box 7.2 Sample Middle School Cognitive Concepts

**Motor Learning**

*Concept: How do people get better at motor skills?*

*Sixth grade:* Different skills require different physical abilities that can be developed through training programs.

*Eighth grade:* Motor skills that are learned well enough to be kept in long-term memory are kept for a long period of time.

**Biomechanics**

*Concept: How is force generated?*

*Sixth grade:* Muscles are arranged in functional pairs that can move our body segments in opposite directions.

*Eighth grade:* Muscles with a large cross-sectional area can produce more force than smaller muscles.

**Motor Development**

*Concept: How does physical development influence motor performance?*

*Sixth* grade: Some children begin puberty earlier than others, resulting in dramatic physical differences between same-age individuals.

*Eighth grade:* Physical abilities contribute to one's potential in motor abilities and level of participation.

*Concept: What characterizes a safe and productive muscular strengthening and stretching program?*

*Sixth grade:* The principles of muscle strength, endurance, and flexibility (adequate stretch)

include overload, individual differences, progression, regularity, and specificity.

*Eighth grade:* Hold stretches for major muscle groups for 30–60 seconds.

**Sport Psychology**

*Concept: How can people improve their sense of self through physical activity?*

*Sixth grade:* Setting and achieving goals based on personal strengths and weaknesses creates a sense of personal responsibility for one's own learning.

*Eighth grade:* Consistent use of short-term goals and self-evaluation when learning a new skill makes it easier for people to recognize and appreciate the things they are doing well.

**Aesthetics**

*Concept: What factors help determine criteria for judging the aesthetic quality of movement in one's own and other cultures?*

*Sixth grade:* Aesthetic guidelines for movement activity make meeting the goals of that activity easier.

*Eighth grade:* People understand the expressive qualities of movement experience through their kinesthetic sense.

*From:* Mohnsen, B. (ed.). (2003). *Concepts and Principles of Physical Education: What Every Student Needs to Know.* Reston, VA: National Association of Sport and Physical Education.

## Standard 3: Participates regularly in physical activity.

Standard 3 focuses on developing patterns of participation in physical activity. In many respects Standard 3 is a "new" program goal for physical education. In spite of the fact that we have always seen our jobs as preparing students for physical activity, we have not recognized our responsibility for helping them make the transition from what we do in our classes to what they do outside of class. In one sense Standard 3 is the goal of all the standards. It is identified as a separate focus as well to underscore its importance and the responsibility of physical educators for the physical activity patterns of students outside the physical education class.

**Box 7.3 The Difference Between Affective Objectives That Are Intended to Be *Caught* and Those That Are *Taught***

*Objective:* **The student will work coopera- tively with others who may be different from themselves.**

*Caught:*    The teacher places students in groups with mixed gender, race, and skill level for an activity and tells the students to "work together" as a "team."

*Taught:*    The teacher discusses issues of why it is natural for people to gravitate toward those who are the same as they are and why it is important

to have the skills to work with those who are not. The teacher has students create a list of how you know when people are really working together: What behaviors can you see? The teacher then places students in groups with mixed gender, race, and skill level for an activity. After the class each student records what others did to them that they felt was supportive or not supportive and what they did to others in the group.

Middle school students are in more control of their time than most elementary students. This is true not only for the unscheduled times in their day, but for the scheduled times as well. They get to choose to be physically active or inactive and they have more opportunities to participate in a wide variety of both structured and unstructured activities. This makes the middle school years an ideal time develop- mentally to help these students choose wisely in terms of the amount of physical activity they acquire on a regular basis. The emphases in this area should be related to helping this student:

■  Understand the importance of being physically active on a daily basis.

■  Participate in physical activity on a daily basis.

■  Understand their own interests and abilities in terms of physical activity.

■  Make lifestyle choices to be physically active.

From a curricular perspective, the content of Standard 3 can be dealt with in many ways, including separate units on lifestyle physical activity or integrat- ing this content with other units. One of the more effective ways to focus on physical activity outside of the physical education class is to ensure that stu- dents know where and when they can be a participant outside of class in all of the activities that are taught in the curriculum. This standard can be taught much more effectively if programs would begin to establish stronger relation- ships with community resources. For instance, in a basketball unit the teacher can facilitate students joining community leagues and intramural programs. Golf pros from local golf courses would be very happy to come to a class and share with students their love for the activity and the potential opportunities for middle school students to play golf. School programs that provide voluntary opportunities before, after, and during school can also facilitate the develop- ment of this standard.

Programs that not only talk about participation but monitor participation outside of class have a better chance of students being participants. Learning experiences that include student logs and other types of records of participation help students make the connection between what you say and what they do. When students are asked to identify whether their participation is organized activity, unstructured play activity, or a lifestyle activity (walking someplace rather than riding), they begin to understand the issues involved in their personal decision making. Students of this age are also beginning to make decisions about their own participation. Helping these students understand where their interests may lie should be a part of every program.

## Standard 4: Achieves and Maintains a Health-Enhancing Level of Physical Fitness

Standard 4 designates health-related physical fitness as a primary goal of physical education for the middle school student. Many middle school students are not fit. They do not have the cardiovascular endurance or muscular strength and endurance needed to be considered healthy. Fast food diets and an increasing lack of physical activity for many of these students are major obstacles to developing and maintaining fitness. Students at this age level should:

- Be able to set personal fitness goals and assess the extent to which they have achieved those personal goals.
- Have the skills to assess their own cardiovascular endurance.
- Meet the standard for fitness identified for their age group.
- Identify the relationship between regular participation in physical activity and fitness.
- Identify the health-related benefits of physical activity and fitness.
- Be very comfortable with identifying and using the components of fitness to talk about their own fitness status and to identify what they can do to improve or maintain their own personal fitness levels.

Many middle school programs will test fitness levels and conduct separate fitness units. Many elementary students will come to the middle school having participated in fitness testing and having been introduced to the components of fitness and taking their own heart rate. Middle school programs should build on these experiences and not duplicate them. If student fitness records can move to the middle school with the student, then students who need special help in developing an acceptable level of fitness can be identified and helped early in the program.

Many middle school programs do not have the program time to develop or maintain fitness within physical education class time without using a disproportionate amount of their time on this goal. Even though developing fitness may not be the best choice of in-class program time, teachers will want to focus their efforts on helping students to develop personal fitness programs, monitoring those programs periodically throughout the year, and holding students accountable for achieving fitness outside of the class, at home or at school.

## Standard 5: Exhibits Responsible Personal and Social Behavior That Respects Self and Others in Physical Activity Settings

Because of the active and interactive nature of physical education programs, physical education is a potential laboratory for either the positive or negative social and emotional development of students. For the middle school student, these unstable areas of development make it essential that the experiences the student gets in physical education are positive ones. Sometimes adults look at the middle school age as being one giant step backward in responsible behavior. Although there might appear to be some truth to that statement, middle school students are actually experimenting with a newfound independence from adult thought and control, and they don't always make good decisions about how to handle that independence. The intent of Standard 5 is to help students act in responsible ways. Standard 5 is designed to identify the specific responsibilities of physical educators to ensure that students:

- Interact with others in a positive way regardless of skill level, gender, or status within the group.
- Accept responsibility for conducting himself/herself in a safe and productive manner in class.
- Work independently.
- Demonstrate respect for self and others.

Middle school students are capable of understanding the reason for rules and procedures and are capable of participating in the process of developing rules and procedures. They are also capable of reflective behavior, which makes helping them identify and evaluate how they feel about situations and how they act in situations an option for teachers to help them accept responsibility for their feelings and actions.

From a curricular perspective the expectations of Standard 5 are usually integrated into other units in the program. One of the more difficult planning problems associated with Standard 5 is to design specific objectives that are actually taught and not intended to be just "caught" in the curriculum. In order to do this the objectives must be very specific and specifically taught as part of the lesson and unit. The example in Box 7.3 contrasts the same objective intended to be just caught and the objective intended to be taught in a class.

## Standard 6: Values Physical Activity for Health, Enjoyment, Challenge, Self-Expression, and/or Social Interaction

The author was a member of the first committee that developed the national content standards for physical education. The committee had identified all of the standards but Standard 6 and was about to proceed to develop the materials to accompany each of the standards. One member of the writing team, an avid golfer, came into a meeting and stated, "I do not play golf for the health of it." He played golf primarily for the opportunity it gave him to interact with others and to be with his friends doing something that was enjoyable to all of them. The committee developing the standards had missed an important part of what needed to be in a good physical education program.

What our golf enthusiast helped us realize is that people participate in physical activity for a variety of different reasons and that understanding why people participate and acting to accommodate that diversity are very important to any program trying to help people be physically active for a lifetime. Some people seek physical activity for the health of it. These people are primarily adults, but more and more adolescents and preadolescents can be convinced that this is a good reason to be physically active. Middle school students primarily engage in physical activity for social reasons. They want to be with and do things with their friends. As they gain the skills and opportunities for participation in a wide variety of different kinds of activities, they can be turned on to the joy of movement and self-expression and the challenge of activities of both an individual and team nature.

Different movement forms and kinds of activities have a greater potential for one or more of these kinds of personal benefits. Middle school programs that

The manner in which competitive activities are conducted determines their value  as an educational exprience.
(© *image100/PunchStock*)

provide an opportunity to experience each of these benefits from physical activity are those that are inclusive of a wide variety of different kinds of activities and that are taught so that students can achieve enough skill and depth with the experience to realize these benefits. What you want to do is to teach the activities so that the student experiences the potential benefits of the activities, with the hope that they will seek additional experience with those activities and similar ones. What you don't want to do is to teach the activities so that you expose the students to what they cannot do and therefore do not want to do again.

Learning for this standard involves helping students to:

- Value physical activity for the positive personal effects of that activity.
- Identify different positive effects of participation in different kinds of physical activity.
- Use movement to express feeling.
- Identify personal likes and dislikes of physical activity in terms of their personal affects and in terms of the kinds of activities that are personally attractive.

Because the middle school student is capable of reflective behavior and is very much interested in "who am I," programs will want to help students experience a wide range of different activities with different potential outcomes, identify and understand their personal feelings toward physical activity, and help them independently seek out experiences that are enjoyable to them. Most of this standard is better integrated into units of different kinds of physical activity, with learning objectives in the unit targeted toward these specific objectives. Teachers can draw attention to the benefits of the activity and help students to understand their own feelings toward the activity.

## Curriculum Issues in the Middle School

There are many issues that surround the development of the middle school program. Among them are whether the program should emphasize depth or breadth in activities, how students should be grouped, whether programs should emphasize competitive or cooperative activities, how programs should be scheduled, and whether students should be given choices in the activities they take in their program. Each of these will be discussed in the following section.

### Depth or Breadth

More than any other level, the middle school program is a balancing act between the need to provide students with a wide variety of activities and the need to give students enough skill and experience with the activity so that they will feel competent enough to want to do it more. Should the middle school curriculum include many activities for a short amount of time, or should fewer activities be taught for a longer amount of time? Advocates of an "exposure" orientation to the issue cite the importance of giving students a wide variety of activities that they can choose to come back to. Advocates of more depth point to the need to give students enough skill so that they can and will want to be participants in that activity outside of the physical education class.

Part of the issue revolves around the issue of competence. How good do students have to be to be competent in the activity at the middle school level? This is where it is important to think about several issues:

**Is this the only experience with the activity or has the activity been taught by the elementary level and will it be taught by the high school level?** The exit criteria for a high school should include the notion that the student should be competent enough in the activity to safely and independently participate in the activity with enough skill to make it enjoyable. If the activity is one that requires the development of a lot of complex motor skills (e.g., tennis), then it is unlikely that the high school alone can develop the competence needed in that activity. That means that the district physical educators would have to work together to decide on the specific activities that they want students to have competence in and plan a sequential K–12 program to accomplish that. For the middle school it may mean that students only get to the level of cooperative play with good basic skills. The high school level would be expected to develop competence in the activity itself.

If the activity is one that a participant can achieve a level of competence without many years of instruction and one that can be played successfully at different levels, then the K–12 curriculum needs to decide whether development of competence should be over several short units or one long unit of instruction. Fundamentals of some units such as wall climbing, bicycle touring, bowling, and in-line skating, for example, can be taught in shorter units and may not have to be repeated for more than one year. Curriculum design requires the designers to look at the whole program and make decisions based upon the entire K–12 program.

**Achieving depth in movement forms.** What should be characteristic of the middle school is depth in the number of different movement forms. While it is not necessary to include lots of different invasion games (e.g., soccer, basketball, field hockey, lacrosse, team handball), a good middle school program will include a variety of movement forms, including aquatics, team, dual and individual sports, dance, self defense, outdoor pursuits, and gymnastics. It is not possible or desirable to offer many different activities from each of these types of activities, but each should be represented in the curriculum in some form.

## Grouping Students

With the passing of Title IX, issues of gender equity led to the abandonment of middle school classes legally assigned by gender. Although the results are not conclusive, more recent research has suggested that based on the unique needs of this age group, there may be merit in scheduling some middle school physical education classes by gender. Differences in the maturity rates of boys and girls, the beginnings of interest in the opposite sex, and the dynamics of the social interaction of this age group has led many to believe that boys and girls may very well learn more and have a more positive experience in physical education if at least some of the time they are taught in separate classes.

There are some middle schools across the country that have moved to assigning boys and girls to different classes in some academic subjects as well as physical education. The decision to do this will probably not be the physical educator's, but hopefully the physical educator in a school will have input into the decision. Because most middle schools are large enough to schedule more than one class during a class period, physical educators will have the option to group within the program even if students are not grouped by gender for other classes. An alternative worth considering is to group some classes homogeneously by gender and some classes heterogeneously. Careful decisions about which classes should be taught separately and which ones taught with both boys and girls would have to be made based on the needs of both genders. For example, the lower skill levels of many girls and the aggressive competitive behavior of many boys in invasion sports are a turn-off for many girls, who might learn more in an instructional environment that could be more tailored to their own skill levels. Girls might be better served by a fitness focus that includes attention to weight issues, and boys by a fitness focus on strength development.

## Physical Activities or Organized Sport

As described in Chapter 2, one of the recent trends in physical education is to replace instructional programs in sport with either a noninstructional program providing physical activity for students or the introduction of instruction in nontraditional activities that are more leisure time pursuits and may not require extensive skill development. While a noninstructional program is not supported by the physical education profession or the author of this text, the introduction of leisure time pursuits may be a means to help students who have little interest in competitive activities get active and stay active.

Nontraditional activities in the middle school would include units in *Project Adventure* and cooperative games and leisure time pursuits such as wall climbing, in-line skating, hiking, bicycle touring, and orienteering. The value of these activities can be determined by assessing their contribution to developing a physically active lifestyle. Are these activities giving students skills they will be able to use to be physically active? Are the units in these activities designed to be instructional with clear objectives that are taught and assessed?

## Competition Versus Cooperation

Some educators have suggested that physical education experiences should be designed to eliminate competition and to emphasize cooperative activities. These voices are particularly strong at the middle school level, where a major developmental focus should be on helping students learn cooperative behavior. The issue is not an easy one and usually quickly gets into a discussion of the value of and the values taught by sport.

Although a lot of the discussion revolves around team sports, many of the activities and nonteam sport activities in physical education encourage self-competition. Improving your fitness score, gymnastics routine, or golf score all involve working to achieve a goal you have set for yourself. Developing positive attitudes of self-competitive behavior is an essential part of helping students to be successful. Many of the most successful people are not competitive with others but rather with themselves.

The reality is that sport and competition have the potential to be either very negative or very positive influences on behavior. Successful players in sport are those who have learned to cooperate with others to achieve team goals. On the other hand, the behavior of many professional athletes is a testament to the potential negative influences of sport. Players can learn self-discipline and the value of working hard to achieve personal goals. They can learn to win and lose and to accept either without blaming themselves or others for the outcome. Sport experiences have the potential to do just the opposite.

Sport is a form of play and, as such, its value lies in the idea that the outcome is unclear. We don't want to participate in games that we know we can win all the time. Neither do we want to participate if we know that we are going to lose all the time. All participants must have a relatively equal chance of winning for the outcome to be unclear and for the competition to be valuable. The problem with many sport experiences for students is that the same people always win and the same people always lose. Under these conditions sport experiences are not valuable for either group.

Many of the negative consequences of participation in sport arise out of issues of what the player has at stake in the game. If losing means that I will lose either self-respect or the respect of my peers or significant adults, then the consequences for participation are great and potentially negative. If everyone can walk away from a competitive experience having enjoyed the participation without losing anything but the game, then participation can be a positive experience for both winners and losers.

It should be clear from this discussion that the manner in which competitive experiences are conducted determines their value to positively or negatively influence the participants. Good middle school programs will be designed so that both competitive and cooperative activities are included. They will conduct competitive activities so that the cooperative nature of these activities is emphasized and so that competition results in a personally challenging and enjoyable experience for all of the participants.

---

**A Time for Reflection**

Choose one of the following and explain why you think it is true.

a. Competition is preparation for life. It is important for students to learn how to win and lose.

b. Competition against others creates an ego-oriented individual who has difficulty valuing his/her own performance or the performance of others.

## Scheduling

Many high schools are now scheduling students for classes using alternative formats such as the AB plan and the 4 × 4. Both of these scheduling formats extend the length of the class period to about 90 minutes. The AB plan schedules each class every other day for the whole year, while the 4 × 4 plan schedules students for a class every day but only for a semester. The ideal would be for every student to have physical education every day for 90 minutes. In most school settings this is not possible given the number of subject areas that have to be scheduled in the student's day. The 90-minute period is actually a good format for physical education classes. By the time students dress for class and dress after class, there is usually not much time left for instruction in the traditional class format. Most classes just get started when it is time for them to end and send students back into the locker room. The AB plan has the advantage of distributed practice over the 4 × 4 plan. More can be accomplished and expectations for learning motor skills can be higher with class every other day for the whole school year rather than every day for just one semester of the school year.

While many teachers do not get to choose the scheduling plan for their classes, again they should have a role in the decision. Physical education programs should be scheduled in a manner that best meets the requirements of the subject matter and the needs of the students.

## Student Choice

Student choice of activities has been highly recommended as a curriculum innovation in the high school (see Chapter 9). A wide variety of different classes are scheduled and students choose the classes that they want to take. For example, students may sign up for weight training or golf, and the class would meet for a quarter of the year and sometimes for a semester. The rationale for choice programs is that by the time students get to high school, they have real preferences for certain types of activities and need time to develop competence in the activities of their choice.

It has been suggested that middle school students as well be given the opportunity to choose among a variety of activities. Giving students choices increases student motivation and interest in a class because they have made a decision to be there and to engage in that activity. However, while high school students should be informed consumers of activity because they had a broad range of different kinds of activities in their middle school program, middle school students may not be informed consumers if given totally free choice between many different activities.

The middle school program is beginning to work on many different specialized movement forms for the first time. If a middle school program can structure a choice program so that students have to participate in a balanced program of different movement forms over the three-year period and gain some competence in those movement forms, then there may be merit in offering a choice program. If however, the program results in students leaving the middle school with no experience or skill in many different movement forms, then the program will not serve the middle school student.

# Check Your Understanding

1. How are middle school children different from elementary school students?

2. Why is middle school physical education so critical to developing a physically active lifestyle?

3. Describe both the generic and unique characteristics of a good middle school physical education program.

4. What characterizes appropriate motor skill content for the middle school student?

5. For each of the national standards, describe at least two specific areas of content that are appropriate for the middle school child.

6. Based on your own perspective of the needs of the middle school child, should the middle school curriculum provide depth in a more limited number of experiences or breadth in a variety of experiences? Why?

7. Based on your own perspective of the needs of the middle school child, should middle school students be grouped in single gender or mixed gender classes? Why?

8. Based on your own perspective of the needs of the middle school child, should the experiences provided the middle school student be concerned with skills for sport or skills for more leisure time pursuits?

9. Based on your own perspective of the needs of the middle school child, should competition be greatly reduced or eliminated in the middle school program?

# References

Carnegie Council on Adolescent Development (2000). *Turning Points: Preparing American Youth for the Twenty-First Century.* New York: Teachers College Press.

National Association for Sport and Physical Education (NASPE). (2001). *Appropriate Practices for Middle School Physical Education.* Reston, VA: NASPE.

National Association for Sport and Physical Education (NASPE). (2004). *Moving Into the Future: National Content Standards for Physical Education.* Reston, VA: NASPE.

Mohnsen, B. (ed.). (2003). *Concepts and Principles of Physical Education: What Every Student Needs to Know.* Reston, VA: National Association for Sport and Physical Education.

# Suggested Reading

Dougherty, N. (2002). *Physical Activity & Sport for the Secondary School.* Reston, VA: National Association for Sport and Physical Education.

Lund, J., & Kirk, M. (2002). *Performance Based Assessment for Middle and High School Physical Education.* Champaign, IL: Human Kinetics Publishers.

Metzler, M. (2000). *Instructional Models for Physical Education.* Boston: Allyn and Bacon.

Mitchell, S., Oslin, J., & Griffin, L. (2006). *Teaching Sport Concepts and Skills.* Champaign, IL: Human Kinetics Publishers.

Mohnsen, B. (2003). *Teaching Middle School Physical Education.* Champaign, IL: Human Kinetics Publishers.

National Association for Sport and Physical Education (NASPE). (2005). *Physical Best Activity Guide: Middle and High School Levels.* Reston, VA: NASPE.

Siedentop, D., Hastie, P., & van der Mars, H. (2004). *Complete Guide to Sport Education.* Champaign, IL: Human Kinetics Publishers.

# CHAPTER 8

# Designing the Middle School Program

The purpose of this chapter is to help you take what you learned in Chapter 3 on designing a curriculum and what you learned in Chapter 7 on the issues involved in middle school curriculum and help you actually design a middle school curriculum. You will be encouraged to design programs with well-articulated program objectives.

## OUTCOMES

- Describe the issues that should be part of the philosophy statement for a middle school curriculum.
- List appropriate objectives for the middle school consistent with each of the national standards.
- Sequence objectives for the middle school program.
- Describe several content frameworks that might be appropriate for the middle school.
- Place program objectives into a content framework for a middle school program.
- Describe alternative assessment plans for program evaluation in the middle school.

The task of putting together all the parts of the written curriculum can seem like an overwhelming task. Like all seemingly overwhelming tasks, it is easier if you consider it to be a series of smaller steps. Although the middle school curriculum is just one part of a K–12 program, many schools will take the more general outline of a K–12 guide and develop curriculum material specific to their level. The purpose of this chapter is to help you take the information from Chapter 7 and actually construct a curriculum from the decisions that you have made.

The curriculum writing process was outlined in Chapter 3 of this text. A full curriculum should include:

1.  A statement of philosophy that describes the purpose of your program and the rationale for including your program in the school curriculum.
2.  The specific goals of your program drawn from your philosophy and your understanding of your students that describe the skills, knowledge, and dispositions you want your students to have when they leave your program.
3.  A sequence of objectives/outcomes by grade level that take the learner from where they are at the beginning of your program to the specific goals you have established for the end of your program.
4.  A content framework that organizes the objectives that you have for your program by content area into units or themes and describes what will be taught in each grade.
5.  A yearly block plan for a grade level that describes what content area will be taught in which lessons.
6.  An assessment plan that will be used to determine if the goals of the program have been achieved (Chapter 9).

Most districts will have one curriculum and all the parts of the full curriculum do not have to be duplicated for each school level. However, the full curriculum should include the specifics for each school level. Each of these parts of the full curriculum will be discussed with samples of development for the middle school level. Also, each part of the sample curriculum will be integrated with the parts that both precede and follow it. There is no intent to dictate a specific curriculum here, but rather to illustrate how the parts of the curriculum need to be integrated so that they are compatible with each other. For example, the ideas you express in your philosophy should be reflected in the other parts of the curriculum and your assessments should be consistent with your goals and objectives.

## Step 1: Statement of Philosophy

The statement of philosophy for the middle school level should include your perspective on the kinds of experiences middle school children need and a description of what you feel to be appropriate physical education experiences for the middle school student. In chapter 7 we described some of the issues involved in planning a middle school program, including:

■ What activities need to be taught?

■ Should the curriculum emphasize depth or breadth in terms of the activities being taught?

■ How should the students be grouped?

■ Should the programs emphasize physical activities or organized sport?

■ Should the programs emphasize competition or cooperation?

■ How should the program be scheduled?

■ How much choice should the students have in the curriculum?

Your position on these issues should be reflected in your philosophy statement. The philosophy statement in Box 8.1 is a sample of one school's perspective on these issues.

---

## Box 8.1    Sample Middle School Philosophy Statement

The purpose of the middle school physical education program is to give students the skills, dispositions, and knowledge to (1) be active preadolescents, (2) prepare students for the choice high school program, and (3) establish a base to be active adults. Middle school students are in a transitional stage between childhood and adolescence. While they desire independence from adults, they need adult guidance to help them through this process. Middle school students will need lots of opportunities to consider choices, to make choices, and to be held accountable for the choices they make. The great diversity in growth and development in all domains makes it essential that the program be conducted to meet the needs of this diverse group. Students will need opportunities to work in cooperative settings with others and compete in challenging ways with themselves and others.

The sixth-grade program should ensure that all fundamental manipulative patterns are developed to a level of competence in simple settings. Students at this age should be introduced to a variety of specialized sport skills in different movement forms and use them in very simplified conditions. Students should have the opportunity to develop several leisure activities not developed in the elementary school. Dance and gymnastics work should culminate in routines and an opportunity to perform. Sixth graders should be active participants in "play" activities outside of school and should be encouraged to join structured community activity programs. They should develop an awareness of their own fitness level and recognize the value of being physically active.

Seventh graders should continue work in sports and activities developed at the sixth grade that have not been developed to an acceptable level of competence. Students can be introduced to other activities. Programs should have a good balance of activities in all of the movement forms. Work should be in small-sided cooperative and competitive settings in team, individual, and dual activities. Seventh graders can begin to choose an activity to improve specific components of fitness and should be required to monitor their physical activity levels.

Eighth graders should continue to develop basic skills of activities already introduced and to use those skills in modified situations with more complexity than the program of the seventh graders. Programs should continue to be balanced in terms of movement forms. More attention can be paid to developing personal fitness programs and to improving lifestyle choices to promote physical activity. An awareness of opportunities in the community to be a participant should be developed with some accountability for outside participation.

## Step 2: The Specific Goals of Your Program

The specific goals of a middle school program are the exit outcomes for the eighth-grade program, if that is the last grade in that school setting. In Chapter 3 we talked about using the national standards to describe the goals of your program. Box 8.2 describes potential middle school goals from the emphasis of the national standards. Goals should be selected that you are willing to make priorities in your program.

---

## Box 8.2   Middle School Program Goals

**Standard 1: Demonstrates Competency in Motor Skills and Movement Patterns to Perform a Variety of Physical Activities**

■ Demonstrate competence in modified versions of a variety of movement forms.

**Standard 2: Demonstrates Understanding of Movement Concepts, Principles, Strategies, and Tactics as They Apply to the Learning and Performance of Physical Activities**

■ Identify critical elements of sport-specific games and activities that characterize good performance.

■ Identify basic tactics of both invasion and net activities and how to use them effectively in modified game situations.

■ Know the basic principles of conditioning for a sport or activity.

■ Identify principles of good practice.

■ Use information from the disciplines as well as feedback from others to improve performance.

**Standard 3: Participates Regularly in Physical Activity**

■ Understand the importance of being physically active on a daily basis.

■ Be a participant in physical activity on a daily basis.

■ Understand their own interests and abilities in terms of physical activity.

■ Make lifestyle choices to be physically active.

**Standard 4: Achieves and Maintains a Health-Enhancing Level of Physical Fitness**

■ Be very comfortable with identifying and using the components of fitness to talk about their own fitness status and to identify what they can do to

improve or maintain their own personal fitness levels.

■ Be able to set personal goals and assess the extent to which they have achieved those personal goals.

■ Have the skills to assess their own cardiovascular endurance.

■ Meet the standard for fitness identified for their age group.

■ Identify the relationship between regular participation in physical activity and fitness.

■ Identify the health-related benefits of physical activity and fitness.

**Standard 5: Exhibits Responsible Personal and Social Behavior That Respects Self and Others in Physical Activity Settings**

■ Interact with others in a positive way regardless of skill level, gender, or status within the group.

■ Accept responsibility for conducting himself/herself in a safe and productive manner in class.

■ Work independently.

■ Demonstrate respect for self and others.

**Standard 6: Values Physical Activity for Health, Enjoyment, Challenge, Self-Expression, and/or Social Interaction**

■ Value physical activity for positive personal effects of that activity.

■ Identify different positive effects of participation in different kinds of physical activity.

■ Use movement to express feeling.

■ Identify personal likes and dislikes of physical activity in terms of personal affects and in terms of the kinds of activities that are personally attracting.

Your philosophy will determine whether you think in-line skating is appropriate content for your middle school.
(© *Karl Weatherly/Getty Images*)

## Step 3: Sequence Objectives/Outcomes by Grade Level

One of the problems with looking at curriculum design from a linear framework is that the process is really not linear. When you get to the sections of your curriculum that identify a sequence of objectives for each grade level and plug those outcomes into a content framework, you will find that these two sections need to be developed together. You will move back and forth from one to the other to ensure that your objectives are consistent with the goals you have established and that you can accommodate all of your goals and objectives in the content framework you have chosen.

The national standards do not describe specific objectives for a grade level. They give guidance but intentionally do not describe specifically what each student should know and be able to do in respect to the goals of the program. You will have to decide just what these are to be. Box 8.3 describes content

## Box 8.3  Sequence of Objectives by Grade Level

**Standard 1: Demonstrates Competency in Motor Skills and Movement Patterns to Perform a Variety of Physical Activities**

*Sixth-Grade Objectives*

- Use an overhand and underhand throw pattern with good form.
- Strike a ball continuously against the wall with a paddle or racket with good forehand form.
- Demonstrate good basic skills and tactics for an invasion sport in a 2-versus-1 situation.
- Demonstrate the basic skills of a leisure activity or outdoor pursuit (e.g., in-line skating, orienteering, bicycle touring).
- Combine traveling, balancing, and rolling actions into a smooth sequence with good form.
- Perform a dance from two different types of dances (line, square, folk, aerobic, creative, and jazz) expressively with good form.

*Seventh-Grade Objectives*

- Demonstrate good basic skills and tactics for an invasion sport in a 2-versus-2 situation.
- Demonstrate the basic skills of a net activity (volleyball, badminton, tennis, racquetball) in a cooperative setting.
- Demonstrate the basic skills of a target activity (e.g., archery, golf, bowling).
- Design a dance in any dance form.
- Demonstrate the basic skills of a marshal art or self-defense activity.

*Eighth-Grade Objectives*

- Demonstrate good basic skills and tactics for an invasion sport in a 3-versus-3 situation.
- Demonstrate the basic skills and tactics of a net activity in a modified situation.
- Use the skills of a target activity competently in the context of the activity.
- Use the skills of a marshal art or self-defense activity in the context of the activity.
- Demonstrate the skills of an outdoor pursuit (canoeing, kayaking, rock/wall climbing, hiking).

**Standard 2: Demonstrates Understanding of Movement Concepts, Principles, Strategies and Tactics as They Apply to the Learning and Performance of Physical Activities**

*Sixth-Grade Objectives*

- Identify the critical elements for striking, throwing, and catching/collecting patterns used in each activity.
- Recognize that invasion and net activities have different tactics.
- Recognize that different physical abilities are necessary for participation in different sports/activities.
- Recognize that the more one skill is related to the other, the better the transfer of skill from one to the other.
- Recognize that puberty occurs at different times in different people and causes dramatic changes in all areas of development.
- Recognize that spin occurs on an object when force is not applied through the center of gravity of the object.
- Recognize that the optimum angle of release for most objects for maximum distance is 45 degrees.
- Recognize that muscles are arranged in functional pairs that move body segments.
- Recognize that longer and heavier bats, rackets, or clubs tend to produce more force.
- Recognize that the principles of cardiorespiratory endurance involve FITT (how often, how hard, how long, what kind).
- Recognize that achievement is directly related to the effort put forth.
- Recognize that movement qualities (time, weight, space, and flow) contribute to the aesthetic dimension of movement.

*Seventh-Grade Objectives*

- Perform lifts and exercises in a slow and controlled fashion.
- Recognize that performing isotonic, isometric, and isokinetic exercises every other day improves muscular strength.
- Recognize that inherited, familial, and cultural factors influence the size and shape of your body.

- Recognize that working productively in cooperative and competitive settings establishes purpose.
- Recognize that setting and achieving goals based on personal strengths and weaknesses creates a sense of personal responsibility for one's own learning.
- Recognize that problems of conflict in games and sports can be resolved with the principles of conflict resolution.
- Recognize that good practice requires attention and effort to perform your best.
- Exercise 20–30 minutes three days per week, to a maximum of 50–60 minutes every other day at the target heart rate.
- Hold stretches in a muscle group 30–50 seconds.
- Recognize that teams that practice inclusion do better.
- Recognize that people pass through developmental sequences at different speeds.

### *Eighth-Grade Objectives*

- Recognize that motor skills that are learned well enough to be stored in long-term memory are retained for a long time.
- Recognize that closed skills require consistency of performance.
- Recognize that most skills should be practiced as a whole so that you can maintain the rhythm of the skill.
- Recognize that transfer of practice to the game depends on how gamelike the practice is.
- Recognize that a variety of activities that require different physical abilities will maintain function throughout life.
- Recognize that the greater the size of the force and the distance from the center of rotation, the greater the torque.
- Recognize that larger muscles produce more force than smaller ones.
- Always face the object you are lifting so that you do not have to bend or twist to the side.
- Use short-term goals and self-evaluation as a process to learn a new activity.

### Standard 3: Participates Regularly in Physical Activity

#### *Sixth-Grade Objectives*

- Identify opportunities in the school and community to be physically active.
- Participate in health-enhancing physical activity of a structured or unstructured nature on a regular basis.
- Identify the critical aspects of a physically active lifestyle.

#### *Seventh-Grade Objectives*

- Use an activity log to assess weekly physical activity levels.
- Participate in health-enhancing physical activity of a structured or unstructured nature on a regular basis.
- Identify opportunities to be a participant outside of class in activities covered in the curriculum.

#### *Eighth-Grade Objectives*

- Set goals and achieve a personal level of physical activity.
- Identify three things to do to make a lifestyle change to enhance a personal level of physical activity.
- Participate in health-enhancing physical activity of a structured nature on a regular basis.

### Standard 4: Achieves and Maintains a Health-Enhancing Level of Physical Fitness

#### *Sixth-Grade Objectives*

- Identify personal fitness levels in each of the fitness components.
- Self-assess cardiovascular fitness levels.
- Use appropriate technique when performing exercises.
- Meet the age and gender expectations for health-related fitness on the Fitnessgram.

#### *Seventh-Grade Objectives*

- Identify both exercises and activities that can be used to develop each of the components of fitness.

*(continued on next page)*

*(continued from previous page)*

- Identify the effects of being fit on the heart.
- Meet the age and gender expectations for health-related fitness on the Fitnessgram.

### Eighth-Grade Objectives

- Meet the age and gender expectations for health-related fitness on the Fitnessgram.
- Plan and conduct a personal fitness program to improve or maintain personal fitness levels consistent with the FITT principles.
- Work independently in the pursuit of fitness goals.

### Sixth-Grade Objectives

- Identify and participate in the establishment of safe rules for an activity.

### Standard 5: Exhibits Responsible Personal and Social Behavior That Respects Self and Others in Physical Activity Settings

- Cooperate with disabled peers to create a supportive environment.
- Identify responsible behavior and assess personal responsibility in class situations.

### Seventh-Grade Objectives

- Remain on task without close supervision.
- Demonstrate respect for people of different ethnic, gender, and skill backgrounds.

### Eighth-Grade Objectives

- Make the right decision when confronted with peer pressure to do otherwise.
- Develop/work with an activity to make it inclusive.
- Demonstrate cooperative behaviors with a group to achieve a common goal.

### Standard 6: Values Physical Activity for Health, Enjoyment, Challenge, Self-Expression, and/or Social Interaction

### Sixth-Grade Objectives

- Identify the benefits of participating in different kinds of activities.
- Recognize that everyone does not enjoy activity for the same reason.

### Seventh-Grade Objectives

- Participate in a "new" activity outside of class.
- Identify personal feelings about an activity.

### Eighth-Grade Emphasis

- Appreciate aesthetic and creative performance of self and others.
- Assess personal likes and dislikes for activity based on the intrinsic values of the activity.

objectives for a sixth-, seventh- and eighth-grade program based on the goals described in Box 8.2. When you first look at these lists they may seem overwhelming. However, it must be remembered that each of those lists by standard represents one year of work.

The sequence of objectives by grade level represents the scope and sequence of your curriculum. The objectives are organized by standard and by grade level. What is critical to understand in developing a scope and sequence is that the objective for a grade level does not mean that previous grade levels or grade levels that follow that objective cannot teach to that objective. In order to reach that objective in the designated grade where it appears, students will need to have prior experiences with that objective. The scope and sequence below is designed to illustrate the idea of progression. Two curricular goals are developed through the grade levels in the psychomotor area for the middle school. In each case the assumption is that previous objectives are met before new ones are introduced.

## Scope and Sequence of Invasion Sports and Net Games

| Goal | Grade 6 | Grade 7 | Grade 8 |
|---|---|---|---|
| Competence in an invasion activity | Basic skills and tactics in 2 vs. 1 | Basic skills and tactics in 2 vs. 2 | Basic skills and tactics in 3 vs. 3 |
| Competence in a net activity | Strike a ball continuously against the wall with a racket | Use the skills of a net activity cooperatively | Demonstrate the basic skills of a net activity in a modified situation |

# Step 4: Choosing a Content Framework for the Curriculum

A content framework is the scaffolding for the curriculum. It will allow you to organize your content into units or themes. The objectives of your curriculum will then be placed into the units. From the objectives identified in the previous section you should recognize that the outcomes of the middle school program are inclusive of all the domains of learning—cognitive, affective, and psychomotor. A good content framework is one that best facilitates the teaching and learning of all the program objectives. The most common organizing framework for most secondary programs in physical education is an activity framework. Units are identified by the activity being taught, and all objectives in all three domains are taught within that framework. Several pure activity content frameworks that could potentially be used in the middle school are illustrated below. In the first sample just the name of the activity is used. In the second sample the content is organized by movement form to describe the number of activities included in each movement form.

## Activity Content Frameworks

| Sample One | Sample Two |
|---|---|
| Soccer | *Invasion Games* |
| Gymnastics | Soccer |
| Line dancing | Basketball |
| Basketball | *Net Activities* |
| Pickle ball | Pickle ball |
| Golf | Volleyball |
| Fitness | *Dance* |
| Volleyball | Line Dancing |
| | *Individual Sports—Target Activities* |
| | Golf |
| | *Individual Activities* |
| | Gymnastics |
| | Fitness |

Although many programs are organized in this way, they do not have to be. Content frameworks that use other domains emphasize different parts of the program. For example, content can be organized by types of psychomotor content as in skill themes, by cognitive discipline knowledge, or by affective concerns.

## Skill Themes

A skill theme content framework is very common at the elementary school level (see Chapter 6). Many middle school programs will use a skill theme approach, particularly at the sixth-grade level. The framework described below illustrates a skill theme approach that might be used at the middle school. Using this approach the program would emphasize the basic skills of different sports and the transfer of fundamental patterns to these basic skills. Striking would be taught as a concept and then applied to different sport activities that use striking. Advocates of this kind of framework cite the value of teaching concepts for their transfer value. If students can see the relationship between similar skills, they will be equipped to better learn new skills. This framework has the advantage of making the transition from the elementary emphasis on fundamental skills to the sport-specific skills of the secondary programs. There are many alternative ways to organize skill theme content. Most of the time skill theme content frameworks are organized according to fundamental patterns, as shown in the sample below.

**A Skill Theme Content Framework for the Middle School**

*Striking Skills*
> Batting
> Tennis
> Volleyball

*Throwing and Catching Skills*
> Basketball

*Kicking*
> Soccer

*Expressive Movement*
> Creative dance
> Folk dance

*Body Management*
> Rolling
> Balancing
> Weight Transference

## Discipline-Oriented Content Frameworks

Like a skill theme approach, a discipline-oriented content framework organizes content by concepts. The specific activity is chosen based on what activity best helps to teach the cognitive content. The example below illustrates a potential content framework based on the emphasis and objectives identified for the middle school. Advocates of this framework believe that cognitive learning in physical education is part of "learning how to learn" and is a better use of students' time because of the transfer value of the knowledge to new experiences, both in and outside the school setting.

### A Sample Discipline-Oriented Content Framework

*How to Develop and Maintain Fitness*
　　Fitnessgram
　　Lifestyle physical activity

*Strength and Flexibility*
　　Gymnastics

*Cardiorespiratory Endurance*
　　Soccer
　　Team handball

*How to Learn Motor Skills*
　　Pickle Ball

*Understanding Force Production and Reduction*
　　Golf
　　Track and field

*The Aesthetic Qualities of Movement*
　　Dance

*The Cultural Basis of Sport*
　　Olympics

## Affectively Oriented Content Frameworks

Content frameworks that are affectively oriented in nature are those that organize the content around affective concepts. Major concepts appropriate for this age group have been identified under Standard 5 and Standard 6 in the example below. Again, the specific movement experiences used to develop the content using this framework are not as important as the idea that the concept is being taught explicitly.

### An Affectively Oriented Content Framework

*Working with Others to Achieve a Common Goal*
　　Basketball—sport education
　　Volleyball

*Working Independently to Achieve a Personal Goal*
>    Fitness
>
>    Track and Field
>
>    Golf

*Accepting Responsibility to be Supportive of Others*
>    Project adventure
>
>    Cooperative games

*Using Leisure Time Productively*
>    Orienteering
>
>    Bicycle Touring

## The Eclectic Content Framework

Eclectic content frameworks are combinations of several different kinds of frameworks. Whereas each of the above frameworks has an inherent consistency about the types of units that would be taught, an eclectic framework will combine ideas from two or more different kinds of frameworks. It is not uncommon for teachers in the middle school to combine aspects of several of these ideas. You may teach a discipline-oriented cognitive unit from the cognitive framework or affective framework in your activity-oriented content framework. Sixth-grade programs sometimes include units that are organized around activities, skill themes, and cognitive and affective concepts.

We began our discussion of content frameworks with the idea that a good content framework is one that best facilitates the teaching and learning of all the program objectives. Although programs will teach to all of the objectives, many will emphasize some over others according to the value decisions made, beginning with program philosophy. Oftentimes, the content framework chosen by a program reflects the value position of that program toward the importance of the six standards. A good experience for beginning teachers is to begin to experiment with different content frameworks and to keep an open mind about the potential for the more nontraditional approaches to organizing your content. What makes physical education unique from other content areas is that movement experiences are used to teach all of the content. Regardless of the framework chosen to organize the content, the total program should result in competence in all of the standards.

## Step 5: A Yearly Block Plan

The yearly block plan describes the content that will be taught for a year for each grade level. In a sense the yearly block plan is a calendar and should give you information on what units are being taught, when, and for how long. Box 8.4 describes a yearly block plan for a middle school program that consists of 36 weeks with physical education every day for 50 minutes. The program is divided so that the first unit described in a week meets for three days and the second unit meets

How would a basketball unit look different if taught using different curriculum frameworks? (© *S. Wanke/Getty Images*)

for two days in the week every other day. You will notice that the content framework for the yearly program is eclectic in that there are several units that have names other then the activity itself. For example, the soccer and ultimate units in the seventh grade are taught together and have invasion game tactics as their focus. The fitness units throughout the three grades each have different focus, moving from ideas of what is fitness, to how it is developed, and in the eighth grade to taking personal responsibility for fitness. Inherent in this content framework is also the idea that net activities with rackets progress from the concept of striking, to badminton, pickle ball, and finally to tennis. Many curriculums that are actually taught in the schools do have an inherent progression that may or may not be made explicit in the outline for the yearly program. Again, the more explicit you can be, the easier it is to plan units that actually accomplish your program objectives.

## Scheduling Issues in Yearly Programs

The yearly program for this school would have to be adjusted for the number of teachers in a school. The availability of facilities and equipment at most schools will not permit every seventh grader scheduled for a class period to participate in

## Box 8.4 Yearly Block Plan: Summerset Middle School

| Week | Sixth Grade | Seventh Grade | Eighth Grade |
|------|-------------|---------------|--------------|
| 1 (8/22) | Orient/Lockers/Cooperative Games | Orient/Lockers/Fitness | Orient/Lockers/Fitness |
| 2 (8/29) | Throwing and Catching | Soccer/Ultimate—Invasion Tactics | Bowling/Team Handball |
| 3 (9/5) | Striking with a Racket | Soccer/Ultimate—Invasion Tactics | Bowling/Team Handball |
| 4 (9/12) | Soccer/In-line Skating | Soccer/Ultimate—Invasion Tactics | Bowling/Team Handball |
| 5 (9/19) | Soccer/In-line Skating | Soccer/Ultimate—Invasion Tactics | Bowling/Team Handball |
| 6 (9/26) | Soccer/In-line Skating | Soccer/Ultimate | Bowling/Team Handball |
| 7 (10/3) | Soccer/In-line Skating | Pickle Ball/Wall Climbing | Tennis/Wall Climbing |
| 8 (10/10) | Soccer/In-line Skating | Pickle Ball/Wall Climbing | Tennis/Wall Climbing |
| 9 (10/17) | Badminton/Lifetime Fitness (What Is Fitness?) | Pickle Ball/Wall Climbing | Tennis/Wall Climbing |
| 10 (10/24) | Badminton/Lifetime Fitness (What is Fitness?) | Pickle Ball/Wall Climbing | Tennis/Wall Climbing |
| 11 (10/31) | Badminton/Lifetime Fitness (What is Fitness?) | Pickle Ball/Wall Climbing | Tennis/Wall Climbing |
| 12 (11/7) | Badminton/Lifetime Fitness (What is Fitness?) | Pickle Ball/Wall Climbing | Tennis/Wall Climbing |
| 13 (11/14) | Badminton/Lifetime Fitness (What is Fitness?) | Pickle Ball /Wall Climbing | Tennis/Wall Climbing |
| 14 (11/21) | Gymnastics/Basketball | Gymnastics/Basketball | Marshal Arts/Volleyball |
| 15 (11/28) | Gymnastics/Basketball | Gymnastics/Basketball | Marshal Arts/Volleyball |
| 16 (12/5) | Gymnastics/Basketball | Gymnastics/Basketball | Marshal Arts/Volleyball |
| 17 (12/19) | Gymnastics/Basketball | Gymnastics/Basketball | Marshal Arts/Volleyball |
| | **CHRISTMAS HOLIDAY** | | |
| 18 (1/2) | Volleyball/Dance | Lifetime Fitness (How Do You Develop Fitness?) | Lifetime Fitness—Personal Responsibility |
| 19 (1/9) | Volleyball/Dance | Lifetime Fitness (How Do You Develop Fitness?) | Lifetime Fitness—Personal Responsibility |

the same activity at the same time. There are several ways in which this can be handled depending on the constraints of climate. First, fall and spring units can be switched so that some teachers will teach some units in the fall and other teachers will teach the same units in the spring. If you are fortunate enough to be in a climate where the weather stays good for a long period of time in the fall and spring, then units can be reversed within the same season. The number of teaching stations and the inclusion of winter sport activities in the winter months will determine how best to handle the program when classes have to be indoors.

| 20 (1/16) | Volleyball/Dance | Lifetime Fitness (How Do You Develop Fitness?) | Lifetime Fitness—Personal Responsibility |
| 21 (1/23) | Volleyball/Dance | Volleyball/Dance and Aesthetic Movement | Lifetime Fitness—Personal Responsibility |
| 22 (1/30) | Volleyball/Dance | Volleyball/Dance and Aesthetic Movement | Lifetime Fitness—Personal Responsibility |
| 23 (2/6) | Volleyball/Dance | Volleyball/Dance and Aesthetic Movement | Basketball/Dance |
| 24 (2/13) | Pickle Ball/Wall Climbing | Volleyball/Dance and Aesthetic Movement | Basketball/Dance |
| 25 (2/20) | Pickle Ball/Wall Climbing | Volleyball/Dance and Aesthetic Movement | Basketball/Dance |
| 26 (2/27) | Creative Dance | Volleyball/Dance and Aesthetic Movement | Basketball/Dance |
| **STATE TESTING (3/6)** | | | |
| 27 (3/20) | Pickle Ball/Wall Climbing | Softball/Orienteering | Archery |
| 28 (3/27) | Pickle Ball/Wall Climbing | Softball/Orienteering | Archery |
| 29 (4/3) | Pickle Ball/Wall Climbing | Softball/Orienteering | Archery |
| **SPRING BREAK** | | | |
| 30 (4/17) | Project Adventure/Track and Field | Softball/Orienteering | Golf/Project Adventure |
| 31 (4/24) | Project Adventure/Track and Field | Softball/Orienteering | Golf/Project Adventure |
| 32 (5/3) | Project Adventure/Track and Field | Project Adventure | Golf/Project Adventure |
| 33 (5/10) | Project Adventure/Track and Field | Project Adventure | Golf/Project Adventure |
| 34 (5/17) | Project Adventure/Track and Field | Project Adventure | Golf/Project Adventure |
| 35 (5/24) | CLOSING | CLOSING | |

# Step 6: Placing Program Objectives into the Curriculum Framework

After your content framework and yearly plan have been established, you will want to take the program objectives you have established and place them in your content framework before you begin to plan your units. Box 8.5 describes both the sixth-grade program objectives and the sixth-grade content framework. At this point in your planning you will decide where best to teach each of the program objectives.

## Box 8.5  Middle School Objectives Assigned to Units

**Sixth-Grade Objectives Assigned to Units**

*Cooperative Games*

- Puberty occurs at different times in different people and causes dramatic changes in all areas of development.
- Participate in health-enhancing physical activity of a structured or unstructured nature on a regular basis.
- Identify and participate in the establishment of safe rules for an activity.
- Cooperate with disabled peers to create a supportive environment.
- Identify responsible behavior and assess personal responsibility in class situations.
- Identify the benefits of participating in different kinds of activities.
- Recognize that everyone does not enjoy activity for the same reason.

*Throwing and Catching*

- Identify the critical elements for striking, throwing, and catching/collecting patterns used in each activity.
- Use an overhand and underhand throw pattern with good form.
- The more one skill is related to the other, the better the transfer of skill from one to the other.
- The optimum angle of release for most objects for maximum distance is 45 degrees.

*Striking with a Racket*

- Identify the critical elements for striking, throwing, and catching/collecting patterns used in each activity.
- The more one skill is related to the other, the better the transfer of skill from one to the other.
- Spin occurs on an object when force is not applied through the center of gravity of the object.
- Strike a ball continuously against the wall with a paddle or racket with good forehand form.
- Longer and heavier bats, rackets, or clubs tend to produce more force.
- Identify and participate in the establishment of safe rules for an activity.

*Soccer*

- Demonstrate good basic skills and tactics for an invasion sport in a 2-versus-1 situation.
- Different physical abilities are necessary for participation in different sports/activities.
- Identify opportunities in the school and community to be physically active.
- Use appropriate technique when performing exercises.
- Achievement is directly related to the effort put forth.
- Identify the benefits of participating in different kinds of activities.
- Recognize that everyone does not enjoy activity for the same reason.
- Identify opportunities in the school and community to be physically active.
- Identify and participate in the establishment of safe rules for an activity.

*Badminton*

- Invasion and net activities have different tactics.

*Lifetime Fitness*

- Use appropriate technique when performing exercises.
- Achievement is directly related to the effort put forth.
- Participate in health-enhancing physical activity of a structured or unstructured nature on a regular basis.
- Muscles are arranged in functional pairs that move body segments.
- Identify the critical aspects of a physically active lifestyle.
- The principles of cardiorespiratory endurance involve FITT (how often, how hard, how long, what kind).
- Self-assess cardiovascular fitness levels.
- Participate in health-enhancing physical activity of a structured or unstructured nature on a regular basis.

### Gymnastics

- Combine traveling, balancing, and rolling actions into a smooth sequence with good form.
- Different physical abilities are necessary for participation in different sports/activities.
- Puberty occurs at different times in different people and causes dramatic changes in all areas of development.
- Muscles are arranged in functional pairs that move body segments.
- Movement qualities (time, weight, space, and flow) contribute to the aesthetic dimension of movement.
- Identify opportunities in the school and community to be physically active.
- Achievement is directly related to the effort put forth.
- Identify and participate in the establishment of safe rules for an activity.

### Basketball

- Demonstrate good basic skills and tactics for an invasion sport in a 2-versus-1 situation.
- Identify opportunities in the school and community to be physically active.
- Self-assess cardiovascular fitness levels.
- Cooperate with disabled peers to create a supportive environment.
- Identify responsible behavior and assess personal responsibility in class situations.
- Identify the benefits of participating in different kinds of activities.
- Recognize that everyone does not enjoy activity for the same reason.

### Volleyball

- Spin occurs on an object when force is not applied through the center of gravity of the object.

### Dance

- Perform a dance from two different types of dances (line, square, folk, aerobic, creative, and jazz) expressively with good form.

- Movement qualities (time, weight, space, and flow) contribute to the aesthetic dimension of movement.

### Pickle Ball

- Strike a ball continuously against the wall with a paddle or racket with good forehand form.
- Longer and heavier bats, rackets, or clubs tend to produce more force.

### Wall Climbing

- Demonstrate the basic skills of a leisure activity or outdoor pursuit (e.g., in-line skating, orienteering, bicycle touring).
- Identify and participate in the establishment of safe rules for an activity.
- Cooperate with disabled peers to create a supportive environment.
- Identify responsible behavior and assess personal responsibility in class situations.
- Identify the benefits of participating in different kinds of activities.
- Recognize that everyone does not enjoy activity for the same reason.

### Creative Dance

- Movement qualities (time, weight, space, and flow) contribute to the aesthetic dimension of movement.

### Project Adventure

- Identify and participate in the establishment of safe rules for an activity.
- Cooperate with disabled peers to create a supportive environment.
- Identify responsible behavior and assess personal responsibility in class situations.

### Track and Field

- The optimum angle of release for most objects for maximum distance is 45 degrees.

In some cases an objective will be taught in more than one unit and in some cases only one unit. After this point you will be able to plan unit objectives.

You will notice that there are 29 program objectives for the sixth grade that would cover all of the standards (Box 8.3). Box 8.5 takes these program objectives and assigns them to a unit. It does not mean that you cannot teach any of these program objectives in other units as well. Also, what it does not mean is that these objectives are the unit objectives. What it does mean is that the program objective assigned to a unit must be taught explicitly in the unit to which it is assigned. There will be additional unit objectives that are very specific to the activity. Assigning program objectives to a unit in a yearly program ensures that they will be taught somewhere in the program.

## Step 7: Developing an Assessment Plan for the Middle School Curriculum

An assessment plan determines the extent to which you have reached the goals for your program. Unlike the assessment of each student, an assessment plan for a program determines how well a program is helping students to reach all of the objectives of a program. As described in Chapter 12, there are many approaches that can be taken to assessing your program. In the sections above, we identified 29 program objectives for the middle school program. It is difficult and probably not desirable to assess every student in all of the 29 objectives in a formal way. A better strategy is to identify critical objectives, sometimes called performance indicators, and to assess some classes in each grade level on the performance indicators. For example, a critical set of performance indicators for the sixth grade might be:

*Psychomotor*
1. Use an overhand and underhand throw pattern with good form.
2. Strike a ball continuously against the wall with a paddle or racket with good forehand form.
3. Demonstrate good basic skills and tactics for an invasion sport in a 2-versus-1 situation
4. Demonstrate the basic skills of a leisure activity or outdoor pursuit (e.g., in-line skating, orienteering, bicycle touring).
5. Combine traveling, balancing, and rolling actions into a smooth sequence with good form.
6. Perform two dances

*Cognitive*
1. Identify the critical elements for striking, throwing, and catching/collecting patterns used in each activity.
2. Identify the offensive and defensive tactics for invasion and net activities.
3. Identify the different physical abilities for two different sports/activities.
4. Know that puberty occurs at different times in different people and causes dramatic changes in all areas of development.

5. Know that spin occurs on an object when force is not applied through the center of gravity of the object.

6. Know that the optimum angle of release for most objects for maximum distance is 45 degrees.

7. Know that muscles are arranged in functional pairs that move body segments.

8. Know that longer and heavier bats, rackets or clubs tend to produce more force.

9. Identify the principles of cardiorespiratory endurance.

10. Recognize that achievement is directly related to the effort put forth.

11. Understand the movement qualities (time, weight, space, and flow) contribute to the aesthetic dimension of movement.

12. Identify opportunities in the school and community to be physically active.

13. Identify the critical aspects of a physically active lifestyle.

14. Using a personal Fitnessgram score identify personal fitness levels in each component of fitness.

15. Explain how to self-assess cardiovascular endurance.

16. Identify the safe rules for an activity.

### *Physical Abilities*

Meet the age and gender expectations for health-related fitness on the Fitnessgram.

Using this set of performance indicators for your classes, you might give a written test to some of the classes with some of the questions and to another class with other questions. You might not assess every class in a formal way on all of the psychomotor objectives. Program assessment should help you determine whether you are able to achieve your program objectives with all of your students. If you cannot, then one of two things has to change. Either you have to revise your objectives or change the way you conduct your program so that you can reach these objectives.

## Check Your Understanding

1. What issues should be addressed in a statement of philosophy for a middle school program?

2. How should middle school objectives be related to the national standards?

3. List two objectives for the middle school that might fall under each of the national standards.

4. Choose an eighth-grade objective and show what that objective might look like in the sixth and seventh grade.

5. Describe three different content frameworks that might be used in middle school physical education.

6. Identify several scheduling issues that might be factors in planning the middle school curriculum.

7. What factors need to be considered in developing an assessment plan for a middle school curriculum?

# Reference

National Association for Sport and Physical Education (NASPE). (2004). *Moving Into the Future: National Content Standards for Physical Education.* Reston, VA: NASPE.

# Suggested Reading

Corsoo, M. & Stewart, A. (1995). "Middle School Successes." *Strategies, 9*(3), 26–29.

Lund, J. & Kirk, M. (2002). *Performance Based Assessment for Middle and High School Physical Education.* Champaign, IL: Human Kinetics Publishers.

Mohnsen, B. (Ed.). (2003). *Concepts and Principles of Physical Education: What Every Student Needs to Know.* Reston, VA: NASPE.

Mohnsen, B. (2003). *Teaching Middle School Physical Education.* Champaign, IL: Human Kinetics Publishers.

Siedentop, D., Hastie, P., & van der Mars, H. (2004). *Complete Guide to Sport Education.* Champaign, IL: Human Kinetics Publishers.

# CHAPTER 9

# Foundations of the High School Curriculum

## OVERVIEW

The high school level is the last opportunity that we have as a profession to influence the extent to which the high school student will lead a physically active lifestyle. This chapter provides the foundation for developing a program that will meet the unique needs of this student. The chapter provides a brief overview of the characteristics of high school students and their needs in terms of physical education. The notion of *a good program* is explored from both the guidelines established by the national professional organization and the content standards established for this school level. The chapter concludes with a discussion of the issues that surround developing a good high school program.

## OUTCOMES

- Identify the characteristics of the high school student and the implications of those characteristics for establishing a high school program.
- Identify the generic and unique characteristics of a good high school physical education program.
- Identify appropriate expectations for the high school student for each national standard.
- Describe and take a position on the issues involved in the development of a high school physical education program.

The high school years present a unique opportunity for physical educators to capture student attention to both health-related fitness and developing an interest in adult physical activities. Students are most interested in their appearance. Unlike elementary and middle school students, high school students have a great deal of independence to decide what to do with their free time. Most high school students have more discretionary time than they will ever have as adults. Many have access to cars and other forms of transportation that allow them to travel to community facilities to be physically active.

Unfortunately, this great potential is often squandered when ineffective programs fail to capture the interest of a very diverse population of high school students. The independence that high school students experience both facilitates and hinders their participation in physical activity. It is a facilitator because they can make their own choices and can access many opportunities to be physically active. It is a hindrance because physical activities are also competing with an increased opportunity to participate in a wide array of nonphysical activities.

## The High School Student

A great deal of development takes place from the freshman year to senior year in high school for most students. Developmentally, high school students are adolescents. Adolescents by their very nature are making the transition from childhood to adulthood. They have more experience to draw on and an increased knowledge base. Although educators often talk about high school students as though they were all the same, they are not. Ninth-grade students are significantly different than twelfth-grade students and one ninth or twelfth grader is likely to be very different from another ninth or twelfth grader.

### Physical Development

If they have not done so in the middle school years, high school students will be experiencing a period of rapid physical growth. This tends to occur earlier for girls and later in these years for boys. Most students will attain an adult body by the time they graduate. While boys will gain more muscle than fat, girls will gain more fat than muscle. Adolescents continue to lose flexibility without efforts to maintain it, although girls remain more flexible than boys.

Adolescent males and females have more potential to increase muscle strength and endurance than adults. Strength training for both genders in this age group has beneficial effects, but because the bones are still growing, great care must be taken not to put too much stress on the growth plates. Endurance training will produce a training effect in adolescents and should emphasize increasing repetitions and not weight.

Physically there are two periods in our physical development where we experience a rapid increase in fat tissue. The first is at six months of age and the second during adolescence. Students who are physically active at this time will not increase the fat levels of their body composition. Students who are not active will.

Adolescents will have most of the physical abilities of adults in terms of perceptual and motor skills. They are capable of learning a wide variety of activities and sports and participating as adults.

## Social and Emotional Development

High school students are beginning to break away from their reliance on peer groups experienced by middle school children and are becoming more autonomous. Most are exploring relationships with the opposite gender and trying on personal belief systems. Most importantly, they can be expected to choose and display appropriate social behavior and formulate ideas based on experience.

## Cognitive Development

Sometime during the adolescent years, students attain adult cognitive functioning, including increases in their ability to use language, increasing ability in terms of memory, and an increasing interest and capacity to deal with abstract thinking and problem solving. The time line for this development varies greatly from student to student.

# What Is a Good High School Program?

There is an abundance of literature that talks about how poor most physical education programs are for high school students, that they are a turnoff for most students rather than a turn-on to physical activity. There are poor programs out there that do tend to be little more than supervised play. There are also a lot of good ones. What characterizes the good programs? The NASPE publication *Appropriate Practices for High School Physical Education* (2004) makes some of the following points about effective high school curriculum:

A good high school physical education program:

- Is a planned program based on state and national standards.
- Provides a variety of different kinds of activities that address the diverse needs of all students (kinds of activity and level of competition).
- Is challenging yet presented to promote success for all students.
- Is appropriate for a broad range of skill abilities and interests.
- Uses the discipline knowledge to facilitate student learning and understanding of movement and fitness.
- Develops and maintains fitness.
- Provides a safe and positive physical and emotional learning environment.
- Reinforces a positive social environment.
- Teaches with the intent to facilitate positive interaction between students who are different from each other (racial, ethnic, skill, gender).
- Provides extracurricular assignments that extend in-class experiences.

Several things are unique about the high school program. By the time students get to high school, their interests in physical activity are often established in terms of those they find enjoyable and those that they may even be reluctant to participate in. For instance, it is not difficult to find students who simply do not want to deal with the aggressive nature of many invasion games (soccer, basketball, lacrosse). It doesn't mean that these students don't like to participate in physical activity. It means they don't want to be forced to play soccer or some other sport. High school programs must find ways to meet these diverse interests by offering a broad range of different kinds of activities and by giving students choices.

The second unique characteristic of high school physical education programs is the emphasis on discipline knowledge (for example, motor learning, biomechanics, or exercise physiology), particularly for programs that have more than a semester or year of physical education. The intention is not to make physical education an academic subject, but rather to use discipline knowledge to facilitate student learning and understanding of movement and fitness for a lifetime of physical activity.

# What Is Appropriate Content for the High School Student?

The high school years are the last opportunity physical education teachers have to influence the physically active lifestyles of both students and the adults they will become. The national standards are, in and of themselves, outcomes for a high school program. The broad nature of the content of the high school programs can best be understood by understanding the high school emphases for each of the national standards. The major emphases are illustrated in Box 9.1. What follows is a discussion of the content expectations for high school students by standard.

# Discussion of the Implications of Content Standards for the High School Program

### Standard 1: Demonstrates Competency in Motor Skills and Movement Patterns Needed to Perform a Variety of Physical Activities

■   Perform basic and advanced skills and tactics to participate in one activity from three of the following types of physical activities: aquatics, team sports, dual sports, individual sports, outdoor pursuits, self-defense, dance, and gymnastics.

Standard 1 for high school students and the emphasis chosen for this standard clearly indicate that students should leave high school competent in at least three different kinds of activities. High school physical educators who are responsible for designing a program to do this are faced with many decisions, some of which are discussed below.

## Box 9.1   High School Content Emphases for Each of the National Standards

**Standard 1: Demonstrates *Competency* in Motor Skills and Movement Patterns to Perform a Variety of Physical Activities**

- Perform basic and advanced skills and tactics to participate in one activity from three of the following types of physical activities: aquatics, team sports, dual sports, individual sports, outdoor pursuits, self-defense, dance, and gymnastics.

**Standard 2: Demonstrates Understanding of Movement Concepts, Principles Strategies, and Tactics as They Apply to the Learning and Performance of Physical Activities**

- Understand and increasingly apply discipline-specific knowledge to enhance performance.

- Design a personal activity plan to improve health-related fitness based on scientifically based knowledge.

**Standard 3: Participates Regularly in Physical Activity**

- Understand the relationship between physical activity and a healthy lifestyle through the lifespan.

- Possess the skills, knowledge, and disposition to maintain a high level of physical activity independently.

- Participate regularly in physical activity.

- Identify community resources for participation in physical activity.

**Standard 4: Achieves and Maintains a Health-Enhancing Level of Physical Fitness**

- Independently apply training principles to maintain or improve a level of fitness.

- Assess personal fitness status.

- Meet the health-related fitness standards as defined by Fitnessgram.

- Achieve personal fitness goals after a period of training.

**Standard 5: Exhibits Responsible Personal and Social Behavior That Respects Self and Others in Physical Activity Settings**

- Positively influence the behavior of others in physical activity settings.

- Develop a personal philosophy of participation that is inclusive of others of different ages, ability, gender, race, ethnicity, socioeconomic status, and culture.

- Hold themselves personally responsible for safe practices, settling conflicts in a positive way, and establishing rules, procedures, and etiquette in physical activity settings.

**Standard 6: Values Physical Activity for Health, Enjoyment, Challenge, Self-Expression, and/or Social Interaction**

- Can identify the potential values of different kinds of activities.

- Can identify the activities that provide personal pleasure and why they provide pleasure.

- Willing to learn new activities.

## What Is Competency in an Activity for High School Students?

High school is the last opportunity to give students enough skill to independently participate in an activity. We know that most people do not participate in an activity if it is not an enjoyable experience and we usually associate an enjoyable experience with being both skillful at that activity and confident in that activity, but how skillful?

What we are trying to do is to identify the skill level of the *participant;* not the athlete, but a person who can independently and safely participate in an activity with enough skill to make it an enjoyable experience. Students should leave high school with the skill level of a participant.

## How Can Teachers Handle the Problem of Student Diversity in Skill and Interest?

One of the major changes in the way we think about expectations for students is the change from objectives being directional—meaning they are targets we don't expect all students to reach—to expectations being minimal outcomes for *all* students. This is a significant change in thinking that may pose problems for teachers if they think about the idea of getting all students to a participant level of competence in activities. Can all students achieve competence in all activities? Maybe if we had the time and they were willing to work at it long enough. For most situations, students are not interested in attaining competence in all activities, and programs don't have the time to get them to a level of competence. So how can high school curriculums handle this problem?

One way to deal with the problem of student diversity in interest and skill level is to design your program so that you have enough different kinds of activities to capture the interest and skill level of all students and to give students a choice of activities. There are many frameworks that can be used to talk about the idea of different kinds of motor skills. The one used in the emphases for this standard categorizes activity in terms of:

- Aquatics
- Team sports
- Dual sports
- Individual sports
- Outdoor pursuits
- Self-defense
- Dance
- Gymnastics

You should be able to identify several activities to include under each of these headings.

Many high school programs have been dominated by team sports that require high levels of control of very complex motor skills. In many cases team-sport-dominated programs have been a big turnoff for many lesser skilled students and students who simply don't enjoy highly competitive and aggressive activities. These programs have alienated the very students we need most to capture in terms of developing and maintaining a physically active lifestyle. The broad inclusion of nonteam sport activities and lifetime/leisure activities has a much better chance of capturing the interest of a large population of high school students.

Not every student is interested in team sports.
(© *PhotoLink/Getty Images*)

Most students have likes and dislikes in these categories. The standard says that students should be competent in at least one activity in at least three of the categories by the time they leave high school. The assumption is that students should have experience in a variety of different activities so that they can better choose those that are more enjoyable to them. Some teachers feel that experience in a variety of activities should come in the middle school and perhaps the ninth grade, and students should be able to choose completely the activities they take in high school. It is not unrealistic to think that some students may want to take a beginning and advanced level of the same activity or perhaps take an activity twice to achieve competency without being put at a disadvantage for the decision.

---

**A Time for Reflection**

If you could have taken any activities in your high school program, how would you have chosen to satisfy the requirement that you be competent in at least one activity from three different kinds of activities? Would your choice be different now than it was as a high school student?

---

## What Level of Complexity Should a Sport/Activity Take?

The level of complexity of the activity involves the number of players, the size of the play space, the type of equipment, and the nature of the rules and how they are enforced. Does competence in an activity require that the student be prepared to play the full game with all the rules or participate in the sport or activity in its *real* context? Increasingly in our society there has been a gradual change from more complex forms of sport to less complex forms with lower levels of organization. Adults play indoor soccer with fewer people, they play paddle ball, deck hockey, beach volleyball, and Ultimate and disk golf. Although some would argue the point, most of these activities require less skill than the *full form* of the sport from which they are derived. Should physical educators aim for this level of the activity, or should students at the high school level be prepared to play the full sport?

Whether students should play the *full* sport in high school depends on their skill level. If the game can be rigorous and continuous when the full game is played, then there is no reason that a full game cannot be played. However, students usually get less of an opportunity to participate when the full game is played rather than small-sided games. Several more aggressive students usually dominate the play in full-sided games. Many adult forms of sports and activities have reduced the number of players. Teachers need to be guided by the answer to the question, "What experience is more likely to prepare and encourage students to participate in this activity as an adolescent and as an adult?"

> **A Time for Reflection**
> Think about students that you had in your high school classes who were not highly skilled. As a professional, what kind of program would you recommend that would motivate these students to want to participate and perhaps be engaged in physical activity outside of school as well?

## Standard 2: Demonstrates Understanding of Movement Concepts, Principles, Strategies, and Tactics as They Apply to the Learning and Performance of Physical Activities

The high school emphases for Standard 2 are rather specific. Students should be learning discipline knowledge that they can apply, and they should be able to design an appropriate personal activity program to maintain or improve their health-related fitness levels.

- Understand and increasingly apply discipline-specific knowledge to enhance performance.
- Design a personal activity plan to improve health-related fitness based on scientifically based knowledge.

The major guide for what is appropriate discipline knowledge for this age group comes from the text *Concepts and Principles of Physical Education: What Every Student Needs to Know* (Mohnsen, 2003). Box 9.2 describes key ideas from each of the disciplines that should be part of a high school program. Most of these concepts should be taught in conjunction with an activity and not apart from it, except perhaps for some of the exercise physiology concepts that may

## Box 9.2   Sample High School Cognitive Concepts

### Motor Learning

- Short-term improvement in motor skills can be achieved without learning if there is enough practice.

- Open skills are performed in an unpredictable and unstable environment and should be practiced in variable conditions.

- Good practice plans allow game players to spend the majority of practice working to get better at combining and adapting skills.

- Although there is no such thing as general motor ability, there is a set of perceptual motor skills related to performance of different motor skills. Those abilities may impose limits on individual performance and may account for why some students seem to be good at many skills.

### Motor Development

- Training (after puberty) can help emphasize physical attributes.

- Increased activity levels reduce the slowing of reaction time in the elderly.

- Accumulating 30–60 minutes of activity most days of the week can improve self-esteem; decrease stress, anxiety, and depression; and improve health.

### Biomechanics

- Forcefully stressing a muscle immediately before a concentric contraction increases the force of that contraction.

- In general, the greater the force required, the greater the speed, range of motion, joint extension, and number of moving segments you will want to use.

- Buoyancy increases with the volume/weight ratio of the submerged body.

### Exercise Physiology

- Regular aerobic activity releases endorphins that allow people to enjoy and sustain commitment to their fitness program.

- People need to adjust their fitness activity as they age and mature.

- Design strength training programs for individuals based on body composition, current strength, and specific requirement of the activity.

### Historical Perspectives

- Understanding the purpose and history of a sport around the world helps people better understand different cultures and appreciate contributions of different people.

- During war times, fitness is emphasized in physical education programs

### Social Psychology

- Developing numerous strategies for preparing to succeed in movement challenges (visualization, positive self-talk, or relaxation exercises) can help people become successful in an activity.

- Constructive communication (active listening, empathy, paraphrasing, questioning, and clarifying) builds shared understanding and appreciation of diverse view points.

### Aesthetic Experience

- Aesthetic criteria can describe progress toward achieving physical competency.

- Understanding aesthetic experience in physical activities enhances pleasure for participants and observers.

need to be studied separately and then applied to an activity. Teachers will be asked to place each concept in the unit that they feel is the most appropriate unit for that concept. For instance, you would want to place the biomechanics concept of buoyancy in a swimming unit and the motor development concept about the usefulness of training for different age groups in a weight training unit.

## Standard 3: Participates Regularly in Physical Activity

In one sense Standard 3 is the purpose of all the standards. It was identified as a separate standard so that it would not only be taught as an inherent component of the other standards but would be taught more directly on its own, with the emphases described below. When they leave their physical education program, high school graduates should:

- Understand the relationship between physical activity and a healthy lifestyle throughout the lifespan.
- Possess the skills, knowledge, and disposition to maintain a high level of physical activity independently.
- Participate regularly in physical activity.
- Identify community resources for participation in physical activity.

There was a time when physical educators thought that if they gave students motor skills and talked about how good physical activity was for you, that they had done their job in terms of preparing students for a physically active lifestyle. We now know that we need to do more than that. We have to teach participation in physical activity directly and deliberately. The teacher is going to have to help the student make links to the community and to participating outside of class, perhaps even requiring students to find an interest in a physical activity and stay with it for a period of time. Teachers have to be facilitators between the community and the student. They can bring in community representatives for different kinds

Basketball can be a lifetime activity for some young adults and adults. (© *PhotoLink/Getty Images*)

of activities, require students to visit community sites, and even help students sign up and become involved in different community activities. As the need for more opportunities to be physically active grows in a community, more facilities and opportunities for participation will develop.

## Standard 4: Achieves and Maintains a Health-Enhancing Level of Physical Fitness

There are two approaches to health-related fitness. One is a training approach and one is an activity approach. The student needs to be prepared in both. The emphases in this standard emphasize the skills and knowledge needed for the training approach to being fit.

- Independently apply training principles to maintain or improve a level of fitness.
- Assess personal fitness status.
- Meet the health-related fitness standards as defined by Fitnessgram.
- Achieve personal fitness goals after a period of training.
- Identify the specific benefits of being fit.

The assumption is that every student should leave a high school physical education program with the ability to assess his or her own fitness level, design a personal fitness program, and achieve fitness goals independently through a training program. Although some programs integrate fitness into all of their units, many high schools have units on personal fitness. There are several good textbooks written specifically for high school students devoted to the material in the emphases above. Programs that have a classroom will find it easier to teach many of the concepts before they are applied.

## Standard 5: Exhibits Responsible Personal and Social Behavior That Respects Self and Others in Physical Activity Settings

Students coming into high school still may show signs of immature and irresponsible behavior. Most students will leave high school with a significant increase in maturity and responsible behavior. Because physical education tends to be a laboratory for the development of social and personal skills, the physical education program can play a major role in this development.

Such a program can:

- Positively influence the behavior of others in physical activity settings.
- Help develop a personal philosophy of participation that is inclusive of others of different ages, ability, gender, race, ethnicity, socioeconomic status, and culture.
- Influence students to hold themselves personally responsible for safe practices, settling conflicts in a positive way, and establishing rules, procedures, and etiquette in physical activity settings.

Responsible personal and social behavior is developmental but not automatic. Unfortunately, a lot of affective behavior is taught when the student does something wrong and the teacher then talks about it. Teachers must design experiences that specifically address these skills and reinforce them. Students need to be taught the appropriate behavior for a variety of physical activity settings, how to handle conflict, and how to participate safely. Just as noninclusive behavior is learned, so is inclusive behavior. Largely this is done when teachers plan objectives in these areas, place those objectives into appropriate units, design specific experiences to teach them, and reinforce what is taught.

### Standard 6: Values Physical Activity for Health, Enjoyment, Challenge, Self-Expression, and/or Social Interaction

Standard 6 addresses why people may want to participate in different physical activities. High school students should be aware of lots of opportunities for participation in a large number of different kinds of activities. They should know why people are attracted to these activities, and they should have a very clear idea of what kinds of activities they are attracted to. These students should be able to:

- Identify the potential values of different kinds of activities.
- Identify the activities that provide personal pleasure and why they provide pleasure.
- Be willing to learn new activities.

Although good health is an outcome of participation in physical activity, for most high school students and for many adults, that is not the reason they choose to participate. By the time students leave high school physical education, they should be connected with the kinds of activities that they find pleasurable, and they should be able to identify what it is about the activity they do find pleasurable. In a sense this is the argument for being competent in three types of activity. Although students may prefer one type of activity to others, Standard 1 ensures that students at least have had the opportunity to participate in different kinds of activity, and can therefore make better choices.

## Curriculum Issues in the High School

With all of the literature calling for change in high school physical education programs, you would think that there would be many alternative models to a multiactivity model of curriculum, but there are not many that veer too far from units of sports, fitness, and other physical activities. Nevertheless, within this model there are many decisions that must be made regarding what to teach, some of which are discussed below.

### Competency or Proficiency?

In the 1995 version of the national standards, Standard 1 set an expectation for competency in many activities and proficiency in a few (NASPE, 1995). The current standards call for competency in at least one activity in three different kinds of activities. In the current edition the expectation for proficiency has been removed.

Why? Most likely because the authors determined that the role of physical education was not necessarily to make students proficient at an activity. The assumption is that competency is required for participation and not proficiency. If students want to be proficient they will need to join a school team, community leagues, or other means to long-term training and participation. The argument for proficiency is that high school students should be able to specialize in an activity in physical education, to take it as part of their physical education program for more than one unit. The elementary and middle school programs should provide and require a broad range of different kinds of activities. High school students should be allowed to specialize in the activities they most enjoy and get good at them, perhaps even proficient.

As discussed above there are really two related issues here that you will have to decide on when you plan your program. You are going to have to decide whether you think students should be allowed to specialize in an activity or whether they need to get competent in at least three different kinds of activity. If you decide to allow students to specialize, perhaps even in addition to the three-different-kinds-of-activity requirement, you will have to decide whether they need to develop proficiency in that special activity. Your decisions will have broad implications for the design of your program.

## Choice/Selective Program

One of the most recommended changes in the high school physical education program is to allow students to choose the activities that they want to take in physical education. The assumption is that if students choose the activity that they want to take, they will be more motivated to do well and will enjoy their physical education experiences a great deal more. This makes sense, but there are many ways to give students choices.

The most effective way to give students a choice is to design the program so that students actually register/sign up for the class they want when they do their schedule for academics. In order to do this, the school computerized schedule must list more than physical education. It must list each activity that is available as a separate course. Students then sign up for the activity of their choice. In many school programs physical education provides the flexibility in scheduling that makes it easier for students to get the classes they need. If it doesn't make any difference when students have physical education, then they can take it where it fits into their academic schedule. With today's computerized scheduling programs it is much easier to arrange for students to sign up for the physical education class that they want to take, but it will require that physical educators work with the guidance counselors and administration.

If it is not possible to schedule physical education as separate classes, there are still other ways to give students choices of activities. More than one physical education class meets at one time in most schools. Although teachers usually are assigned a class list of "their" students, it is possible to reshuffle the students into different classes when they get to physical education. If two teachers teach at the same time, you can have two choices for each unit; if three teachers teach at the same time, students can be given three choices; and so forth.

Many programs that give students choices of activities limit those choices to different movement forms. For example, if there are four nine-week units the student is given the opportunity to schedule, the student would have to choose one fitness activity, one team sport, and one individual/recreational activity for the year. Programs that have more than a year of required physical education can offer students more opportunity to choose.

## Block Scheduling

High school schedules are usually designed in one of three formats. The typical format is a 45- to 55-minute period for each subject taught all year. Many schools have moved to a 90-minute format, which reduces the number of different periods in the school day and therefore the number of subjects a student can take in one day. There are two scheduling formats that use the 90-minute period. In the first, called the AB format, students take a subject every other day for 90 minutes for the whole year. In the second, students take a subject every day for one half of the year and then take an entirely different set of courses the second semester.

Most high school teachers prefer the 90-minute period because students actually get more physical education time during this period. Two 45-minute periods are not the same amount of physical education time as one 90-minute period because of the dressing and locker room time involved. The 90-minute period allows teachers to teach and apply material, do fitness and skill development, and provide academic work and activity all in the same period. When given a choice, most physical education teachers will support the 90-minute period. In the AB program students get physical education all year every other day. This is preferable to half a year every day for our subject area, both in terms of skill development as well as the need for physical activity on a regular basis.

## Outside Experiences as Physical Education

Some schools have experimented with the idea that students can satisfy their physical education requirement by participating outside the school. Students can acquire certification as lifesavers to get credit for part of their physical education course. They can participate on a community or school team. In some cases part of the coursework is computerized so that students can complete it at their leisure. At first glance this idea seems a real threat to good physical education programs. If however, program requirements are written as measurable expectations that can be attained outside of school rather than just participation in activity, it is easier to support this direction for special cases. One of the advantages of having standards and measurable performance outcomes for those standards is that it is easier to make a case for not accepting just anything for physical education. It is unlikely that students would be able to satisfy all of the requirements of a good physical education program with extracurricular activities, but it is reasonable to expect that some of the requirements can be achieved.

## Length of Units

For a very long time physical education programs at the high school level were designed to expose students to many activities but not necessarily develop any skill or proficiency in any of them. Most *exposure* models have been replaced with programs designed to develop competence in activities under the assumption that high school students will need some skill if they are to participate in that activity outside of school. This changing orientation has brought with it the need to increase the amount of time devoted to each unit so that there is enough time for students to develop competence. This means that students can take fewer activities but will take them for a longer period of time. The amount of time will vary with the activity or sport but will not be the two- and three-week units of the exposure curriculum. Many students in high school physical education programs in Europe and other parts of the world are involved in a unit for half of an academic year. Many programs trying to develop competence have increased the length of most units to at least half a semester or quarter of the year.

## How Much Cognitive Material?

While most educators think that cognitive material in both fitness and other disciplines should be part of a good high school program, there is by no means agreement on the extent of that involvement. At the very least, cognitive concepts should be integrated into most units and teachers should decide ahead of time what concepts

Important cognitive material at the high school level may need to be taught formally as academic content. (© *image100 Ltd.*)

are going to be taught in what units. Another orientation to cognitive material is to teach the cognitive material as the primary content and to use activities as the medium through which the concepts are taught. There potentially could be entire units that focus on biomechanics, exercise physiology, or sport psychology. These units would not be of the depth of your college coursework, but would be deliberate attempts to create understanding of the concepts that are foundational to our field.

### The Physical Activity Director of the School

High school students need to be physically active every day. Most students do not have physical education every day of every year. One of the newest roles the physical educator needs to play is that of the physical activity director of the school, whereby the school is responsible for providing opportunities within the school for faculty and students to be active during the day outside the structured physical education class. In order to do this many schools have started thinking about providing facilities that teachers and students can use when they have "free" time before, during, or after school. They have also started thinking about providing opportunities for students and faculty to participate in special before- and after-school programs beyond intramural-type events and weekend opportunities. What makes these programs different from previous before- and after-school programs is that the emphasis is not necessarily on sport and competition (athletics), but on being physically active. The emphasis is not necessarily on attracting people with skill, but rather on people who want and need to be physically active on a regular basis.

## Check Your Understanding

1. How do high school students differ from middle school students and adults?
2. What are the most important characteristics of a good high school program?
3. For each of the national standards describe two emphases appropriate for the high school program.
4. What are the advantages of a choice program for this age group?
5. What school scheduling format is best for a high school program?

## References

National Association for Sport and Physical Education (NASPE). (1995). *Moving Into the Future: National Content Standards for Physical Education*. Reston, VA: NASPE.

National Association for Sport and Physical Education (NASPE). (2004). *Appropriate Practices for High School Physical Education*. Reston, VA: NASPE.

National Association for Sport and Physical Education (NASPE). (2004). *Moving Into the Future: National Content Standards for Physical Education*. Reston, VA: NASPE.

Mohnsen, B. (Ed.). (2003). *Concepts and Principles of Physical Education: What Every Student Needs to Know*. Reston, VA: National Association for Sport and Physical Education.

# Suggested Reading

Dougherty, N. (2002). *Physical Activity & Sport for the Secondary School*. Reston, VA: National Association for Sport and Physical Education.

Lund, J., & Kirk, M. (2002). *Performance Based Assessment for Middle and High School Physical Education*. Champaign, IL: Human Kinetics Publishers.

Metzler, M. (2000). *Instructional Models for Physical Education*. Boston: Allyn and Bacon.

Mitchell, S., Oslin, J., & Griffin, L. (2006). *Teaching Sport Concepts and Skills*. Champaign, IL: Human Kinetics Publishers.

National Association for Sport and Physical Education (NASPE). (2005). *Physical Best Activity Guide: Middle and High School Levels*. Reston, VA: NASPE.

Pennington, T., & Krouscas, J. (1999). "Connecting Secondary Physical Education to the Lives of Students." *JOPERD*. 70,1, 34–40.

Siedentop, D., Hastie, P., & van der Mars, H. (2004). *Complete Guide to Sport Education*. Champaign, IL: Human Kinetics Publishers.

# CHAPTER 10

# Designing the High School Program

## OVERVIEW

T his chapter will help you design a high school curriculum using the steps of curriculum design presented in Chapter 3. In order to do this you will need to have a clear position on the issues related to planning high school curriculum that were discussed in Chapter 9. The purpose of this chapter is to get very specific about your intended program outcomes. The level of specificity should permit you to design materials to conduct and assess your program.

## OUTCOMES

- Describe the issues that should be part of the philosophy statement for a high school curriculum.
- List appropriate objectives for a high school program consistent with each of the national standards.
- Sequence objectives for the middle school program.
- Describe appropriate content frameworks for the high school program.
- Place program objectives into a content framework for a high school program.
- Describe alternative assessment plans for program evaluation in the high school.

I n one sense the high school program is easier to design than the other school levels. This is because the outcomes of the national or state standards you are using as a guide should be the outcomes of the high school program. By the time students leave high school they should be able to meet the national standards and/or others that your school has decided are appropriate. In a K–12 program the elementary and middle school programs should prepare students for high school expectations. The task of putting together all the parts of the written curriculum can seem like an overwhelming task. Although the process is not totally a linear process, it helps if you think about developing the parts of the curriculum in steps.

The curriculum writing process was outlined in Chapter 3 of this text. A full curriculum should include:

1. A statement of philosophy that describes the purpose of your program and the rationale for including your program in the school curriculum.
2. The specific goals of your program drawn from your philosophy and your understanding of your students that describe the skills, knowledge, and dispositions you want students to have when they leave your program.
3. A sequence of objectives/outcomes by grade level that takes learners from where they are at the beginning of your program to the specific goals you have established for the end of your program.
4. A content framework that organizes your program objectives by content area into units or themes and describes what will be taught in each grade.
5. A yearly block plan for a grade level that describes what content area will be taught over which lessons.
6. An assessment plan that will be used to determine if the goals of the program have been achieved (Chapter 9).

Most districts will have one curriculum. If this is the case, all the parts of the full curriculum do not have to be duplicated for each school level. However, the full curriculum should include the specifics for each school level. Each of these curriculum parts will be discussed with samples of development for the high school level. As the chapter is developed, each part of the sample curriculum will be integrated with the parts that both precede and follow it. There is no intent to dictate a curriculum with this sample, but rather to illustrate how the parts need to be integrated so that they are compatible with each other. For example, the ideas you express in your philosophy should be reflected in the other parts of the curriculum. What you evaluate should be consistent with your goals and objectives. This is called curriculum *alignment*.

## Step 1: Develop a Statement of Philosophy

The statement of philosophy for the high school level should reflect your perspective of an appropriate physical education program for this age level, particularly addressing some of the issues presented in Chapter 9, such as:

■ How competent should students be in an activity?
■ What activities are "required" and what are student choices?
■ What activities should programs offer?
■ What approach to fitness will be stressed or taught in your program?

- Should students be required to participate outside of the physical education class?
- How much knowledge do students need about fitness and other disciplines in our field and how should this knowledge be acquired?

Box 10.1 is a sample statement of philosophy for a high school program.

## Step 2: Determine the Specific Goals/ Objectives of Your Program

The specific goals of your program are the exit outcomes for the high school. If your program ends at the ninth grade, then your program goals will reflect what you think you can accomplish in a one-year program. If your program ends at the twelfth grade, then the specific goals should reflect what you think you can accomplish in a four-year program. A major source of program goals should be the

Is it reasonable to expect high school students to choose to be active outside of physical education class and hold them accountable for doing so? (© *PhotoLink/Getty Images*)

## Box 10.1    Sample High School Statement of Philosophy
## Meadowbrook High School

The high school physical education program serves a critical role in the education of students and has as its primary goal the development of a physically active lifestyle. We believe that students who are prepared to live a physically active lifestyle have the skills, knowledge, and dispositions to do so. Students will need the following:

### Motor Skills

Students will need to be competent and confident participants in physical activities. *Competence* is defined as the ability to independently and safely participate in an activity with enough skill to make that participation enjoyable. We recognize that students will need experiences in a variety of different movement forms but will also need the opportunity to choose and to specialize in activities of their own choosing; therefore, both program aspects need to be accommodated over the four years. Program offerings will need to be broad (including team sports, individual sports, lifetime activities, leisure activities, fitness activities, and dance) to capture the interest of a very diverse group of students. The early high school years should be devoted to giving students skills in at least two different movement forms of their choice. The latter part of the high school program should permit students to specialize in an activity of their own choosing if they desire. Unit size will need to be long enough to develop competence in the activity and will vary with the activity.

### Fitness and Physical Activity

We believe that in order to prepare students for a lifetime of physical activity, students will need to be prepared with both a training approach as well as an activity approach to fitness. Student fitness will be monitored and students with teacher support will design individual fitness programs that include both exercise as well as physical activity components. Goals will be established for each student and opportunities outside of the physical education class both inside and outside of the school will be made available for students to work on those goals. Students with low levels of fitness will be encouraged to sign up for classes that take a training approach to the development of fitness.

A critical part of preparing students for a lifetime of physical activity is establishing the knowledge base to recognize why physical activity and a health-related level of fitness is important, and how to develop and maintain fitness with both an activity and a training approach to fitness. Students will be responsible for acquiring this knowledge by the sophomore year.

We believe it is the responsibility of the physical education program to help students make the transition from physical education class to participation in physical activity outside of the school. Therefore, the physical education program will both bring the community to our program and bring the students to the community.

content emphases for a grade level under each of the national standards. These are presented in Chapter 9, Box 9.1, on page 165. The program goals for the sample Meadowbrook High School are described in Box 10.2. These goals reflect the national standards but are modified for the specific needs of this school. Our sample high school is a four-year program. Box 10.3 describes what might be appropriate goals for a school having a one-year high school physical education requirement. The goals that a program establishes should be attainable and not just broad statements of desirable outcomes. When program time is limited the selection of what content is most important from many good choices is perhaps the most difficult thing for curriculum designers to do.

## Box 10.2 Specific Goals of a Four-Year Program Meadowbrook High School

**Standard 1: Demonstrates *Competency* in Motor Skills and Movement Patterns to Perform a Variety of Physical Activities**

- Be competent in three different activities in two different movement forms.

**Standard 2: Demonstrates Understanding of Movement Concepts, Principles Strategies, and Tactics as They Apply to the Learning and Performance of Physical Activities**

- Know why physical activity is important.
- Use both a training approach and an activity approach to maintain or improve fitness.
- Design a personal activity plan to improve health-related fitness based on scientifically based knowledge.
- Use discipline-specific and activity-specific knowledge to improve performance and learning.

**Standard 3: Participates Regularly in Physical Activity**

- Understand the relationship between physical activity and a healthy lifestyle through the lifespan.
- Possess the skills, knowledge, and disposition to maintain a high level of physical activity independently.
- Participate regularly in physical activity.
- Identify community resources for participation in physical activity.

**Standard 4: Achieves and Maintains a Health-Enhancing Level of Physical Fitness**

- Independently apply training principles to maintain or improve a level of fitness.
- Assess personal fitness status.
- Meet the health-related fitness standards as defined by Fitnessgram.
- Achieve personal fitness goals after a period of training.

**Standard 5: Exhibits Responsible Personal and Social Behavior That Respects Self and Others in Physical Activity Settings**

- Positively influence the behavior of others in physical activity settings.
- Develop a personal philosophy of participation that is inclusive of others of different ages, ability, gender, race, ethnicity, socioeconomic status, and culture.
- Hold themselves personally responsible for safe practices, settling conflicts in a positive way, and establishing rules, procedures, and etiquette in physical activity settings.

**Standard 6: Values Physical Activity for Health, Enjoyment, Challenge, Self-Expression, and/or Social Interaction**

- Identify the potential values of different kinds of activities.
- Identify the activities that provide personal pleasure and why they provide pleasure.
- Be willing to learn new activities.

## Step 3: Sequence the Specific Goals/ Objectives by Grade Level

From your goals you will need to establish more specific objectives that are for the most part measurable and will be placed into your content framework to establish your units. Actually, this is the point where work with program goals, your content framework, and the specific objectives of your program are aligned. You

## Box 10.3   Specific Goals of a One-Year High School Program

**Standard 1: Demonstrates *Competency* in Motor Skills and Movement Patterns to Perform a Variety of Physical Activities**

■ Be competent in two different activities in two different movement forms.

**Standard 2: Demonstrates Understanding of Movement Concepts, Principles, Strategies and Tactics as They Apply to the Learning and Performance of Physical Activities**

■ Know why physical activity is important.

■ Use both a training approach and an activity approach to maintain or improve fitness.

■ Design a personal activity plan to improve health-related fitness based on scientifically based knowledge.

**Standard 3: Participates Regularly in Physical Activity**

■ Understand the relationship between physical activity and a healthy lifestyle through the lifespan.

■ Participate regularly in physical activity for a period of nine weeks.

■ Identify community resources for participation in physical activity.

**Standard 4: Achieves and Maintains a Health-Enhancing Level of Physical Fitness**

■ Assess personal fitness status.

■ Meet the health-related fitness standards as defined by Fitnessgram.

■ Design a personal fitness program.

**Standard 5: Exhibits Responsible Personal and Social Behavior That Respects Self and Others in Physical Activity Settings**

■ Positively influence the behavior of others in physical activity settings.

**Standard 6: Values Physical Activity for Health, Enjoyment, Challenge, Self-Expression, and/or Social Interaction**

■ Identify the potential values of different kinds of activities.

■ Identify the activities that provide personal pleasure and why they provide pleasure.

■ Be willing to learn new activities.

will establish an objective from looking at your program goals, and you will want to place it into your content framework. You may find that it may need to be modified to meet the needs of your content framework. You may also find that you have designed your expectations for what you can actually achieve in your program too high.

Although some of them do, most of the national standards do not get specific enough for you to pull your objectives from this source. You will have to take the program goals and decide specifically what exactly you want students to do. Box 10.4 describes the specific objectives for Meadowbrook High School.

One issue in developing a curriculum for the elementary and middle school levels was that of sequencing objectives through the grade levels. At these levels there is an identified progression of difficulty. Although some high school programs do designate some activities and content by grade level, most high schools do not have students for more than a one- or two-year program and do not designate a "sequence" of objectives beyond offering certain activities for certain grade levels or by making some courses required in the early high school years and giving

# Box 10.4  Goals Translated into Specific Objectives for Meadowbrook High School

**Standard 1: Demonstrates *Competency* in Motor Skills and Movement Patterns to Perform a Variety of Physical Activities**

■ Be competent in three different activities in two different movement forms.

*Specific Objective*

1. Demonstrate competence in three different activities from two of the following:
   a. Team sports—basketball, volleyball, lacrosse, soccer, field hockey
   b. Individual/Dual Sports—gymnastics, bowling, archery, tennis
   c. Outdoor Pursuits—canoeing, backpacking, kayaking, wall climbing
   d. Fitness and Training—weight lifting, jogging, aerobic dance
   e. Dance—line and folk dance, modern, African
   f. Martial arts—yoga, tae kwon do; karate

**Standard 2: Demonstrates Understanding of Movement Concepts, Principles, Strategies and Tactics as They Apply to the Learning and Performance of Physical Activities**

■ Know why physical activity is important.

■ Use both a training and an activity approach to maintain or improve fitness.

■ Design a personal activity plan to improve health-related fitness based on scientifically based knowledge.

■ Use discipline- and activity-specific knowledge to improve performance and learning.

*Specific Objectives*

1. Can describe the benefits of participation in physical activity.

2. Can plan a program to improve fitness using a training and activity approach.

3. Can identify the safety, rules, and tactics of the activities chosen for competence development.

4. Can describe one principle of learning and one principle of biomechanics that would improve performance in each activity taken.

**Standard 3: Participates Regularly in Physical Activity**

■ Understand the relationship between physical activity and a healthy lifestyle through the lifespan.

■ Possess the skills, knowledge, and disposition to maintain a high level of physical activity independently.

■ Participate regularly in physical activity.

■ Identify community resources for participation in physical activity.

*Specific Objectives*

1. Can identify the major sources of physical activity and community resources for people of different ages.

2. Participates for at least nine weeks in a structured physical activity outside of school.

3. Participates at least three times a day in moderate to vigorous physical activity outside of a physical education class.

**Standard 4: Achieves and Maintains a Health-Enhancing Level of Physical Fitness**

■ Independently apply training principles to maintain or improve a level of fitness.

■ Assess personal fitness status.

■ Meet the health-related fitness standards as defined by Fitnessgram.

■ Achieve personal fitness goals after a period of training.

*Specific Objectives*

1. Meet the health-related fitness standards as defined by Fitnessgram.

2. Independently apply training principles to diagnose, set goals, and establish a personal fitness program to maintain or improve levels of fitness.

*(continued on next page)*

*(continued from previous page)*

### Standard 5: Exhibits Responsible Personal and Social Behavior That Respects Self and Others in Physical Activity Settings

- Positively influence the behavior of others in physical activity settings
- Develop a personal philosophy of participation that is inclusive of others of different ages, ability, gender, race, ethnicity, socioeconomic status, and culture.
- Hold themselves personally responsible for safe practices, settling conflicts in a positive way, and establishing rules, procedures, and etiquette in physical activity settings.

*Specific Objectives*

1. Be inclusive in their relationships with others in physical activity settings.

2. Know how to be an independent and responsible participant in a wide variety of physical activity settings.

### Standard 6: Values Physical Activity for Health, Enjoyment, Challenge, Self-Expression, and/or Social Interaction

- Can identify the potential values of different kinds of activities.
- Can identify the activities that provide personal pleasure and why they provide pleasure.
- Is willing to learn new activities.

*Specific Objectives*

1. Can identify the potential values of different kinds of activities.
2. Can identify the activities that provide personal pleasure and why they provide pleasure.
3. Demonstrates a willingness to learn new activities by their selection of activities in the program.

students choices during the later years of the program. Students still need to be competent in the activity, but the activities differ by grade level.

When schools do have physical education all four years of high school, the issue of sequence needs to be revisited. Students can take more advanced work in some activities, and programs can manipulate what students can choose to fit the needs of different age groups. What would be most affected by more years of physical education would be the cognitive and affective objectives of the program, which could be identified by grade level.

## Step 4: Establish a Content Framework for the Curriculum

The content framework for the high school program describes its units of study. Sometimes units are organized around cognitive concepts or other themes that reflect cognitive or affective concerns (see Box 10.5). The multiactivity model is used overwhelmingly by current programs, in spite of the fact that many different content frameworks have been proposed for the high school. In the multiactivity model, units are identified by the sport or activity that is their focus (i.e., basketball, weight training, fitness).

Most programs recognize that there are different *forms* of sport and activity (i.e., team sports, individual activities). These different forms or categories of sports and activities in one sense become a content framework of sorts for the high school program. Many different content frameworks for activities have been proposed.

---

## Box 10.5    Concept Frameworks for High School

**Example A**

*Becoming fit:*    The why, the how, and the process of maintaining and obtaining fitness

*Physical activity and the community:*    Exploring community offerings

*Lifetime low-skill activities:*    Recreational activities

*Learning to compete and cooperate:*    Team sports

*Learning how to learn:*    Individual sports

*Sport as expression and aesthetics*

**Example B**

Force production

Cooperation

Balance

Responsibility

Force reduction

Fitness

---

Several are described in Box 10.6. To some extent, the categories you choose reflect the breadth of your program. Programs that include more types of activities are usually broader in scope and have a better chance of meeting the needs of a very diverse population of students. Some programs as suggested in the national standards and illustrated in the goals for Meadowbrook High School expect that students have competence in more than one of these movement forms. Perhaps that is the biggest issue to be resolved by high school program planners. Should high school students have to be competent in more than one kind of movement, or can the program permit them to develop competence in the kinds of activities they like? For instance, some students really like team sports and some students really like dance or individual kinds of activities. How important is it for students to be competent in activities they may not enjoy as much? Obviously the argument against being competent in different activities is that personal interest is a big factor in

---

## Box 10.6    Frameworks for Activity Forms

**Example A**

*Team sports:*    volleyball, basketball, lacrosse, soccer

*Aquatics:*    beginning swimming, intermediate swimming, life guarding

*Dance:*    line dance, modern dance

*Individual/dual sports/activities:*    archery, bowling, wall climbing, tennis

*Outdoor pursuits:*    kayaking, rappelling

*Fitness:*    weight training, jogging, aerobic dance, fitness training

**Example B**

*Dance:*    social dance, jazz

*Team sports:*    ultimate, basketball, team handball

*Individual sports:*    golf, tennis, racquetball

*Martial arts:*    Tai chi, karate

*Lifetime activities:*    paddle tennis, recreational activities, bicycle touring

*Fitness:*    aerobic dance, weight training, fitness training

enjoyment and motivation to become competent. Students at the high school level should be able to meet their interest needs. The argument for competence in different activities is that students may not ever try new activities unless they are required to and being willing to learn new activities is an important part of developing a physically active lifestyle.

The advantages and disadvantages of a totally required and totally elective high school program is the reason why many programs that have more than one year of required physical education try to combine the two. Beginning students are required to take certain kinds of activities. As students progress in the program they are given more opportunities to choose the activities they will take.

## Step 5: Place Your Curriculum Framework into a Yearly Block Plan for Each Grade Level

After you have established the content framework for your program you will want to place the "units" of the framework into a block plan for a year. The block plan is the calendar for the school year and what you will teach each week. Table 10.1 shows a sample block plan for Meadowbrook High School. The block plan indicates that students will be required to choose one of four different blocks of activities in the freshman year. The intent here is to make sure that every student experiences different movement forms for the year. At the sophomore, junior, and senior year, students may freely choose from a variety of different movement forms for each unit time block in the year. It is conceivable that some students may choose mostly team sports, although they would be encouraged not to.

**Table 10.1** | Sample Block Plan for Meadowbrook High School

| Week | Freshman Year | Sophomore Year | Junior Year | Senior Year |
|------|---------------|----------------|-------------|-------------|
| 1 | Orientation/ Lockers | Orientation/ Lockers | Orientation/ Lockers | Orientation/ Lockers |
| 2–10 | Choice of soccer, basketball, ultimate | Choice of tennis, archery, lacrosse | Choice of tennis, archery, lacrosse | Choice of tennis, archery, lacrosse |
| 11–18 | Personal fitness and recreational activities | Choice of bowling, modern dance, basketball | Choice of bowling, modern dance, basketball | Choice of bowling, modern dance, basketball |
| 19–26 | Choice of archery, bowling, golf | Choice of karate, golf, personal fitness | Choice of karate, golf, personal fitness | Choice of karate, golf, personal fitness |
| 27–34 | Choice of dance, gymnastics, karate | Choice of flag football, kayaking, line and folk dancing | Choice of flag football, kayaking, line and folk dancing | Choice of flag football, kayaking, line and folk dancing |
| 34–35 | Lockers and program evaluation | Lockers and program evaluation | Lockers and program evaluation | Lockers and program evaluation |

## Scheduling Issues in Creating a Block Plan

There are very practical considerations that teachers must consider when developing a block plan of what they will teach. Some of these are discussed below:

**Weather.**   You will want to schedule activities that need outdoor space when the weather is suitable. Cold weather in the north and hot weather in the south have to be considered.

**Number of indoor and outdoor teaching stations.**   Many programs have limited indoor or outdoor teaching stations, which means all classes scheduled for one class period cannot be either indoors or outdoors at the same time. This means that you need to consider using the indoor stations when it is nice outside and using the outside stations when perhaps the weather is a little cold.

**Number of sections of each activity you will need.**   The number of activity sections that you will need to schedule during any one time frame for a unit depends

Block scheduling enables programs to travel to community facilities (© *Jiang Jin/SuperStock*)

on the number of students who want that activity. In the Meadowbrook High School block plan, soccer, basketball, ultimate, tennis, archery, and lacrosse are all being offered the first unit time frame. Teachers can do a survey to find out how many sections they will need to offer of each activity. If Meadowbrook High School has four teachers and they are on a block schedule, each teacher can teach three classes a day. That would mean that there are potentially 12 sections being offered every unit time period and six different activities. Some activities may require only one section being offered and some may require more than two. With the six activities offered during that first unit time frame, three of them are field sports and would need to be scheduled at different times.

## Step 6: Place Your Program-Specific Goals/ Objectives into Your Content Framework

At this point in your curriculum design you are getting ready to assign the specific objectives to units. Box 10.7 takes the objectives identified in Box 10.4 for Meadowbrook High School and in Table 10.1 places them in the curriculum framework identified for this school. If you have done a good job with your objectives you will have a good start on developing your units. One of the problems with offering a choice program is the difficulty of ensuring that each student is accomplishing the objectives of the program. If a student chooses basketball, will he or she have an opportunity to meet the program objectives? High school objectives are written at a more general level of specificity so that they can be applied to different activities. For instance, Meadowbrook High School has an objective that says: Use discipline- and activity-specific knowledge to improve performance. This has been placed in each activity unit. It is likely and desirable that each different activity will actually teach different knowledge and apply it. When students sign up for different activities they will not be applying the same discipline- or activity-specific knowledge. When you have a choice program you have to accept the idea that you cannot dictate specifically what students will get from the program because they each will be learning different things.

## Step 7: Establishing an Assessment Plan for Your Program

A program assessment plan identifies the extent to which a program meets its objectives. Fifteen objectives across the six standards were identified for Meadowbrook High School. The assessment plan has to devise a method of measuring the extent to which the students in the program meet these objectives. Assessment used to evaluate the achievement of each student should be a part of each unit. Help in devising a good assessment plan is provided in Chapter 12. It is important to understand that when you do program assessment you don't have to assess every student in every objective to identify the extent to which the program is accomplishing its objectives.

# Box 10.7    Program Objectives Placed into Content Framework for Meadowbrook High School

## Soccer, Basketball, Ultimate, Lacrosse, Flag Football

Team sport units will include the following program objectives:

1. Demonstrate competence in team sports.
2. Identify the safety, rules, and tactics of the activities chosen for competence development.
3. Describe one principle of learning and one principle of biomechanics that would improve performance in each activity taken.
4. Be inclusive in their relationships with others in physical activity settings.
5. Know how to be an independent and responsible participant in a wide variety of physical activity settings.
6. Identify the potential values of different kinds of activities.
7. Identify the activities that provide personal pleasure and why they provide pleasure.
8. Demonstrate a willingness to learn new activities by their selection of activities in the program.

## Bowling, Archery, Tennis, Golf, Gymnastics

Individual sport units will contain the following program objectives:

1. Demonstrate competence in individual sports.
2. Identify the safety, rules, and tactics of the activities chosen for competence development.
3. Describe one principle of learning and one principle of biomechanics that would improve performance in each activity taken.
4. Be inclusive in their relationships with others in physical activity settings.
5. Know how to be an independent and responsible participant in a wide variety of physical activity settings.

## Modern Dance, Line and Folk Dancing

Dance units will contain the following program objectives:

1. Demonstrate competence in individual sports.
2. Identify the safety, rules, and tactics of the activities chosen for competence development.

3. Describe one principle of learning and one principle of biomechanics that would improve performance in each activity taken.
4. Be inclusive in their relationships with others in physical activity settings.
5. Know how to be an independent and responsible participant in a wide variety of physical activity settings.

## Karate, Kayaking

Martial arts and outdoor pursuit units will contain the following program objectives:

1. Demonstrate competence in martial arts or outdoor pursuits.
2. Identify the safety, rules, and tactics of the activities chosen for competence development.
3. Describe one principle of learning and one principle of biomechanics that would improve performance in each activity taken.
4. Be inclusive in their relationships with others in physical activity settings.
5. Know how to be an independent and responsible participant in a wide variety of physical activity settings.

## Personal Fitness

The personal fitness unit will contain the following objectives:

1. Describe the benefits of participation in physical activity.
2. Plan a program to improve fitness using a training and activity approach.
3. Identify the major sources of physical activity and community resources for people of different ages.
4. Participate for at least nine weeks in a structured physical activity outside of school.
5. Participate at least three times a week in moderate to vigorous physical activity outside of physical education class.
6. Meet the health-related fitness standards as defined by Fitnessgram.
7. Independently apply training principles to diagnose, set goals, and establish a personal fitness program to maintain or improve levels of fitness.

## Check Your Understanding

1.  What are the critical issues to take a stand on in a high school curriculum philosophy statement?
2.  For each of the national standards list what might be appropriate objectives for the high school level.
3.  Describe a sequence of experiences leading to one of the objectives you have listed above.
4.  Describe two appropriate content frameworks for the high school program.
5.  What strategy might you use to assess a high school physical education program?

## References

National Association for Sport and Physical Education (NASPE). (2004). *Appropriate Practices for High School Physical Education*. Reston, VA: NASPE.

National Association for Sport and Physical Education (NASPE). (2004). *Moving into the Future: National Content Standards for Physical Education*. Reston, VA: NASPE.

Mohnsen, B. (Ed.). (2003). *Concepts and Principles of Physical Education: What Every Student Needs to Know*. Reston, VA: National Association for Sport and Physical Education.

## Suggested Reading

Couturier, L., Chepko, S., & Coughlin, A. (2005). "Student Voices—What Middle and High School Students Have to Say About Physical Education." *The Physical Educator.* Early Winter, 170–177.

Hastie, P. (2003). *Teaching for Lifetime Physical Activity Through Quality High School Physical Education.* San Francisco: Benjamin Cummings.

Kinchin, G., & O'Sullivan, M. (1999). "Making Physical Education Meaningful in Schools." *JOPERD, 70,* no. 5, 40–44.

Wallstrom, T. (2005). "Developing a Lifetime Adventure-skills Curriculum." *JOPERD, 76,* no. 6, 36–39.

# CHAPTER 11

# The Process of Developing and Implementing the Curriculum

## OVERVIEW

C hapter 3 described the sections of the curriculum guide and what goes in each section. The goal of this chapter is to outline a process that will give you the skills to write good curriculum and the means to implement it in a way that increases the chances that the curriculum will actually be delivered to the students as conceived by the curriculum writers.

## OUTCOMES

- Identify the tasks that must be completed before a curriculum writing team meets.
- Identify the order in which the sections of the curriculum guide should be written.
- Describe the process of working with a writing team who has been assigned to write a curriculum.
- Identify the role of faculty and administration not on a curriculum writing team.
- Identify the factors that must be considered in developing a plan for implementation of a curriculum.
- Describe several alternative strategies for implementing a curriculum.
- Describe how a curriculum committee might obtain the support and develop the skills of teachers not on the curriculum committee.

Many curriculum experts think that the real value in developing a curriculum is not the product of the guide itself, but the process that is used to develop and implement it. Developing a curriculum requires the designers to think through what they want to do and how they want to do it. This process is in and of itself a growth-producing activity for the participants. Unfortunately many curriculum products (guides) sit on a shelf to collect dust. They are really never implemented. The process has been a valuable one for the participants on the writing team, but little change is evident in the program actually delivered to students. Knowing the problems of implementation and having some strategies to deal with them increases the likelihood that the materials that are designed will actually be used. This chapter discusses the processes of planning and implementing a curriculum.

## The Planning Process

The administration of your school district has decided that they want a curriculum guide for physical education. They have asked you for suggestions about doing this and have also asked you to take the lead on the project. You are supportive of the task because the district does not have an applied curriculum—the one that sits on the shelf is not integrated throughout the school levels.

There are many tasks related to the planning process that take place prior to the time that the school curriculum committee even meets. You will need to obtain administrative support for the project and decide on the size of the committee and committee members. You will need to have a plan for what the final product of your work will be and how it will be disseminated. In addition, you will need to know what programs are already implemented and you will need to gather resources to facilitate the work of the committee. These are all tasks that need to be accomplished before the committee meets for the first time; they are summarized in Box 11.1.

### Administrative Support

One of the first things you need to do when asked to lead a curriculum writing team is to determine the amount and kind of administrative support for the project you are likely to receive. The amount of participation you get depends

---

### Box 11.1   Preparation for Writing Curriculum

- Determine the extent to which the project will be supported by the administration.
- Determine who should be on the committee.
- Have a vision of what the final product will look like.

- Determine what programs are already doing.
- Have a vision/plan for what the process will be.
  Identify and collect the resources you will need.

mainly on the administration's interest in what you are doing. If the sense of the district teachers is that the curriculum will make a difference to them, then you are more likely to get support. Will the administration provide support for the writing team in terms of release time, additional compensation, and consultants? You need to know before you start what kind of support the committee will get and what is likely to happen to the materials that you do develop in terms of accountability and support for using them.

## Forming the Committee

The composition of the curriculum committee is critical to it success. The choice as to how many and who should be on the committee is likely to be a joint decision involving both the administration and the teachers involved.

**Size of group.**   The more participation that you are able to elicit in the process, the more support you are likely to get in implementing your decisions. However, the larger the committee, the more difficult and unwieldy the process becomes and the more difficult it is to get consensus. One way to maintain the advantages of larger participation and avoid the disadvantages of a large group is to begin the process with a larger group for input (perhaps focus groups at each level) and to use a smaller group to deal with the details of design and writing. When smaller writing groups are formed, it will be important to seek input throughout the process and make sure to keep the larger group as well as all the teachers the curriculum will affect informed. E-mail and electronic copies of all work will facilitate this process.

**Who should be on the committee?**   In the best of circumstances you would have at least one representative from each of the schools in the district if the district is not too large. These people would want to be there and would be willing to do the work needed competently to get the job done. In some cases district curriculum administrators are also members of the committee, often playing a facilitator role.

Sometimes it is recommended that parents and students be represented on the committee. There are advantages and disadvantages to having these groups represented. The advantage is that they provide a unique perspective that is important to the process. The disadvantage is that they do not have the expertise in the field that teachers have and may considerably slow down the process, while only making a limited contribution to it. An alternative is to seek the perspective of these groups ahead of time and apply it during the development of the curriculum.

The district administration may be willing to hire consultants from a local university to help you get started. If so, use them, as they are likely to put you in touch with resources that would be helpful. In any case all schools should be invited to attend, and teachers you know who have added skills needed for the writing process should be extended special invitations to be on the committee.

## A Vision of the Final Product

Before you embark on a journey you need to know where you are going. As a curriculum leader you will want to have a clear idea of what the final product is going to be. You will also want to share this vision with the members of the committee. The previous chapters of this text were designed to help you understand the parts of a good curriculum guide. It would also be helpful to look at the work of other districts that are considered good models as well as to obtain a copy of the Physical Education Curriculum Evaluation Tool (PE-CAT; see Chapter 12) that describes criteria for evaluating school physical education curriculum guides. As a group leader you should be prepared to outline the task of the committee in terms of the final product and to describe to the committee the criteria for each part of the product.

## Information on What Programs Are Already Doing

Not only do you need to know where you are going, but you also need to know where you are at the beginning of a journey. One of the more useful strategies to use before beginning a curriculum project is to seek objective information on what current programs are already doing. A lot of teachers think they already know this information, and many times their perceptions are wrong. Schools can be surveyed as to what objectives and content they are already teaching or they can be asked to submit objectives and yearly block plans for each grade level.

Teacher surveys and questionnaires work best in situations where no written materials are available or when teachers are reluctant to share those materials. Surveys can also be used to determine teacher values and beliefs prior to commencing a project. It helps to know if there is consensus and where the lack of consensus might be before you begin to work with a group.

## A Vision of the Process

As a leader you will need to have a clear idea of the process that is going to be used to develop the curriculum, and you will want to share this with the administration ahead of time so that they understand and support what you are doing. Most participants in curriculum design underestimate the time and effort needed to develop curriculum, which often results in a poor product. When materials are not good they are not used, and their development has been wasted effort. For most district curriculum projects a two-year commitment is not unreasonable.

## Resources You Will Need

Before you begin the process of developing a curriculum you should begin collecting resources. Some helpful resources are listed below. Faculty in your district may already have some of these resources. If not, the administration should be willing to obtain them for you.

- State and district curriculum guides and assessment materials.
- Assessment resources (national materials, published materials, and materials from other districts and states are good sources).

If you are the leader of the curriculum project, you will have to prepare resources for the committee. (© *image100 Ltd.*)

# Steps in the Writing Process

Chapter 3 outlined the parts of the curriculum guide. At first glance it would seem to make sense to start with the first part (the philosophy statement) and work your way through the development of the guide. However, experienced curriculum designers will tell you that the process of developing curriculum is not an entirely linear process. Major ideas in the philosophy statement may only become clear after program goals and objectives are developed, which means that the philosophy statement should probably be written later in the process. Program objectives may only become entirely clear after a scope and sequence of content is developed for each school level, which means that you may want to save refining your objectives until after the scope and sequence is developed. Knowing that the process is not a linear one ahead of time and that you will have to go back to previous sections as you work through later sections will help facilitate the process.

## Orienting the Committee

One of your first tasks as a group curriculum leader will be to orient the committee to the task. They will need to know what the final product is going to be and how you intend to get there. They will also need to have input into these decisions.

Sharing curriculum guides and materials from other districts that are considered good ones and proposing a strategy to get there as a point of departure for a discussion will facilitate the process. As part of this orientation the responsibilities of each of the members of the committee should be made clear. In some cases it may be necessary to have participants formally acknowledge their willingness to meet those responsibilities.

## Defining Program Goals

A good strategy to use as you begin work with a committee is to keep ideas more global in the beginning part of the process. Be prepared with materials that the group can read ahead of time. Use resources for this first step, particularly the state and national standards to determine if they are what you support as a group. Work to define the goals of the K–12 program, which will largely be the exit outcomes for the high school program. Talk about the implications of those goals for what students should know and be able to do at all grade levels. Share with the committee what the position of the administration is on the implementation process and the established accountability for implementation.

## Establishing a Review Process

At this point it is be helpful to decide what your role in the group is going to be. Although group consensus is a goal, the lead person is responsible for articulating that consensus and putting it down on paper. Sometimes this process results in one person writing parts of the curriculum and committee members taking on less and less responsibility. A good rule to establish from the very beginning is to establish every member of the committee as a working reviewer. That means that you (or whoever puts ideas in the project down on paper) seek input on the drafts of materials and use that input. It also means that every member of the committee must take seriously his or her role in writing and reviewing the materials. If the members of the group do not function well with reviewing the materials as an outside assignment, then the first part of every meeting for which new materials are available should be spent in a review process. Teaming group members up as partners in your meetings is likely to be more successful than working as individuals.

## Defining Program Objectives

Once you have defined the broad goals (or standards) of the program, then you need to get more specific with objectives for each school level. This is the heart of the curriculum. Again, provide resources for the group to read ahead of time. The exit performance indicators for each school level should be defined from the objectives. The materials that accompany this text include sample objectives and performance indicators designed to help you with this process. The national standards, performance indicators, assessment material developed by NASPE (1995, 2004) are good resources for this level. There are also textbooks written that describe curriculum for different school levels. It helps to know ahead of time which of the orientations to curriculum (curriculum frameworks) each of the schools is presently using, if they are using one.

You might start with having each school level review textbooks and determine which of the frameworks inherent in each are most supported by the group.

It should be clear to all the participants that these exit objectives and performance indicators are achievement expectations for all students with few exceptions. They are not just directional goals, but should be what each teacher is willing to hold him- or herself accountable for in terms of student achievement at the end of the school program. If curriculum guides are to be useful, then the program objectives must be selected with great care. Teachers are expected to teach to these objectives and performance indicators and assess program effectiveness based largely on the extent to which students achieve them.

One of the issues that frequently arises when planning objectives has to do with the very practical realities of resources. Objectives should be written so that all the schools in a district have the resources to teach to those objectives. Many times some schools have better resources than others. One strategy to use is to write objectives so that there are choices of content within that object. For example, in the middle school, instead of saying that students should be able to use a tennis racket to keep a ball going continuously across a net, you might say that students should be able to use a racket to keep an object going across a net. This flexibility allows the program to use either tennis rackets, pickle ball, badminton rackets, or paddle ball rackets.

In order to work on school level exit-performance indicators, you may want to initially divide the group by school level. Each school group should be assigned to develop objectives and performance indicators that are exit criteria for their school level. When school groups are working independently, you will need to assign a group leader who is willing to call the meetings and facilitate the work of the group. You should spend some time training these group leaders on how best to facilitate the process. If the leadership in the school groups is not there, then you might consider working with these groups independently.

The total committee will need to come back as a group to make sure that the exit performance indicators that the elementary level has identified will appropriately feed into the middle school program and that the middle school program performance indicators will feed into the high school program. At this point there is likely to be a discussion about whether or not the goals of the total program are feasible. If they are not, then you may need to go back and revise the exit criteria for the high school program. This will also be a time when the group as a whole will need to consider the specific curriculum activities. If students have no striking experience before a high school tennis class, it is difficult for high school teachers to give students the competence they need. Likewise, if elementary school students are learning to take their heart rate, it makes no sense to include this in the middle school or high school experience.

## Aligning Objectives with Goals

After you have developed your objectives you will want to go back and make sure that the objectives are aligned with the goals (standards) of the program. If the objectives are met, will the goals be achieved? If not, then either the goals or the objectives will need to change. The objectives should describe what students need to know and be able to do in order to reach the program goals.

## Developing a Philosophy Statement

If you haven't worked on a philosophy statement up to this point, then this would probably be a good time to do it, before the scope and sequence is developed. Chapter 3 described the importance and parts of the philosophy statement. This statement should describe what you believe a program should do in your district and why you believe it is important for your students and your situation. Philosophy statements can be generic (fitting any district in the state) or specific to the conditions in your school. They are better if they communicate that you have considered the needs of your specific situation. Once your goals and objectives are aligned, the group should be in a better position to know what they really want to do with their program and why.

## Developing Scope and Sequence

When you have a set of objectives and performance indicators for each school level that are consistent with the goals the group has decided are the most important goals, then each school level group is ready to develop a scope and sequence of materials for their school level. The section of this text on writing a scope and sequence (Chapter 3) and evaluating the curriculum (Chapter 12) are good sources to make available to the committee. There are also good textbooks and online resources that should be of some help that should be made available to the group.

The scope and sequence will take a great deal of time to do. If good initial models are developed with the format clearly delineated, then the responsibility for writing a scope and sequence for different content areas can be shared with members outside of the curriculum committee as well. Within each school level group different faculty can be assigned to develop a first draft for different content areas to be reviewed by others in the group. Prior to this step, however, the specific content that is to be developed and the format that is going to be used should be decided by the entire group.

Ideally, the scope and sequence of content should be piloted before it becomes part of the guide. Different teachers in the district can be asked to try to use the materials that are developed and to provide input into their revision. One of the reasons that a lot of guides are unsuccessful in their implementation is that the materials were not tested before they become part of the guide. Nobody thought to see if they worked or were achievable. This step is the most time-consuming but perhaps the most important in the process. Piloting the materials will not only tell you whether the materials are appropriate content for students, the process will also tell you whether teachers who are expected to use the materials can use them.

## Developing Assessment Material

There will be two kinds of assessment material needed in your guide. The first is the assessment material designed to measure your objectives and performance indicators. The second kind is the assessment material and a plan for assessment needed to assess the goals of the curriculum. These are described in Chapters 3 and 12, respectively.

The advantage of writing the assessment material with the objectives and the scope and sequence is that oftentimes when you are forced to determine how an objective is going to be assessed, you gain insight into how the objectives and performance indicators, as well as the scope and sequence, need to be revised. In other words, it helps if you align all three with each other so that your intent is what you teach and is what you assess. Good assessment materials for physical education standards are becoming increasingly available from NASPE (1995, 2002, 2004) and commercial publishers in physical education. State professional groups, such as the South Carolina professional group (SCAHPERD), and the State of Kentucky have also worked hard to produce appropriate assessment materials that should be available for your use. Again, once you have selected the assessment materials, they need to be piloted to make sure they are appropriate measures of the objectives that you are trying to assess.

## Assessing Your Work

As you move through each part of the guide, your work should be assessed using a set of criteria established to evaluate that part of the guide. The previous chapters of this text as well as the PE-CAT tool are good places to look for criteria to evaluate your work before it becomes a final product. Continuous and ongoing assessment of the materials will increase the probability that the final product will be used by the teachers in the district.

# The Implementation Process

One of the biggest mistakes often made by school district curriculum committees is to finish the writing process and then give the document to teachers with a directive to use it. No planned implementation process takes place, which almost ensures that the materials will not be used. Having a plan for implementing the curriculum is just as important as having a plan for writing one. Table 11.1 outlines a plan for implementation of a curriculum.

## Curriculum as Policy

District school boards approve curriculum in most states. When the physical education curriculum is completed and teachers in the district have had an opportunity for input and revisions of the work of the committee, the guide should be approved by the district school board. Approval of the school board makes the curriculum policy. It is unlikely that many board members understand what their physical education programs are trying to do. Physical educators should seek the opportunity to present the curriculum to the board. This presentation should be considered an opportunity for program advocacy and should be done well.

There is a lot of advocacy material available from NASPE, some of which is available online to members free of charge, that can help you determine the critical points to make in supporting your program. What you will want to do is to share the need for your program (why physical education is important) as well as the

**Table 11.1** | A Sample Curriculum Implementation Plan

| Task | Date | Responsibility | Assessment and Feedback |
|---|---|---|---|
| Disseminate curriculum to the school board, all teachers, and administrators. | August Year 1 | Curriculum writing team with administrator support. | Provide a feedback sheet should they want to provide input into the material before it becomes official. |
| Seek board approval of the curriculum. | October Year 1 | Curriculum writing team. | — |
| Confirm administrative policy toward implementation. | October Year 1 | Curriculum writing team. | — |
| Present curriculum to all teachers at a district in-service day. Present time line for implementation. | September Year 1 | Lead administrator, curriculum writing team, and other teachers who have participated in the writing. | Seek preliminary information on what teachers initial perceptions and support are for the document (what they like and don't like about what they see). |
| Teacher development in one content area to be implemented; including objectives, development of content, and assessment. | October Year 1 | Expand presenters to those teachers who actually developed the units that will be implemented first. | Provide opportunity for teachers to provide feedback on the unit before it is implemented. |
| Implement one unit at each grade level with assessment materials. | January Year 1: assessment material and feedback sheet returned March Year 1 | All teachers. | Provide feedback sheet for teachers who have used each unit. |
| Revise unit and other materials if necessary. | April–June Year 1 | Curriculum writing team. | — |
| Teacher development in other content areas. | November–May Year 1 | As large a number of teachers as possible should be presenters at different sessions. | Provide feedback sheet for teachers to evaluate sessions. |
| Curriculum writing team meeting to make any necessary revisions and plan teacher development and implementation for following year. | July–August Year 1 | Curriculum writing team and any teacher interested in being a participant. | — |
| Develop materials to share expectations with students and parents. | July–August Year 1 | A committee of teachers and administrators. | — |
| Teacher in-service on revisions and plan for full implementation. | September Year 2 | Curriculum writing team and as many teachers as possible. | Provide feedback sheet for teachers to evaluate sessions. |
| Teacher in-service with choices of content. Teachers should have options at each in-service to attend sessions on the content areas they are less comfortable teaching and assessing. | October–June Year 2 | Curriculum writing team and as many teachers as possible; consider bringing in experts in the content areas outside of the school district. | Provide feedback sheet for teachers to evaluate sessions. |

*(continued on next page)*

**Table 11.1** | *(continued from previous page)*

| Task | Date | Responsibility | Assessment and Feedback |
|---|---|---|---|
| Teachers submit baseline data on student performance for selected areas of the curriculum. | June Year 2 | Committee established to collect and report data. | Reports of the data should be given to school administrators and the teacher only; initial data should not be public. |
| Teacher in-service on content identified by teachers and data collection as having low student achievement scores. Focus on how to improve student achievement. | August–June Year 3 | Curriculum writing team and as many teachers as possible; consider bringing in experts in the content areas outside of the school district. | |
| Teacher collection of data on a three-year rotating basis. Some parts of the curriculum should be assessed every year. | Years 3–5 | A district assessment team, or outside team, should be responsible for receiving, monitoring, and reporting the data. | Data should be reported to teachers, administrators, and if desired, to the public. |

program goals of your curriculum in terms of expectations for student achievement. You may want to give a rationale for why you selected the goals and how they compare to the national or state standards. If the decision of the committee is that you were not able to meet the national OT or state standards because of limited resources or program time, then you need to share with the board what it would take to fully implement the higher level of standards.

## The Role of the Administration

Full implementation of a curriculum is difficult if not impossible without administrative support. Administrative support is necessary to provide resources for implementation as well as to provide some level of accountability for implementing the curriculum. State assessment programs in all content areas of the curriculum have largely changed what teachers do with students because they not only make clear what students are to learn, they also hold students and teachers accountable for learning that defined content. Accountability for teaching what is expected can be developed in different ways but must be a part of any successful implementation process.

The best situation is for the administration to support a policy that requires programs to provide evidence that students are learning what the curriculum says they should be learning. If the assessment materials part of the curriculum are good, then teachers can be required to use the materials to provide evidence of student achievement. Some districts require teachers to indicate in their planning which standards and objectives they are working on in a unit or lesson. This level of accountability is better than no accountability but not as effective as evidence provided in terms of student achievement.

## Dissemination of Materials

At the completion of the development of the curriculum materials, they should be disseminated to all of the physical education teachers and school administrators in a district. The curriculum committee should have the opportunity to meet with all of the district teachers and administrators to explain the project and "walk" them through the document and its use. Materials should be made available as electronic copies. Many districts are creating CDs that allow teachers to make modifications in the materials and to print out assessment materials and scopes and sequences of content as they are needed. As teachers develop units for content areas, they can be asked to share those units with other teachers and record them on the CD.

## A Strategy for Implementation

There are different theories on how a new program should be implemented. A program can:

- Ask a few teachers or schools to pilot the program, and then revise it;
- Ask all teachers to phase in a part of the program; or,
- Ask all teachers to begin the total program.

Under the best of circumstances all three strategies would be used. Often, however, there is neither the time nor resources to do all three. Each has its advantages and disadvantages.

If you have piloted each of the content areas as you have developed them in the objectives and scope and sequence, it may not be as important to pilot the entire program before implementing it. Waiting for a pilot of the entire program often decreases the momentum of a project because it only involves a few teachers or programs. A better strategy might be to implement parts of the program across all schools. This allows all teachers to be involved and allows you to train teachers more specifically in the content.

Even when you decide to have all teachers implement a part of the program, you still have to decide which parts to implement in what order. There are several ways that you can phase in a program. You can start with all the content for one or two grade levels or you can start with some content across grade levels. Both are effective ways to phase in a curriculum. Phasing in some content across all grade levels allows you to create a better understanding of the development of content across grade levels and makes teacher development opportunities easier to plan while maintaining the involvement of all of the teachers. Phasing in a program by grade levels makes the expectations for student achievement more realistic.

A strategy and time line for implementation should be published and made available to both teachers and administrators. Teachers should have the opportunity to make a case for any new equipment or materials that are essential to implement the curriculum. However, it is best to seek these resources prior to the point in the process in which they are indispensable to meeting program objectives and expectations for student achievement.

Regardless of the strategy you use for initial curriculum implementation, teachers need to be able to provide feedback on the materials to the committee. At this point in the process most of the feedback should be about the usefulness of the materials and not the appropriateness of the content. No matter how much time a curriculum committee puts into the development of materials, there are always changes that need to be made to help teachers better use the materials the way they were intended to be used.

## Teacher Development Opportunities

One of the most critical steps in implementation process is helping teachers to understand, value, and implement the curriculum you have designed. This means that you not only have to help them understand the material and give them the skills to implement it, you first have to help them support the effort. Educational change takes far more time than most of us are willing to accept. Fully implementing a new program may take up to five years.

**Seeking teacher support for the curriculum.**   One of the most often neglected steps in trying to produce educational change is getting the support of the people whom you are asking to change. It is difficult for those who have worked on a project for a long time, in many cases years, to understand that the teachers you are expecting to implement the project do not have as much invested in what you have done. They may initially see change as threatening and in some cases may even be unsupportive of the direction you have taken. Some may even be hostile to the effort. Finding a way to make advocates of the teachers who will ultimately have to implement your work requires understanding of the process of change as well as planning.

There has been a lot of research done on the process of change. Most of it begins with the premise that people will adopt change at different rates. Early adopters are likely to be those who have been most involved in the process of change as well as those who can most identify with the changes you want to make. Some of this group has already probably made the kinds of changes you would like to see. What you are asking them to do does not mean they have to give up what they are doing, nor will it take a great deal of effort. There will be teachers who are not already doing what is compatible with the curriculum who will also begin to change within a short amount of time. These teachers are oftentimes highly involved professionally and committed at least to the need for change. They will spend the necessary time to determine what needs to be done in their own programs and will begin the process of implementing what you have asked them to.

For the majority of teachers within a school district you are going to have to "sell" the importance of the curriculum and teaching to it. This will be easier if there is administrative support for the changes and some accountability for "getting on board." If teachers have been active participants in the review process and some part of the writing process, it will also be easier to solicit their support. Sharing your philosophy and rationale for the decisions that you have made will help. It will also help if teachers can see that they have many options for implementing the curriculum and it doesn't mean that every teacher has to be teaching the same thing in the same way. Slowly implementing the curriculum will also make the changes less threatening.

### Time Line for Implementation

A time line for implementing the curriculum should be developed and shared with teachers and administrators. A sample time line is presented in Table 11.1. You will notice that full implementation of the guide upon which this time line is based took three years after the writing team completed its work. The dates for completion of different phases in this time line are realistic estimates given the part-time nature of the writing team and the time needed for teachers to establish new units in their teaching. Most of the time for implementation is designed to provide in-service opportunities for teachers with the content. The process is facilitated by districts that provide monthly opportunities for teachers to get together for planning and teacher development.

### Sharing Expectations with Students and Parents

When a new curriculum is being implemented, students should be informed of the changes and what those changes might mean for student achievement expectations. This is particularly true for upper elementary and secondary students. When there is a choice in the guide for specific activities such as which racket sport a school will choose to teach, students should have input into those decisions. Students can be informed with handouts or can go online to look at the new offerings and expectations. They can also be provided with links to find out about those activities.

Many parents are unaware of what their children do in physical education. The introduction of a new curriculum presents a great opportunity to educate parents and solicit their support for what you are doing. Program goals and student achievement expectations, particularly in relation to grading and other policy issues, should be part of the materials shared with parents.

## Check Your Understanding

1. What information do you need from the administration before you begin writing a curriculum for a school or district?
2. What factors should you consider when choosing the size of a curriculum writing team?
3. Why do you need information on what programs are already doing before you change a written curriculum?
4. Where should you go for resources for developing a curriculum?
5. Describe the order in which sections of the curriculum should be written.

6.  What role should schools in the same district but with different resources play in the design of a curriculum?

7.  What kinds of assessment material should be included in a curriculum guide?

8.  Outline a plan to implement a curriculum.

9.  How do you make the implementation of your curriculum policy?

10.  What are alternative strategies for a time frame for implanting curriculum?

## References

National Association for Sport and Physical Education (NASPE). (1995). *Moving into the Future: National Standards for Physical Education.* Reston, VA: NASPE.

National Association for Sport and Physical Education (NASPE). (2004). *Moving into the Future: National Standards for Physical Education (*2nd ed.). Reston. VA: NASPE.

## Suggested Reading

Belka, D. (2007). *Games Stages and Assessment.* Reston, VA: NASPE.

Cone, T. & Cone, S. (2005). *Assessing Dance in Elementary Physical Education.* Reston, VA: NASPE.

Doolittle, S. & Fry, T. (2002). *Authentic Assessment of Physical Activity in High School Students.* Reston, VA: NASPE.

Fitzpatrick, J., Sanders, J., & Worthen, B. (2003). *Program Evaluation: Alternative Approaches and Practical Guidelines* (3rd ed.). Boston: Addison-Wesley.

Gredler, M. (1996). *Program Evaluation.* New York: Prentice Hall.

Grosse, S. (2005). *Assessment of Swimming in Physical Education.* Reston, VA: NASPE.

Holt Hale, S. A. (1999). *Assessing and Improving Fitness in Elementary Physical Education.* Reston, VA: NASPE.

Holt Hale, S. A. (1999). *Assessing Motor Skills in Elementary Physical Education.* Reston, VA: NASPE.

Lund, J. & Kirk, M. (2002). *Performance-Based Assessment for Middle and High School Physical Education.* Champaign, IL: Human Kinetics.

Mitchell, S. & Oslin, J. (1997). *Assessment in Games Teaching.* Reston, VA: NASPE.

Mohnson, B. (2004). *Assessing Concepts: Secondary Biomechanics.* Reston, VA: NASPE.

O'Sullivan, M. & Henninger, M. (2007). *Assessing Student Responsibility and Teamwork.* Reston, VA: NASPE.

Seidel, K. (2001). *Assessing Student Learning: A Practical Guide CD-Rom.* Reston, VA: NASPE.

Stark, S. (2007). *Assessing Gymnastics in Elementary School Physical Education.* Reston, VA: NASPE.

Steffen, J. & Grosse, S. (2003). *Assessment in Outdoor Adventure Physical Education.* Reston, VA: NASPE.

Townsend, J. S., Mohr, D., Rairigh, R., & Bulger, S. (2003). *Assessing Student Outcomes in Sport Education.* Reston, VA: NASPE.

# CHAPTER 12

# Evaluating the Curriculum

## OVERVIEW

Physical educators make many assumptions about the value of their programs. Many times these assumptions are not accurate. This chapter provides a rationale and process for the collection of objective information on the planned and implemented curriculum and the outcomes of the curriculum.

## OUTCOMES

- Value curriculum evaluation as a critical component in developing and implementing an effective curriculum.
- Identify the different purposes for which curriculum evaluation may be conducted.
- Develop a rationale for conducting curriculum evaluation.
- Outline a procedure for evaluating the planned curriculum.
- Outline a procedure for evaluating the implemented curriculum.
- Outline a procedure for evaluating curriculum outcomes.
- Identify the appropriate kinds of data for the planned and implemented curriculum and the outcomes of curriculum.

Not too long ago the author was invited to be a participant at the United States Department of Education in a discussion about getting legislative support at the national level for physical education. About 10 people from all over the country were invited. We talked in general for a while about how important physical education is and all the things it can do for children. The Department representative, who was not a physical educator, innocently asked,

"And what evidence do you have that physical education programs can do all of these things?" There was total silence in the group.

Physical educators have largely resisted defining their outcomes and assessing what they do. Sometimes this resistance comes from an assumption that the needs of students in different schools are different, and that curriculum ought to be very different in each school. Such a perspective, for the most part, has not led to programs with different objectives but to programs with no objectives. Other false assumptions that have shielded the profession from clearly defining and assessing outcomes is, first, the assumption that teachers already know how their students are doing and, second, that time taken out to do assessment is wasted time. A lot of research would indicate that teacher perceptions of student ability are usually inaccurate without the collection of more systematic and objective data. It is also true that time taken out for assessment improves the quality of what teachers do with instructional time.

We are living at a time when accountability for performance is driving educational practice and policy. Programs that cannot articulate their outcomes and measure the extent to which they meet those outcomes have an uncertain future. The curriculum planning process is designed to help educators articulate their outcomes and describe the way in which those outcomes will be measured. While most of this text has focused on the process of articulating outcomes in preparation for the instructional process, this chapter will focus on assessing the extent to which the curriculum achieves those outcomes. School programs and curriculum can be assessed in many ways depending upon what you want to know and what you want to do with what you find out.

## Who Wants To Know?

With the increased involvement of the federal and state governments in educational policy, there has been an increasing need to provide legislators and other policy makers with evidence of impact. Legislators want to know if their resources are being used appropriately. For educational programs the acid test for impact is student performance. While educational programs used to be evaluated primarily "in house" and the results of evaluation kept in house, in many states the results of program assessment is not only shared with policy makers, but with the public. Often the criteria used for these kinds of evaluations are externally imposed and may or may not be consistent with the goals of the school curriculum as articulated by the teachers and administrators of a school district.

External evaluations that are designed to determine the value of a program can be political and threatening depending on what is done with the information collected. Although external evaluations have largely dominated the evaluation scene, there are still many reasons for schools and districts to assess the curriculum as the school defines the objectives of the curriculum. The important idea is that programs need to set up a formal evaluation that collects objective information on the program whether or not external reviewers request that information.

# Why Do You Want to Assess?

While all assessment and evaluation of programs and curriculum may have as their ultimate goal better educational experiences and improved learning for students, internal and external assessments can have very different purposes. Policy makers generally take an accountability perspective toward assessment and evaluation. The purpose of assessment from an accountability perspective is to hold educators accountable for student performance by identifying schools and teachers that do well and those that do not. The intent in identifying poor and weak programs is to improve them, although for many teachers in the position of working with a poor program, negative consequences imposed from above can be both real and imagined. Evaluation imposed externally is usually outcome based and on a smaller scale than evaluations done within an institution.

When educators assess internally they not only want to look at outcomes, they usually want to improve the delivery of the curriculum. If the program is not producing the desired outcomes, then either the desired outcomes must be changed or the program needs to be redesigned to develop those outcomes. Oftentimes a major assumption of a perspective that asks questions about the delivery of a program is that if the program is delivered as planned, then the outcomes will be achieved. Unless objective data is collected to support the idea that the curriculum is achieving its goals, educators cannot make such a claim.

# What Do You Want to Assess?

While curricular outcomes are the acid test of program effectiveness, the difficulty of assessing a comprehensive set of outcomes and the need for more information on the conduct of programs has led educators to look to assessments of both the planned and implemented curriculum. When assessing the planned curriculum, you would determine the extent to which the written curriculum guide for a school met a set of criteria. When assessing the implemented curriculum, you would look to see if what the teachers actually taught and the manner in which they taught it was consistent with the goals and plan of the curriculum.

If you want to create accountability for student achievement or if you want to provide evidence of program effectiveness for policy makers, you will want to measure outcomes. Do the programs do what they are supposed to do? Which usually means, do students learn, what they are supposed to learn in that program? School curriculums should clearly articulate the goals and objectives of a program in terms of what students should learn and that is what should be assessed. However, policy makers are usually more interested in short-term evidence of learning rather than long-term goals. For instance, they would want to know if students were fit and not necessarily whether the program produced adults who led physically active lifestyles.

One of the issues playing out in education today is related to the idea that assessment is driving the curriculum. In other words, what is assessed becomes the

The best evaluation of a physical education program is a measure of the extent to which students are active as adults. (*Top left:* © *Crearas/Jupiter Images; top right:* © *Steve Cole/Getty Images; bottom left:* © *PhotoLink/Getty Images;* bottom right: *Steve Mason/Getty Images*).

curriculum and what is not assessed is not taught. The danger is that long-term goals that are achieved over time are lost in the zeal to provide evidence that short-term goals have been achieved.

When high-stakes assessments and accountability systems are put in place from the top, educators are forced to align their curriculums with what is assessed or accept a poor assessment of their program. Most accountability programs are outcome oriented and leave the issues of how to develop those outcomes to the school and teacher. The assessment programs prescribe minimum outcomes in particular areas. Schools are free to develop their own programs and objectives as long as those programs and objectives help students meet those minimum outcomes.

If you want to evaluate a program to improve it or to find out if it is doing what it is supposed to do, you will want to not only collect data on outcomes, but on the intended (written) curriculum and the delivered curriculum (instructional process). Collecting information on a program is usually called program evaluation.

## Evaluating the Physical Education Curriculum

The type of evaluation you design depends on the questions you want to ask and answer and the feasibility of answering those questions. All of the questions listed in Box 12.1 are legitimate questions to ask about curriculum. You will notice that the questions are organized into issues related to the planned document, outcomes, and implementation of the curriculum. Each gives you a different perspective on the quality of the program.

## Assessing the Planned Curriculum

One of the quickest and least expensive ways to assess curriculum is to assess the planned curriculum or curriculum guide of a school. External reviewers can do a review of the curriculum guide or documents to determine the quality of the planned document and its congruence with a given set of criteria. If the guide is good, it does not necessarily mean that it is being implemented or that the outcomes are being realized. However, if the planned curriculum is not good or has problems it is unlikely that a good program is being implemented or that appropriate goals and objectives are being realized.

In addition to external reviewers, a content analysis of the curriculum guide using a set of criteria is a good self-study for a faculty. The more specific the criteria used, the more helpful the analysis will be. One of the best tools for self-assessment of the written curriculum in physical education is the Physical Education Curriculum Evaluation Tool (PE-CAT) available at no charge from the Centers for Disease Control and Prevention Web site. What follows are typical criteria used to do a content analysis of written materials.

## Box 12.1   Evaluating the Physical Education Curriculum

**The Planned Curriculum**

- Does the program address the national/state standards?

- Are the goals and objectives of the program clearly stated?

- Is there an articulated scope and sequence to the program?

- Is the content of the curriculum developed in a developmentally appropriate way?

- Are the goals and objectives of the program achievable within the time and resources available?

- Is enough detail provided so that unit development would have a clear direction?

- To what extent is both formative and summative assessment integrated throughout the curriculum?

- Is the program designed to meet the needs of these particular students? Are the goals and objectives appropriate?

**Curriculum Implementation**

- To what extent are teachers using the written curriculum to deliver the program?

- To what extent are the students/parents/administrators aware and supportive of what they are being taught?

- To what extent is the physical education program supported by the school administration?

- Is the curriculum being implemented as planned?

- Are the resources for the curriculum adequate to accomplish the goals and objectives of the curriculum?

- Do teachers meet on a regular basis to plan, implement, and adjust the curriculum?

- Is a clear program of continuous assessment and realignment in place?

- To what extent are students and teachers supportive of the curriculum?

**Curriculum Outcomes and Impact**

- To what extent are the goals of the program being met?

- What are the other outcomes of the curriculum that are not expressed?

- To what extent are the objectives of the program being met?

- What factors are facilitating the attainment of program goals and objectives?

- What factors are a hindrance to the attainment of program goals and objectives?

- To what extent does the program meet the standards established for student performance by the external body/agency over the program?

## Does the Program Address the National/State Standards?

Current best practice in physical education suggests that physical education programs should be designed so that students can meet the national or state content standards for physical education. A lot of teachers have looked at the list of outcomes that are exit criteria and somehow have been able to fit what they already do into those outcomes. The position of this text is that the standards should not be treated as general directions of the program, but as outcomes that are measurable. Teachers should not only teach toward an understanding of fitness, but rather teach toward intended outcomes in regard to fitness. The grade level outcomes should be the basis for planning, both the more comprehensive goals for a grade level and the performance indicators of a grade level. That would mean that the assessment of the curriculum guide using the national standards should use the more specific grade level outcomes to determine whether the guide is addressing the standards. For example, if the national/state standard indicates that students at the end of the fifth grade should be able to dribble and pass a basketball to a receiver, you should see content in the curriculum that addresses dribbling and passing a basketball in the grades 3–5 scope and sequence.

One way to do a content analysis is to take the performance indicators for a grade level and to identify:

1. Is the content included?
2. Is the content included in a context that identifies work on the indicator specifically?
3. Are learning experiences indicated for the content?
4. Are assessment materials included for the content?
5. Is the content developed through the scope and sequence of the entire curriculum appropriately?

## Are the Goals and Objectives of the Program Clearly Stated?

A good curriculum guide clearly identifies the goals and objectives of the program. While goals can be broader and identify long-term directions for the program consistent with the philosophy statement, the written objectives for the curriculum should specify exit outcomes for the program that are in some way measurable and achievable in the context of the school. Objectives that are not achievable and not specific enough to indicate clearly the expected behavior are not helpful.

*Example:*

> *Not helpful level of specificity of objective:* Students will be able to identify concepts in fitness.
>
> *Helpful level of specificity of objective:* Students will be able to identify four components of fitness and at least two activities that might develop that component.

## Is There an Articulated Scope and Sequence to the Program?

The scope and sequence of the curriculum represents the program's perspective on how content is developed throughout the program. Normally a scope and sequence describes what the content is for each grade level and how it is developed across the different grades. There are three important characteristics of a good scope and sequence.

**1. The content is aligned with the program goals and objectives.** While objectives identify where you want to go, the scope and sequence should describe how you plan to get there. The scope and sequence you design should be able to get you to where you want to go. If not, you either have to change your objectives or change your scope and sequence. These two parts of the curriculum need to be aligned, which means they should closely relate to each other.

**2. The content is developed logically.**    Content should be developed logically from one grade level to another. The following example illustrates a logical development of striking skills through the elementary grade levels:

> **Kindergarten:** Strike a balloon upward without letting it hit the floor.
>
> **First Grade**: Strike a large ball with the hand in self-space and against the wall.
>
> **Second Grade**: Strike a lightweight small ball with a paddle in self-space.
>
> **Third Grade**: Strike a lightweight small ball against the wall or with a partner continuously.
>
> **Fourth Grade:** Strike a ball with a paddle in a net activity in a small space, demonstrating basic offensive and defensive skills.
>
> **Fifth Grade**: Use a forehand strike with a paddle to keep a tennis ball or Wiffle® ball going against the wall or with a partner.

Striking with a paddle might not actually be assessed by a national and state assessment until the fifth grade. However, in the example above, striking wasn't first introduced in the fourth or fifth grade, it was developed throughout the grade levels. This kind of thoughtful attention to progression and sequencing of content increases the probability that students will be successful at a more advanced task. You should be able to take this progression into the middle school and high school years.

A common problem in physical education programs is the repetition of content from one grade to another without any significant difference in what is expected or what is taught from one grade to another (example: basketball dribbling, Grades 2, 3, 4, 5, 6, 7, 8). While planned repetition in a program is important, each grade level should take students further in the content.

**3. The content is developmentally appropriate.**    Developmentally appropriate content is appropriate for a particular age level and best practice for the field. You may have a great volleyball progression, but if it starts with students in the first grade learning how to do a forearm pass, it is probably inappropriate. If you include murder ball as an activity in your scope and sequence, it is likewise not appropriate, or it is inappropriate if your fourth-grade games program is largely dodgeball.

### Are the Goals and Objectives of the Program Achievable Within the Time and Resources Available?

Many programs have a limited time with a student, which means that a teacher has to choose the most critical content and objectives. One of the most difficult tasks for a curriculum designer is to choose what is to be taught from among many *good* options. Curriculum guides that do not choose, but rather list, content that can't possibly be taught in the time frame of the program are not helpful. A state middle school guide listed 21 different sports/activities for one grade. Each unit would have less than two weeks in about a 36-week school year and with nothing else being taught. When programs do not accomplish their objectives, it is usually because the objectives are not reasonable expectations for the time period.

### To What Extent Is Both Formative and Summative Assessment Integrated and Aligned Throughout the Curriculum?

A curriculum guide should plan for both formative and summative assessment of program goals and objectives. *When* in the program assessment takes place and *where* assessment takes place should be identified ahead of time. What is assessed should be aligned with what is taught. The reader should recognize at this point that in a good curriculum plan, the objectives, the scope and sequence, and the assessment should all be aligned. You should teach and assess what you intend students to learn.

### Is the Program Designed to Meet the Needs of These Particular Students? Are the Goals and Objectives Appropriate?

Most state and national standards are designed to be minimal expectations that every student should be able to meet. Students who have more opportunities or fewer opportunities to be participants in physical activity may need to have the standards adjusted for their particular needs. Likewise, different geographical areas afford different opportunities to be participants in different kinds of activities depending on the weather and geographical location of a school. For example, schools close to water would want to consider the importance of aquatics, while schools in the northern mountains would want to consider winter sports as options for curriculum. In most cases the standards will not change; the activities that are used to meet those standards might.

## Evaluating the Process—The Delivered Curriculum

The previous section of this chapter focused on the evaluation of the written curriculum. Evaluating the written curriculum is important but is only a first step. Many written curriculums are never implemented. In one sense when you look at the implementation of curriculum you are doing formative assessment and want to know what you can do to improve curriculum delivery. A lot of educational programs are not effective because they simply haven't been implemented as planned. Educators assume ideas or plans don't work when they would if they actually had been implemented.

### How and to What Extent Is the Curriculum Being Implemented?

One of the most basic questions regarding program implementation revolves around issues of whether or not teachers are actually teaching to the objectives of the curriculum and to what extent they are doing so. Related to these questions are:

1. Is the scope and sequence of the curriculum being followed?
2. Are the objectives being addressed and are they being addressed at an appropriate level?

There are many ways in which the curriculum evaluator can obtain this information. You can ask teachers what they are doing or whether what they are doing is consistent with the curriculum. You can ask students what they have done and what they have learned in physical education or, you can have an outside observer review written plans or observe what is being taught directly.

## What Are Student, Teacher, Parent, and Administrator Perceptions in Regard to the Curriculum?

One way to look at the extent to which a curriculum is implemented is to collect information on student, teacher, parent, and administrator perceptions of the curriculum. Their perceptions should match the written curriculum. While the participants' perceptions toward the curriculum can be inconsistent with each other and perhaps wrong, they play an important role in determining the amount of support a curriculum receives. Students, teachers, parents, and administrators are all stakeholders in an educational program. If they are aware of the program goals and are supportive of that goal, implementing a curriculum is easier for educators.

Identifying the level of awareness these groups have of the program objectives and identifying their support and perceptions on the value of the program can help educators make better decisions about how to implement a program. If these groups identify the same goals as the written curriculum and perceive that those goals are being implemented, there is a very good chance that they are being implemented. Primary tools for identifying stakeholder perceptions will be written surveys and questionnaires, along with focus group and interview data.

Students are the primary stakeholders of an education program. Student perceptions can provide teachers and curriculum planners with great insights into differences between the message the teacher thought was being communicated and the message the students are actually receiving. Because educators often fail to communicate objectives and rationales for programs, students are often unaware of the intent of programs and therefore respond in terms of the more immediate effect of a program. What often makes perfect sense to adults who put together programs with a conceptual scheme often goes unnoticed by students.

Many good programs go unsupported because the programs have not been shared with parents. Parents typically do not have a clear understanding of what a good physical education program should be and if they knew what the objectives of a program were, they could be good advocates for it, along with both students and the school administration.

Curriculums that are supported by the participants have a greater chance of being implemented and in a manner that makes them effective. The results of a formal evaluation of outcomes, including performance tests in the psychomotor and fitness areas, written tests, student logs and journals, and student portfolios that are shared with participants can all facilitate student understanding of the expected outcomes of a curriculum. Investigations into participants' perceptions can also identify misconceptions, strengths, and weaknesses essential to improving programs. Typical tools to identify participants' perceptions are questionnaires, surveys, focus groups, and interviews.

## Are the Resources for the Curriculum Adequate to Accomplish the Goals and Objectives of the Curriculum?

A thorough evaluation of the extent to which a curriculum is implemented requires a thorough evaluation of the resources available to implement the curriculum. The best planned curriculum and the most dedicated and competent teachers cannot implement a program without resources. Essential and primary resources include program time, competent teachers committed to the program, class size, dedicated teaching stations, and equipment.

**Program Time.**  We have talked about considering program time as being an essential part of planning. This is perhaps the biggest problem facing teachers today. While the profession works to preserve and increase program time, teachers need to use the program time they have wisely and be clear about what they can and cannot do. While the national organization (NASPE, 2004) calls for daily physical education for every student in all grades, few states come near to that goal. That means there are really two issues in terms of evaluating curriculum program time. The first is how much time is actually devoted to physical education in the school program and whether that time is adequate to meet the expectations stipulated for the program. In other words, are the goals and objectives attainable? The second issue is related to the way in which a program uses the time allotted. Does the program use the time in the school program wisely to accomplish the objectives? Programs should be evaluated on both issues.

Teachers tend to underestimate the amount of time it actually takes to teach content to a level where every student (with few exceptions) can accomplish the objectives of a unit. What the standards movement has done is to set minimal expectations that *every* student should be able to accomplish. That means that in most situations, the amount of content that can actually be achieved in the time given would need to be reduced and more time would need to be spent on less content.

Strong programs have found ways to utilize the time that they do have wisely and creatively. It is always amazing how many physical education classes are put on "time out" when it rains. A soccer unit that cannot be taught inside is replaced with a "free day," meaning that no teaching is going on that day. The reality is that it rains on a regular basis in most parts of the country. Good programs plan to utilize rainy days for different units such as those that might do more classroom work or for units like dance that may not require continuous days or large and specialized facilities to be taught effectively.

**Class size.**  Although some states permit physical education classes to have more students in them than other classes in the school, a good physical education program should not be expected to have more students in a class than other school programs. Physical education teachers tend to be good managers of large numbers of students. Quality instruction, however, cannot be provided in programs in which teachers are forced to do little but manage students. Maximum class sizes are different by state and by district. Teachers should insist that their classes be no longer than what other teachers in the school are asked to teach.

**Competent teachers committed to the program.**   Although a prerequisite for competence in teaching is usually defined by most states as *certified* in the area you are teaching, teacher certification does not guarantee that teachers are either competent or committed to a program. Teacher certification is a necessary but not sufficient condition for competence and commitment. Teachers must demonstrate their competence on a continuous basis through teacher evaluations and their ability to help students meet performance objectives. Teachers also need to support the curriculum they are trying to implement. When teachers play a part in curriculum development and when they are helped to understand a curriculum's goals and objectives, they are more likely to be supportive.

Because physical education programs are so closely aligned with school athletic programs, many programs find themselves saddled with teachers who are committed to athletics and not to the school physical education program. Oftentimes, coaches assert that they cannot do a good job teaching because of their coaching responsibilities. However, some of the most effective teachers we have in physical education are also excellent coaches. In most states and districts coaches are hired first as teachers. Their primary responsibility should be to teaching. If they cannot do both, then adjustments should be made to their teaching or coaching schedules.

**Facilities.**   There should be a dedicated teaching station for each teacher. One large gym or play space with two, three, or four teachers trying to conduct a class without any walls or curtains between them is not adequate. Even when the space is adequate, a learning environment cannot be obtained or maintained in conditions where teachers are trying to shout over the noise created by other classes. The amount of space and the type of space needed by a program usually varies the school level. Specific recommendations for facilities are described in Box 12.2.

## Box 12.2   Specific *Minimum* Recommendations for Physical Education Facilities

**Early elementary grades**

Indoor: 2500 sq. feet, 20 foot ceilings, no windows—per teacher

Outdoor: 50 by 50 yards of grass field space and a hard surface

**Upper elementary grades**

Indoor: 4200 sq. feet, 20 foot ceilings, no windows—per teacher

Outdoor: 100 by 50 yards of grass field space and a hard surface

**High school and middle school***

Indoor: large gym that can be divided, smaller gym, specialized space for mats/dance/wrestling, weight room, classroom

Outdoor: 100 by 50 yards of grass field space, tennis courts, track/jumping pits

*High school and middle school programs require specialized facilities for different activities (climbing walls, weight rooms, paddle tennis, etc.). Each teacher should have a designated teaching station and schools are encouraged to provide facilities for as many different activities as possible.

Adequate space for elementary programs usually means that there is a dedicated gym or all-purpose room used just for physical education, a blacktop area for outside classes, and field space for outdoor activities. Gyms tend to be built around the size of one basketball court. Each teacher should have their own designated teaching station. Indoor spaces in the elementary school need to have minimally a 20-foot ceiling and wall space that can be used to kick, throw, and strike objects. Outdoor space needs to be far enough away from "recess space" so that the teacher can maintain a learning environment when other classes are outside for recess.

Facilities for middle school programs are oftentimes the least adequate of all the school levels. Middle schools do not have the athletic facilities of the high school and yet they have large numbers of classes meeting at one time. Middle school programs need dedicated indoor teaching stations for each teacher. Every teaching station does not have to be a basketball court, but rather, planners need to think about spaces for the entire program so that dance, gymnastics, individual activities, and classroom work can be taught elsewhere when large gymnasiums are not needed. Outside field space and a blacktop area with courts and walls is extremely helpful.

Because high school athletic programs need a variety of different kinds of facilities, high school facilities are normally the least problematic in terms of teaching stations. It is not uncommon to see large gyms that can be divided into at least two teaching stations, weight rooms, classrooms, and several smaller play spaces that can be used for a variety of activities. Many high schools have more than adequate outdoor field spaces and many have outdoor basketball courts, ropes courses, and tennis courts.

**Equipment.**   There are several factors that need to be used in evaluating the adequacy of program equipment. The first is that the equipment is developmentally appropriate for the age level and the second is that there is an adequate amount of equipment to facilitate maximum participation in the activities being taught. Modified regulation equipment is available for beginners of all levels, including high school students, and should be made available for programs. There should be enough equipment so that every student can have a ball, racket, club, or stick. For activities such as weight training or gymnastics, for example, there should be enough equipment so that students do not have to wait for turns to learn the activity.

**Time for planning.**   Teacher schedules should be designed so that teachers have time to plan their classes and also so that teachers within a program have time to meet with each other. Planning is essential for well-designed programs to be conducted effectively. Physical education teachers, like other teachers within the school, should have at least one planning period a day and one of those planning periods each week should be reserved for and used for department planning.

## What Factors Are Facilitating the Attainment of Program Goals and Objectives? And What Factors Are a Hindrance to the Attainment of Program Goals and Objectives?

Many of the factors identified in this section can either facilitate or hinder the implementation of a good program. There are also other factors that may be playing a unique role that are specific to a particular state, district, and school setting. These can be easily identified by asking teachers to identify the factors that they think support what they are trying to do and factors that they feel make it very difficult to run an effective program. When these factors are identified, then it is much easier to resolve the problems and support the facilitators.

# Evaluating the Outcomes of the Curriculum

In this chapter we have talked about the importance of evaluating the written curriculum and the extent to which the written curriculum has been implemented. These are both important factors in determining the effectiveness of a curriculum and program. However, it is the extent to which a program achieves its outcomes that is perhaps most important. There are several issues that arise when we talk about evaluating curriculum outcomes, including the following:

- Do you evaluate short-term objectives or long-term goals of the program?
- Do you evaluate products that are made explicit in the program or those that are implicit as well?
- Do you look for positive as well as negative program outcomes?
- Do you need to measure every student on every outcome?
- What standard do you use to determine program effectiveness?

### Short-Term Objectives or Long-Term Goals?

Physical educators are not accustomed to looking at program outcomes, but it is the evaluation of outcomes that provides the support needed for programs and the means to make programs more effective. The "acid test" for curriculum objectives is whether or not the curriculum accomplishes its purpose and long-term goals. For most physical education programs the question is, are students physically active as students and when they are adults, do they remain physically active? Although few programs are in a position to track students into adulthood, programs can determine the physical activity of their students and the preparation of students for a physically active lifestyle through a variety of ways.

In one sense the six national standards can be directly evaluated as terminal outcomes for a school level. Table 12.1 lists each of the standards and potential ways in which the standard can be assessed. Program evaluation of outcomes normally takes place at the end of a program. However, it is easier and makes more sense for teachers to continuously collect data throughout a program to provide evidence that a program is accomplishing its objectives.

### Do You Evaluate Products That Are Made Explicit in the Program or Those That are Implicit As Well?

Programs that are well planned include all the potential outcomes considered important to the planners. There are, however, many outcomes of an education program that are shared by all programs that become almost "givens" for a school

**Table 12.1** | Evaluating the National Content Standards for Physical Education

| Standard | Potential Evaluation |
|---|---|
| *Standard 1:* Demonstrates competency in motor skills and movement patterns to perform a variety of physical activities. | Skills tests, scoring rubrics of participation, other evidence of competence (e.g., Red Cross swimming card). |
| *Standard 2:* Demonstrates understanding of movement concepts, principles, strategies, and tactics as they apply to the learning and performance of physical activities. | Written tests, observation in authentic activity setting, cognitive tests. |
| *Standard 3:* Participates regularly in physical activity. | Student journals, contracts, and logs. |
| *Standard 4:* Achieves and maintains a health-enhancing level of physical fitness. | Fitnessgram or other standardized tests. |
| *Standard 5:* Exhibits responsible personal and social behavior that respects self and others in physical activity settings. | Peer evaluations, teacher observation, student self-report. |
| *Standard 6:* Values physical activity for health, enjoyment, challenge, self-expression, and/or social interaction. | Written test, participation surveys. |

program and often are not stated explicitly. They are implicit kinds of goals held by many programs. If many teachers were asked they would say things like:

- I want my students to be able to think and solve problems for themselves.
- I want my students to show respect to themselves, others, and me by their behavior.
- I want my students to find ways to resolve problems between them without resorting to violence.
- I want my students to care for and respect the facilities and equipment we have.
- I want my students to feel good about themselves as "movers."

In one respect, if these are truly program goals and objectives, then they should be made explicit and taught for. On the other hand, many teachers assume that these are part of what teachers do. They are often not targeted as explicit objectives unless they become a problem. They often are best evaluated by evidence to the contrary. That is, when students start abusing the equipment, or becoming violent, or clearly do not feel good about their own abilities, teachers feel a need to make the objective explicit in their programs. Collecting evidence that these ideas and others like them are problems or need to be targeted and then planning to change that behavior, should be an explicit process.

## Developing a Plan for Evaluation

Because time is already limited in physical education programs, it is not possible to evaluate every student on everything. Nor is it possible to do the kind of evaluation suggested in this chapter every year. Because teachers have looked at evaluating their programs as an impossible task, most often they have chosen to do no program evaluation. For purposes of program evaluation you do not need to evaluate your program comprehensively every year, and when you are doing program evaluation, you do not need to evaluate every student on every objective. What follows are some ideas on how to approach a plan for evaluating all three dimensions of curriculum evaluation (the curriculum plan, curriculum implementation, and curriculum outcomes).

**Evaluating the planned curriculum.**   Guidelines for evaluating the planned curriculum should be used as a checksheet when you are planning the curriculum and should be used periodically (three to five years) as the planned curriculum has changed to determine if the curriculum as planned is still within those guidelines.

**Evaluating curriculum implementation.**   If the planned curriculum has been evaluated, then one of the biggest challenges is to determine if the plan is being implemented. After a program has begun to be implemented, programs should initially do an evaluation to determine if they are implementing the program as it has been planned. This should take place within two years and then periodically (every three to six years) to determine if it is being implemented.

**Evaluating curriculum outcomes and impact.**   Collecting data on program outcomes and impacts should be ongoing throughout the implementation of a curriculum. Teachers can use data they collect on student assessment as part of this process. All program outcomes need to be evaluated. However, you do not need data every year on every outcome, nor do you need to evaluate every student on every outcome. A more reasonable solution is to collect data every few years on different outcomes and to sample classes for each outcome. You may decide to look at several psychomotor program objectives that are part of Standard 1 and fitness objectives that are part of Standard 4 in one year and to use just several classes to collect the data. Another year you might choose to collect data on student participation in physical activity outside of class and several affective objectives. It would not be unreasonable to assume that it would take you three years to do a full program evaluation of outcomes. In this sense then, evaluation becomes ongoing and manageable.

One of the issues related to evaluating outcomes is the level of achievement that you use to determine program success. If you have written your goals and objectives with enough specificity, you have already defined what success in a goal or objective is to you. If you have not, then interpreting your data is more difficult. The National Association for Sport and Physical Education is developing assessment materials for the standards that should be a great help to practicing teachers. You will still need to modify these expectations either upward or downward for the students in your situation.

## Collecting Data

In the beginning of this chapter we talked about three kinds of evaluation: evaluating the planned curriculum, evaluating the implementation of curriculum, and evaluating the outcomes and impact of curriculum. Table 12.2 describes some suggestions for the kinds of data that can be used for each of these areas of curriculum evaluation.

You will notice that the data seem to fall into several categories. Some of the data are analyses of documents used to both plan and implement the curriculum (curriculum documents, unit and lesson plans, teacher schedules). Some of the data

**Table 12.2** | Curriculum Data and Potential Data Sources

| Type of Evaluation | Potential Types of Data |
|---|---|
| **The Planned Curriculum** | |
| Does the program address the national/state standards? | Physical Education Curriculum Assessment Tool (CDC, 2004); National standards, state standards. |
| Are the goals and objectives of the program clearly stated? | Evaluation of written document in terms of clarity and measurable outcomes. |
| Is there an articulated scope and sequence to the program? | Evaluation of scope and sequence in terms of alignment with goals and objective, logical development, and developmental appropriateness. |
| Are the goals and objectives of the program achievable within the time and resources available? | Analysis of specific allotment of time to each program goal and objective. |
| Is enough detail provided so that unit development would have a clear direction? | Analysis to determine if a "new" teacher could pick up the document and use it. |
| To what extent is both formative and summative assessment integrated throughout the curriculum? | Analysis to determine if assessment is planned to be integrated into instruction, as well as at the end of instruction and the school level. |
| Is the program designed to meet the needs of these particular students? Are the goals and objectives appropriate? | Analysis to determine if plan identifies the specific needs of students in the school and a way to meet those needs. |
| **Curriculum Implementation** | |
| Is the curriculum being implemented as planned? | Analysis of unit and daily lesson plans of the teacher, observation of instruction, interviews with teachers and students, student surveys, and questionnaires. |
| To what extent are the students/parents/administrators aware and supportive of what they are being taught? | Student, parent, administrator interviews, questionnaires, focus groups, and surveys. |
| To what extent is the physical education program supported by the school administration? | Budget analysis administrator interviews and questionnaires. |
| Are the resources for the curriculum adequate to accomplish the goals and objectives of the curriculum? | Analysis of documents, interviews, and surveys to determine class size, number of teachers, and qualifications of teachers, facilities, equipment, and department budget. |
| Do teachers meet on a regular basis to plan, implement, and adjust the curriculum? | Analysis of teacher schedules, interviews, and surveys with teachers. |
| Is a clear program of continuous assessment and realignment in place? | Analysis of documents, teacher interviews, and surveys to determine if a regular program of curriculum audit and program assessment is in place. |
| To what extent are students and teachers supportive of the curriculum? | Teacher and student surveys, questionnaires, and focus groups. |
| **Curriculum Outcomes and Impact** | |
| To what extent are the goals of the program being met? | Evaluations of student participation outside of class, including follow-up of graduates. |
| To what extent are the objectives of the program being met? | Formal evaluation of outcomes, including performance tests in the psychomotor and fitness areas, written tests, student logs and journals, student portfolios, student surveys, projects, and questionnaires. |
| To what extent does the program meet the standards established for student performance by the external body/agency over the program? | Analysis to determine if student achievement meets expected achievement of the standards as described in published materials (NASPE, 2004), including state expectations and district expectations. |

What are the other outcomes of the curriculum that are not expressed?

What factors are facilitating the attainment of program goals and objectives? And what factors are a hindrance to the attainment of program goals and objectives?

Open questions to present and past students regarding what programs have done for them.

Document analysis for implementation section, interviews with teachers and students.

are direct measures of student performance (skill and fitness tests, written tests, student portfolios) or participant attitudes and perceptions (surveys, questionnaires), and some of the measures use more qualitative measures (interviews, observation, focus groups). Each of these data sources can provide different kinds of data that are useful in fully understanding the planning, implementation, and effectiveness of a curriculum.

Teacher competence and commitment can be evaluated through documentation of certification and of effectiveness in producing student performance, observation of instruction, and interviews with teachers about their commitment to a program.

## Check Your Understanding

1. Why is evaluating a curriculum important?
2. What kinds of data are of interest to policy makers?
3. List three questions of importance to evaluating the planned curriculum and identify how you might go about answering those questions.
4. List three questions of importance to evaluating the implemented curriculum and identify how you might go about answering those questions.
5. List three questions of importance to evaluating curriculum outcomes and identify how you might go about answering those questions.
6. What kinds of data might you collect on each of the national standards?

## Reference

Centers for Disease Control and Prevention. (2004). Physical Education Curriculum Assessment Tool, Atlanta, GA: CDC. Available at www.cdc.gov/Healty Youth/PECAT/index.htm

## Suggested Reading

Lund, J., & Kirk, M. (2002). *Performance-Based Assessment for Middle and High School Physical Education.* Champaign, IL: Human Kinetics.

Melograno, V. (1998). *Professional and Student Portfolios for Physical Education.* Champaign, IL: Human Kinetics.

Hopple, C. (2005). *Elementary Physical Education Teaching and Assessment: A Practical Guide.* Champaign, IL: Human Kinetics.

**NASPE Assessment Series**

Baker, D. (2001). *Elementary Heart Health: Lessons and Assessment.* Reston, VA: NASPE.

Belka, D. (2007). *Games Stages and Assessment.* Reston, VA: NASPE.

Buck, M. (2002). *Assessing Heart Rate in Physical Education.* Reston, VA: NASPE.

Cone, T., & Cone, S. (2005). *Assessing Dance in Elementary Physical Education.* Reston, VA: NASPE.

Doolittle, S., & Fry, T. (2002). *Authentic Assessment of Physical Activity in High School Students.* Reston, VA: NASPE.

Grosse, S. (2005). *Assessment of Swimming in Physical Education.* Reston, VA: NASPE.

Holt Hale, S. A. (1999). *Assessing and Improving Fitness in Elementary Physical Education.* Reston, VA: NASPE.

Holt Hale, S. A. (1999). *Assessing Motor Skills in Elementary Physical Education.* Reston, VA: NASPE.

Ignio, A. (2002). *Video Tools for Teaching Motor Skill Assessment.* Reston, VA: NASPE.

Lambart, L. (1999). *Standards-Based Assessment of Student Learning.* Reston, VA: NASPE.

Lund, J. (1999). *Creating Rubrics for Physical Education.* Reston, VA: NASPE.

Markos, N. E. (2007). *Self- and Peer-Assessments for Elementary School Physical Education Programs.* Reston, VA: NASPE.

Melograno, V. (1999). *Preservice Professional Portfolio System.* Reston, VA: NASPE.

Melograno, V. (2000). *Portfolio Assessment for K–12 Physical Education.* Reston, VA: NASPE.

Mitchell, S., & Oslin, J. (1997). *Assessment in Games Teaching.* Reston, VA: NASPE.

Mohnson, B. (2004). *Assessing Concepts: Secondary Biomechanics.* Reston, VA: NASPE.

O'Sullivan, M., & Henninger, M. (2007). *Assessing Student Responsibility and Teamwork.* Reston, VA: NASPE.

Seidel, K. (2001). *Assessing Student Learning: A Practical Guide CD-Rom.* Reston, VA: NASPE.

Stark, S. (2007). *Assessing Gymnastics in Elementary School Physical Education.* Reston, VA: NASPE.

Steffen, J., & Grosse, S. (2003). *Assessment in Outdoor Adventure Physical Education.* Reston, VA: NASPE.

Townsend, J. S., Mohr, D., Rairigh, R., & Bulger, S. (2003). *Assessing Student Outcomes in Sport Education.* Reston, VA: NASPE.

# Sample Basketball Unit Plan (Secondary)

**Objectives:** The student will be able to:

1. **Motor**: Meet the minimum requirements for competency in basketball as defined by the state competency (SC) scoring rubric. (50%)
   Assessment: Self, peer, and teacher assessment using the scoring rubric for basketball.

2. **Cognitive**: Call basic rules infractions fairly and accurately in an officiating role in class basketball games. (10%)
   Assessment: Written test on rules, peer assessment of officials.

3. **Cognitive**: Assess their own ability accurately and set realistic personal goals for improvement. (10%)
   Assessment: Student use of scoring rubric for goal setting.

4. **Motor**: Demonstrate improvement in performance in the game of basketball from the beginning of the unit to the end of the unit. (20%)
   Assessment: Self-assessment using scoring rubric, peer assessment using scoring rubric, teacher assessment using scoring rubric.

5. **Affective**: Work cooperatively with members of a team for the good of the team. (5%)
   Assessment: Team, and self-assessment of cooperative team behavior.

6. **Affective**: Identify and find personal meaning in some aspect of the experience of playing basketball. (5%)
   Assessment: Personal feelings about basketball shared in reflective journal experience and class discussion.

**Grading:**

(50%)  Meet the minimum requirements for competency in basketball as defined by the SC scoring rubric.

(10%)  Call basic rules infractions fairly and accurately in an officiating role in class basketball games.

(10%)  Assess their own ability accurately and set realistic personal goals for improvement.

(20%)  Demonstrate improvement in performance in the game of basketball from the beginning to the end of the unit.

(5%)   Work cooperatively with members of a team for the good of the team.

(5%)   Identify and find personal meaning in some aspect of the experience of playing basketball.

Block Plan

| Monday | Tuesday | Wednesday | Thursday | Friday |
|---|---|---|---|---|
| **1** | **2** | **3** | **4** | **5** |
| ■ BB warm-up. <br> ■ Game play—have students play the game. <br> ■ Look at skilled play on video—what are the differences between your play and skilled play?—small group discussion. <br> ■ Review scoring rubric of expectations. <br> ■ Self-assessment using scoring rubric. <br> ■ Personal goal setting using scoring rubric. | ■ Teach warm-up routine to be used in basketball unit. <br> ■ Basketball as a lifetime activity—review opportunities to play in the community. <br> ■ Offense and defensive stance and drills. <br> ■ 1 vs. 1 practice with offensive and defensive stance. <br> ■ Game play: 1 vs. 1 with shooting. | ■ BB warm-up dribble tag. <br> ■ Dribble with footwork drills. <br> ■ Dribble and pass— dribble and pass drills. <br> ■ Free-throw pre-test— free-throw instruction and practice. <br> ■ Game play: 2 vs. 2 games—modified courts. | ■ BB warm-up—dribble drills with footwork. <br> ■ Dribble and pass drills (simple to active defense). <br> ■ 2 vs. 2 offensive and defensive tactics. <br> ■ 2 vs. 2 games. <br> ■ Set shot pre-test. <br> ■ Free-shooting practice. | ■ BB warm-up. <br> ■ Preseason tournament games—3 vs. 3 mixed-ability teams— emphasis on cooperative learning (skilled players helping less skilled players). <br> ■ Team assessment and goal setting following play. Each team uses major items on the scoring rubric to check those items they need to work on and establish some priorities for working on those items. |
| **6** | **7** | **8** | **9** | **10** |
| ■ BB warm-up. <br> ■ Three-person teams choose dribbling, passing, shooting, or footwork to work on for first 10 minutes of class. At the end of practice teams assess their productivity and ability to work independently. <br> ■ Community opportunities for play—students in class who have played after school report their experiences. <br> ■ Off-the-ball movement and shot defense. (film)—and practice <br> ■ Game play—3 vs. 3. | ■ BB warm-up and dribbling/passing/shooting drills with defense. <br> ■ Player-to-player defense. <br> ■ Offense for person-to-person defense. <br> ■ Three-player teams work on offensive plays and defense at half court. | ■ BB warm-up. <br> ■ Layup shot and layup shot variations (no defense/from a partner pass/defense). <br> ■ Rebounding—foul shot and field goal. <br> ■ Game play—3 vs. 3. <br> ■ Reflective journal experience—what I like/don't like about basketball. | ■ BB warm-up. <br> ■ Teacher discussion of reflective journal ideas. <br> ■ Dribbling/passing/ shooting with layup and set shot—active. <br> ■ Zone defense. <br> ■ Offense against a zone defense. <br> ■ Scrimmage—3 vs. 3 half court. <br> ■ Shooting per assessment test. | ■ BB warm-up. <br> ■ 3 vs. 3 tournament. <br> ■ Self-assessment using scoring rubrics. <br> ■ Self-assessment on standards 5, 6, 7. <br> ■ Personal goal setting using scoring rubrics. Students decide on whether they want to play in highly competitive or not so competitive 5-layer team league. |

| Monday | Tuesday | Wednesday | Thursday | Friday |
|---|---|---|---|---|
| 11 | 12 | 13 | 14 | 15 |
| ■ BB warm-up.<br>■ Conditioning for basketball.<br>■ Basketball safety and consumerism.<br>■ Organization into two leagues (highly competitive and competitive—student choice with five-man teams—mixed gender (students made decision period before/teacher assigned teams).<br>■ Team organization and practice—select captain/equipment manager.<br>■ Rules and officiating—go over rules to be used in class.<br>■ Officiating practice in scrimmage game (five officials per game—discuss calls). | ■ BB warm-up.<br>■ Team practice—team choice.<br>■ Discussion of team practice/independence and productivity of your team.<br>■ 5 vs. 5 scrimmage—half court.<br>■ Team assessment of weaknesses, and goal setting and strategies for improvement. | ■ Written test on rules/officiating. Warm-up.<br>■ Team practice—ball handling/shooting.<br>■ 5 vs. 5 scrimmage—half court.<br>■ Team assessment of performance during the game and goal setting. | ■ BB warm-up.<br>■ Shooting practice—active defense.<br>■ Zone defense—full court.<br>■ 5 vs. 5 tournament play, peer assessment of individual—particular aspects of the scoring rubric for game play. | ■ BB warm-up.<br>■ Team practice—team choice.<br>■ 5 vs. 5 tournament play.<br>■ Self-assessment assignment—students use a videotape of their performance in media center to assess their performance using scoring rubric.<br>■ Peer assessment of officials using officiating scoring rubric. |
| 16 | 17 | 18 | 19 | 20 |
| ■ BB warm-up.<br>■ Teacher shares personal assessments of each team with the team captains.<br>■ Team practice—team choice.<br>■ Teacher workshop (optional)—offensive positions for zone defense.<br>■ Tournament play—5 vs. 5. | ■ BB warm-up.<br>■ Team practice—teacher choice.<br>■ Teacher workshop (optional)—offense and defense for inbounds plays—other students choose what they want to work on at different stations.<br>■ Tournament play—5 vs. 5. | ■ BB warm-up.<br>■ Team practice—team choice.<br>■ Written test.<br>■ Tournament play—5 vs. 5. | ■ BB warm-up.<br>■ Team, peer and self-evaluation of affective standards 5, 6, 7.<br>■ Tournament play. | ■ BB warm-up.<br>■ Tournament play.<br>■ Individual assessment of improvement in the unit.<br>■ Unit assessment discussion with the teacher.<br>■ Peer assessment of officials. |

# Assessment-Scoring Rubric

## Setting:

The following assessment is to be made of the student by observation over a period of time, through a testing situation set up by the teacher, or through a submitted videotape of student performance. The student should play with and against students of similar ability.

## Scoring:

Each indicator is scored on a 1–3 basis according to consistency with which the indicator is observed. All indicators are totaled and averaged to determine a student's score. Students must score 2.0 and above to meet the state criterion.

Level 3:   Uses basic indicators in an extremely consistent manner.

Level 2:   Uses basic indicators with consistency most of the time.

Level 1:   Uses basic indicators with occasional consistency.

## Indicators:

### Rules, Etiquette, and Safety

_____1.   Makes no observable errors in interpreting or applying the rules of the game.

_____2.   Refrains from any action or behavior that would endanger or injure another student.

_____3.   Recognizes and acknowledges good play by an opponent or teammate.

_____4.   Accepts calls from officials without complaint.

## Basic Skills and Offensive and Defensive Play:

_____ 5.   Uses the *appropriate pass* in game situations (i.e., two-hand overhead, chest, bounce).

_____ 6.   Clear evidence of offensive and defensive *rebounding* technique (i.e., box out).

_____ 7.   Makes use of *fakes* to gain an advantage in shooting, passing, or dribbling.

_____ 8.   Can maintain possession of the ball with a *dribble*.

_____ 9.   Can *delay the progress* of the ball by dribbling player.

_____10.   Can *move the ball down* the court quickly with teammates.

_____11.   *Inbound a ball* to a teammate with an effective entry pass.

_____12.   Can shoot four out of five *foul shots* effectively (i.e., score or near miss with good form).

_____13.   Can use a *layup and set shot* effectively in a game situation.

### Use of Game Strategy:

_____**14.** Clear evidence of offensive play that *creates openings and plays* (with and without the ball).

_____**15.** Chooses the *appropriate shot* and makes good decisions about when to shoot.

_____**16.** Moves appropriately with teammates in *one-on-one or zone defenses.*

_____**17.** Clear evidence of the execution of *simple offensive plays.*

_____**18.** Defends an *inbound play* effectively.

_____        Total (Score of 36 necessary to meet the required average)

### Scoring-Rubric Assumptions:

1. The evaluator knows the content.
2. The rubric is based on content that has been taught.
3. Each category in the rubric is clearly defined.
4. The rubric will be used across time.
5. It is applied using players of the same skill.

### Rubric Applications:

1. You need a system of scoring.
2. Record final achievement scores.
3. Record scores on each rubric item for all students in a given class.
4. Pick one skill and observe every student for that skill for a variety of dates.
5. Have students assess themselves (each other).

## Description of Learning Experiences for Selected Lessons

### Lesson 2

**Warm-up routine to be used in basketball unit**   Each class period will consist of a warm-up involving three parts: activities to increase the heart rate, stretching, and ball handling. In some cases the ball handling and heart rate exercises will be the same. Through the unit students should get experiences in all of the heart rate exercises, stretching exercises, and ball handling warm-ups described in the attached material. Each day the warm-up will occupy no longer than 10 minutes and will include a combination of new and old experiences.

**Basketball as a life-time activity**   A handout describing opportunities available for playing basketball will be handed out to students. The handout will include a list of public and private organizations (recreation centers, YWCA/YMCA, churches, etc.) that have organized leagues. The handout will include age groups, dates, expenses, phone numbers, and locations for these opportunities. Students will be encouraged to think about joining some these teams to meet the expectations of Criterion 3. If possible a representative from one of these organizations will come and talk with the class about opportunities provided by the organization.

### Offensive and Defensive Stance

Explanation and demonstration of basic offensive and defensive stances (stationary) and why it is important to take these positions.

Moving in defensive side-step and attack and retreat positions. Practice to cues changing positions according to the direction teacher calls.

Offensive footwork—total class practice drill.

Offensive and defensive shadowing drill.

Full-court offensive and defensive work.

**1 vs. 1 Practice of Offensive and Defensive Footwork**   Students are divided into groups of three and given a boundary (cones or lines), defining a space about one-sixth the basketball court. The third person uses a check sheet of major offensive and defensive footwork cues to give verbal feedback to other two group members. Students switch roles.

**Game Play—1 vs. 1 with Shooting**   Students are given the option to choose their own opponents. Students play for five minutes with one opponent and then must move on to another opponent. Two groups of two at one basket. The focus is on offensive and defensive footwork. The teacher selects several students at the end of the period to demonstrate good footwork during game play.

## Lesson 8

**BB Warm-Up**   Teacher identifies four people to lead the warm-up for the day. Teacher leads students through a ball-handling warm-up—wall-passing stationary and on the move and stationary passing. (All drills are designed for maximum activity—no standing around waiting for a turn.)

**Rebounding**   Students watch a videotape of rebounding techniques. Teacher leads a discussion on why rebounding is important and the characteristics of a good rebounder (emotional, mental, physical, and skill-specific).

- Defensive rebounds—front turn and back turn.
- Offensive rebounds—Teacher demonstrates and students practice with a group of three people (1 vs. 1 with a shooter). Shooter tosses first, throws off backboard and rim second.
- Practice drills for rebounding (1 vs. 2, tipping, alternate hand-tipping, circle rebounding, 2 balls/3 players shooting, passing, and rebounding).

**3 vs. 3 Game Play**   Mixed-ability teams play a modified game with foul shots. Emphasis is on rebounding technique. Official stops the game after a player rebounds after a shot. The team who gets the rebound scores an extra point and puts the ball in play from out of bounds.

**Reflective Journal Experience**   Students sit in a group on the floor or in the bleachers and take out their journals. The teacher leads a discussion of what students like/don't like about basketball. The teacher makes it very clear that there are no right or wrong answers to the question and talks about the different kind of feelings that people get from participation in sport and physical activity. The teacher asks students to write in their journal:

- In general what is it about basketball that you like/don't like?
- Describe a specific incident that happened in the game today that made you feel good/not so good.

## Lesson 11

**BB Warm-Up**   Overview of conditioning requirements for basketball and self-assessment of personal areas of strengths and weaknesses. Teacher leads students through a modified conditioning plan based on the warm-up taught at the beginning of the unit.

After warm-up teacher presents a chart listing the most common causes of injury in basketball (including rough play, water on the floor (sand/oil outside). Teachers and students discuss purchasing balls and shoes for basketball.

**Division into Leagues**   Teacher calls students' attention to posted leagues and teams and the schedule of play for the rest of the unit. Students are divided into teams by the teacher according to the level of play they selected the period before (highly competitive and competitive). Two teams from each league play at a time. One team assumes the role of officials for the game.

**Team Organization and Practice**   Teacher shares with students what the role of the captain is and what characteristics make a good captain. Teacher also defines the role of the equipment manager and the schedule for officiating. Teams meet to elect positions and decide who is going to do what and when for the rest of the unit. The teacher suggests several practices the teams might want to run in the time given (students can select their own if they can justify their response).

**Rules and Officiating**   The teacher hands out a sheet to all students on the rules of basketball and goes over the rules using examples on the floor if necessary to explain each rule. Two teams scrimmage and the teacher officiates, explaining each call and signal. Four teams play and two teams officiate (five officials per game, each official has a whistle). After seven minutes the team officiating rotates into play. After each call made by one of the five officials, the official making the call has to explain to the other officials and the players why the call was made.

## Lesson 16

**BB Warm-Up**   Teacher leads entire class through ball-handling warm-up drills.

**Team Practice—Teacher Meets with Team Captains**    Team captains assign their team a practice for 15 minutes. The teacher meets with each of the six captains and shares:

- Overall strengths and weaknesses observed in play.
- The extent to which each team is using their practice time wisely.
- Team captain perception of strengths and weaknesses.
- Teacher perception of strengths and weaknesses of each team.
- Caliber of officiating.

Teacher asks each team captain to identify two goals for team improvement for the next few days and how they might practice to improve.

**Teacher Workshop (Optional): Offensive Positions for Zone Defense**    Any team that wants to participate in the teacher workshop can. Teams do not have to participate. Teacher identifies three specific plays useful against a zone defense. All participants are active as either offense or defense. Teacher walks students through each play with a "passive defense" until players feel comfortable. Defense is then told to be more aggressive but not yet "full out." Players switch offensive and defensive roles until all have had the opportunity to play both offense and defense.

**Tournament Play—5 vs. 5**    Continue round-robin play with 20-minute games and student officials.

## Goal-Setting Scoring Rubric

**Purpose:** To assess the degree to which students can assess their own skill in basketball using the scoring rubric and set realistic personal goals for improvement.

### Level 4
- Correctly identifies at least three different strengths in playing basketball using the state competency scoring rubric.
- Correctly identifies at least two different weaknesses in playing basketball using the state competency scoring rubric.
- Sets a realistic goal for improvement of weaknesses.
- Identifies a strategy for improvement that is "doable."

### Level 3
- Correctly identifies at least one strength in playing basketball using the state competency scoring rubric.
- Correctly identifies at least one weakness in playing basketball using the state competency scoring rubric.
- Sets a realistic goal for improvement of weaknesses.
- Identifies a strategy for improvement that is "doable."

*Level 2*
■ One of the key factors missing in Level 3 is not there.

*Level 1*
■ More than one of the key factors listed in Level 3 are not there.

## Self/Peer Assessment—Affective Unit Objectives

Members of effective basketball teams are able to work with their teammates for the good of the team. The purpose of this experience is for you to reflect on your own behavior as well as the behavior of your teammates in terms of the degree to which you and they were able to work with the team to accomplish team goals.

Identify one personal incident that has occurred in the basketball unit that would identify you as a cooperative team player.

Identify one personal incident that has occurred in the basketball unit that might identify you as an uncooperative team player.

If 5 meant most cooperative and 1 meant least cooperative, how would you rate yourself on a 1–5 scale? _____

On a 1–5, scale how would you assess the behavior of your teammates in terms of their team cooperation throughout the unit?

Name_____ Rating_____

Name of Official_____ Name of Evaluator _____

Score _____Date _____

# Scoring Rubric—Referee Assessment

## *Level 4*

Has total charge of game—play is safe.

Has respect of players—players do not question calls.

Calls plays with no accuracy problems—clearly knows the rules and can apply them.

Calls plays fairly and evenhandedly between the teams and players.

## *Level 3*

Play is safe but occasionally gets too rough.

Has respect of players—only an occasional call will be questioned by players.

Calls players with few accuracy problems.

Calls plays fairly and evenhandedly between the teams and players.

## *Level 2*

Play is safe but occasionally gets too rough.

Calls are regularly questioned by players.

Calls reflect more than an occasional lack of knowledge of the rules.

Calls plays fairly and evenhandedly between the teams and players.

## *Level 1*

Play is not safe and is too rough.

Calls are regularly questioned by players.

Calls reflect more than an occasional lack of knowledge of the rules.

Several incidences of calling plays unfairly to one team are noticed.

# Basketball Rules: Sample Questions*

1. What is the purpose of the rules?
   *a.* To control the game
   *b.* To provide fair play
   *c.* To give offensive players a chance to score
   *d.* To build breaks into the game
2. The ball is temporarily out of play. What is this called?
   *a.* Dead ball
   *b.* Jump ball
   *c.* Time out
   *d.* Delay of game

---

*From: McGee, R., & Farrow, A. (1987). *Test Questions for Physical Education Activities*. Champaign, IL: Human Kinetics.

3. When does the clock not stop during the game?
   a.  When a player shoots a free throw
   b.  When a goal has been made
   c.  When a player commits a foul
   d.  When a substitute enters the game

4. A player has stopped the dribble. How long can the same player hold the ball when closely guarded?
   a.  3 seconds
   b.  5 seconds
   c.  10 seconds
   d.  No time limit

5. How many seconds may a defensive player stay in the lane?
   a.  3 seconds
   b.  5 seconds
   c.  10 seconds
   d.  No time limit

6. A team must get the ball across the half-court line in how many seconds?
   a.  10 seconds
   b.  8 seconds
   c.  5 seconds
   d.  3 seconds

7. How much time does a player have to pass the ball in bounds?
   a.  3 seconds
   b.  5 seconds
   c.  10 seconds
   d.  An indefinite amount of time

8. When does the clock begin an out-of-bounds play?
   a.  When the ball is handed to the player to throw it inbounds
   b.  When the ball is touched by a player on the court
   c.  When the ball crosses the boundary line
   d.  When the player throwing the ball releases it

9. From what location on the floor is the ball put into play after a field goal?
   a.  From anywhere along the end line
   b.  From a specific spot on the endline
   c.  From anywhere on the sideline
   d.  From a specific spot on the sideline

10. A player making a throw-in from under the basket hits the back of the backboard and the ball rebounds into the court. Who gains possession of the ball?
   a.  Ball is awarded to opponents out-of-bounds at the side line.
   b.  Ball continues in play.
   c.  Ball is awarded to opponents out-of-bounds at the end line.
   d.  Ball is awarded to the same player and the end line play is repeated.

11. How many times may a player tap the ball on a jump ball?
    a. Once
    b. Twice
    c. Three times
    d. Any number of times

12. In which jump ball situation is a violation called on the jumper?
    a. An opposing player touches the ball first, then jumper's teammate controls it.
    b. A teammate enters the circle before the tap.
    c. The opposing jumper controls the ball following a bounce.
    d. The opposing jumper taps the ball twice, and a teammate gains control.

13. In which jump ball situation is a violation called on the jumper?
    a. An opposing player touches the ball first, then the jumper's teammate controls it.
    b. A teammate enters the circle before the tap.
    c. The opposing jumper controls the ball following a bounce.
    d. The opposing jumper taps the ball twice, and a teammate gains control.

14. Which play is legal?
    a. An offensive player fumbles the ball and proceeds to dribble it.
    b. A defensive player kicks the ball in an attempt to block a pass.
    c. An offensive player steps over the sideline when passing the ball inbounds.
    d. A player involved in a jump ball situation taps the ball and then catches it.